HIKING
NEVADA

The North Twin River Trail climbs over a spur to avoid an impassible section of the river canyon (Hike 35).

Fall color at the foot of the Monitor Range

HIKING NEVADA

A GUIDE TO THE STATE'S GREATEST HIKING ADVENTURES

THIRD EDITION

Bruce Grubbs

FALCONGUIDES

GUILFORD, CONNECTICUT

FALCONGUIDES®

An imprint of Globe Pequot

Falcon and FalconGuides are registered trademarks and Make Adventure Your Story is a trademark of Rowman & Littlefield.

Distributed by NATIONAL BOOK NETWORK

Copyright © 2018 Rowman & Littlefield

TOPO! maps copyright 2018 National Geographic Partners, LLC. All Rights Reserved.

Maps © Rowman & Littlefield

All photos by Bruce Grubbs unless otherwise noted.

British Library Cataloguing-in-Publication Information available

Library of Congress Cataloging-in-Publication Data
Names: Grubbs, Bruce (Bruce O.)
Title: Hiking Nevada : a guide to the state's greatest hiking adventures / Bruce Grubbs.
Description: Third edition. | Guilford, Connecticut : FalconGuides, [2017] |
   Includes bibliographical references and index. | Description based on print version
   record and CIP data provided by publisher; resource not viewed.
   Identifiers: LCCN 2017013508 (print) | LCCN 2017014622 (ebook) | ISBN
   9781493027798 (e-book) | ISBN 9781493027781 (pbk.)
Subjects: LCSH: Hiking—Nevada—Guidebooks. | Trails—Nevada—Guidebooks. |
   Nevada—Guidebooks.
Classification: LCC GV199.42.N3 (ebook) | LCC GV199.42.N3 G78 2017 (print) |
   DDC 796.5109793—dc23
LC record available at https://lccn.loc.gov/2017013508

∞™ The paper used in this publication meets the minimum requirements of American National Standard for Information Sciences—Permanence of Paper for Printed Library Materials, ANSI/NISO Z39.48-1992.

Printed in the United States of America

South Twin River (Hike 36)

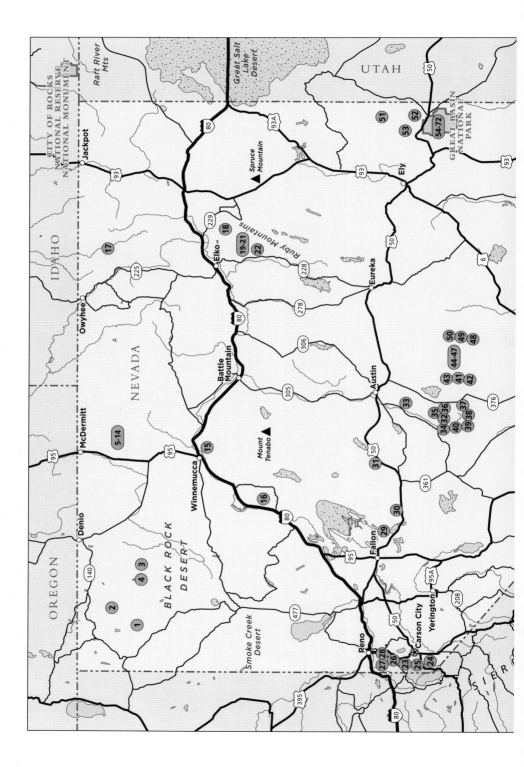

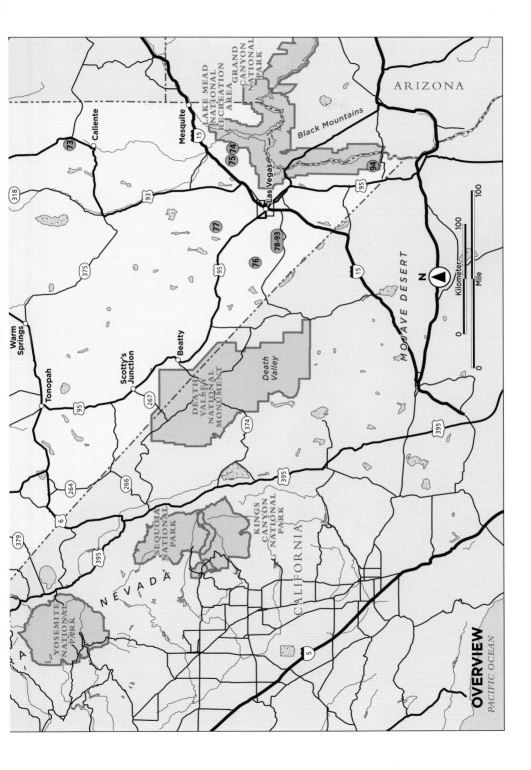

OVERVIEW

PACIFIC OCEAN

ARIZONA

NEVADA

CALIFORNIA

MOJAVE DESERT

Black Mountains

GRAND CANYON NATIONAL PARK

LAKE MEAD NATIONAL RECREATION AREA

DEATH VALLEY NATIONAL MONUMENT

Death Valley

SEQUOIA NATIONAL PARK

KINGS CANYON NATIONAL PARK

YOSEMITE NATIONAL PARK

Las Vegas

Mesquite

Caliente

Warm Springs

Tonopah

Scotty's Junction

Beatty

N

Kilometer

Mile

100

100

100

0

0

73

75

74

94

77

76

78-93

318

375

93

95

95

95

15

15

95

395

395

395

5

6

264

266

267

374

379

Backlit quaking aspen below the cliffs

THE HIKES

MEET YOUR GUIDE	xiii
MAP AND ICON LEGEND	xiv
TRAIL FINDER	xvi
BEFORE YOU HIT THE TRAIL	1
HIKING IN NEVADA	1
GEOLOGY AND GEOGRAPHY	1
NATURAL HISTORY	3
HUMAN HISTORY	4
HIKING TECHNIQUES AND ETHICS:	
LEAVE NOTHING BUT FOOTPRINTS	7
OUR ARCHAEOLOGICAL AND HISTORICAL HERITAGE	9
MAKING IT A SAFE TRIP	10
WATER	10
WEATHER	12
HOW TO USE THIS GUIDE	13
THE HIKES	13
FINDING AND USING MAPS	15

Northwestern Nevada

1. Desert Trail: High Rock Canyon Section	18
2. Desert Trail: Sheldon National Wildlife Refuge Section	23
3. Blue Lakes	29
4. Duffer Peak	32
5. Buckskin Mountain	34
6. Lye Creek Basin	36
7. Granite Peak	38
8. Rebel Creek Trail	41
9. McConnell Creek Trail	45
10. Horse Canyon Trail	46
11. Falls Canyon Trail	48

12. Santa Rosa Summit Trail: Buffalo Canyon   50
13. Santa Rosa Summit Trail: Singas Creek   52
14. Santa Rosa Summit Trail: North Hanson Creek   54
15. Water Canyon   56
16. Star Peak   60

Northeastern Nevada

17. Matterhorn Loop   66
18. Soldier Creek   70
19. Island Lake   73
20. Ruby Crest National Recreation Trail   78
21. Echo Lake   82
22. Overland Lake   85

Western Nevada

23. Hobart Creek Reservoir   90
24. Spooner Lake   93
25. Marlette Lake   96
26. Jones Creek/Whites Creek Trail   98
27. Mount Rose   101
28. Ophir Creek Trail   104
29. Grimes Point Archaeological Area   107
30. Sand Springs Desert Study Area   108

Central Nevada

31. Cold Springs Pony Express Station   112
32. Berlin-Ichthyosaur State Park   114
33. Toiyabe Crest National Recreation Trail   116
34. Arc Dome   122
35. North Twin River Loop   125
36. South Twin River Overlook   128
37. Jett Canyon Trail   130
38. Toms Canyon Trail   132
39. Peavine Canyon Trail   134
40. Cow Canyon Trail   136
41. Mount Jefferson   137

42. Meadow Creek Trail — 142
43. Moores Creek Trail — 144
44. Morgan Creek Trail — 146
45. Mosquito Creek Trail — 149
46. North Mosquito Creek Trail — 152
47. South Mosquito Creek Trail — 154
48. Cottonwood Creek/Barley Creek Trail — 156
49. Green Monster Trail — 160
50. Clear Lake Trail — 162

Eastern Nevada

51. Smith Creek — 166
52. Hendrys Creek — 168
53. Big Canyon — 172
54. Osceola Tunnel — 175
55. Strawberry Creek and Osceola Ditch — 177
56. Osceola Ditch Interpretive Trail — 179
57. Lehman Creek — 181
58. Bald Mountain — 184
59. Wheeler Peak — 188
60. Alpine Lakes — 191
61. Bristlecone-Glacier Trail — 194
62. Mountain View Nature Trail — 198
63. Lehman Cave — 199
64. Baker and Johnson Lakes — 200
65. Timber Creek and South Fork Baker Creek — 205
66. Pole Canyon — 207
67. Can Young Canyon — 209
68. Johnson Lake — 211
69. Dead Lake — 214
70. Snake Creek — 216
71. South Fork Big Wash — 218
72. Lexington Arch — 221

Southern Nevada

73. Cathedral Gorge — 226
74. Mouses Tank — 228

75. White Domes — 231

76. Charleston Peak National Scenic Trail — 233

77. Joe May Canyon — 237

78. Moenkopi Trail — 241

79. Calico Tanks — 243

80. Turtlehead Mountain — 245

81. Keystone Thrust — 247

82. White Rock Hills — 249

83. White Rock Spring — 251

84. White Rock Spring to Willow Spring — 253

85. Lost Creek Loop — 254

86. Willow Spring Loop — 256

87. La Madre Spring — 257

88. Top of the Escarpment — 258

89. Bridge Mountain — 261

90. Ice Box Canyon — 264

91. Pine Creek Canyon — 266

92. Oak Creek Canyon — 269

93. First Creek Canyon — 271

94. Spirit Peak — 272

AFTERWORD: NEVADA'S WILDERNESS CHALLENGE — 275

APPENDICES — 277

HIKERS' CHECKLISTS — 277

RESOURCES — 279

FURTHER READING — 281

HIKE INDEX — 283

MEET YOUR GUIDE

BRUCE GRUBBS has a serious problem—he doesn't know what he wants to do when he grows up. Meanwhile, he's done such things as wildland firefighting, running a mountain shop, flying airplanes, shooting photos, and writing books. He's a backcountry skier, climber, figure skater, mountain biker, amateur radio operator, river runner, and sea kayaker—but the thing that really floats his boat is hiking and backpacking. No matter what else he tries, the author always comes back to hiking—especially long, rough, cross-country trips in places like the Grand Canyon. Some people never learn. But what little he has learned, he's willing to share with you—via his books, of course, but also via his websites, blogs, and whatever works. He has written more than three dozen books, most of them FalconGuides. You can check them out at BruceGrubbs.com.

I wish to thank my friends and hiking companions over the years who suggested new areas to hike and often provided great company in the backcountry.

I wish to thank the personnel of the US Bureau of Land Management, the US Fish and Wildlife Service, the USDA Forest Service, the National Park Service, and the Nevada Division of State Parks for their invaluable assistance with all editions of this book. Thanks also to the readers who commented on the hikes.

Specifically, I wish to thank Ron Kezar for his original description of the Hendrys Creek Trail. Thanks also to Marjorie Sill for the afterword, "Nevada's Wilderness Challenge."

Thanks also to the fine folks at Rowman & Littlefield, and specifically to my editor, Katie Benoit, and to Melissa Baker, map coordinator, for turning my rough manuscript into a finished book.

Warm thanks to Duart Martin for supporting this project and putting up with my long trips to Nevada, and also to Stewart Aitchison for suggesting the original project and providing valuable assistance along the way.

Map and Icon Legends

ICON LEGEND

 BEST PHOTOS

FAMILY FRIENDLY

WATER FEATURES

DOG FRIENDLY

FINDING SOLITUDE

NOTES ON MAPS

Topographic maps are essential companions to the activities in this guide. Falcon has partnered with National Geographic to provide the best mapping resources. Each activity is accompanied by a detailed map and the name of the National Geographic TOPO! map (USGS), which can be downloaded for free from natgeomaps.com.

If the activity takes place on a National Geographic Trails Illustrated map, it will be noted. Continually setting the standard for accuracy, each Trails Illustrated topographic map is crafted in conjunction with local land managers and undergoes rigorous review and enhancement before being printed on waterproof, tear-resistant material. Trails Illustrated maps and information about their digital versions, which can be used on mobile GPS applications, can be found at natgeomaps.com.

MAP LEGEND

15	Interstate Highway		⊿	Campground
6	US Highway		✪	Capital
376	State Highway		✝	Cemetery
709	Local/County/Forest Road		▬	Dam
- - - -	Unpaved Road		⊠	Mine
- - - -	Unimproved Road		Ⓟ	Parking
▪▪▪▪▪▪	Featured Route		⤭	Pass/Gap
- - - - -	Trail		▲	Peak
··········	Off-Trail Route		🎋	Picnic Area
- · - · -	State Boundary		☐	Point of Interest
∿	River/Creek		🏢	Ranger Station/Park Office
∿	Intermittent Stream		⊓	Ruins
▬▬▬	National Park/Forest Boundary		◄	Scenic View
- - - - -	Wilderness Boundary		🔍	Spring
▬▬▬	State Park Boundary		○	Town
∩	Arch		①	Trailhead
▲	Backcountry Campground		⊢⊣	Tunnel
⬠	Cabin/Lodge/Guard Station		?	Visitor/Information Center

Day hiking below Wheeler Peak,
Snake Range (Hike 60)

	BEST PHOTOS	FAMILY FRIENDLY	WATER FEATURES	DOG FRIENDLY	FINDING SOLITUDE
NORTHWESTERN NEVADA					
1. Desert Trail: High Rock Canyon Section					•
2. Desert Trail: Sheldon National Wildlife Refuge Section					•
3. Blue Lakes	•	•	•		•
4. Duffer Peak	•				•
5. Buckskin Mountain	•	•		•	
6. Lye Creek Basin	•	•		•	
7. Granite Peak	•				•
8. Rebel Creek Trail			•		•
9. McConnell Creek Trail			•		•
10. Horse Canyon Trail			•		•
11. Falls Canyon Trail	•		•		•
12. Santa Rosa Summit Trail: Buffalo Canyon	•				•
13. Santa Rosa Summit Trail: Singas Creek	•				•
14. Santa Rosa Summit Trail: North Hanson Creek	•				•
15. Water Canyon			•		
16. Star Peak	•				•
NORTHEASTERN NEVADA					
17. Matterhorn Loop	•				•
18. Soldier Creek	•		•		•
19. Island Lake	•		•		
20. Ruby Crest National Recreation Trail	•		•		

	BEST PHOTOS	FAMILY FRIENDLY	WATER FEATURES	DOG FRIENDLY	FINDING SOLITUDE
NORTHEASTERN NEVADA (CONTINUED)					
21. Echo Lake	•		•		•
22. Overland Lake	•		•		•
WESTERN NEVADA					
23. Hobart Creek Reservoir		•	•	•	
24. Spooner Lake	•	•	•	•	
25. Marlette Lake	•		•	•	
26. Jones Creek/Whites Creek Trail			•		•
27. Mount Rose	•				
28. Ophir Creek Trail			•		
29. Grimes Point Archaeological Area		•			
30. Sand Springs Desert Study Area	•	•			
CENTRAL NEVADA					
31. Cold Springs Pony Express Station	•	•			
32. Berlin-Ichthyosaur State Park	•	•			
33. Toiyabe Crest National Recreation Trail	•				•
34. Arc Dome	•				•
35. North Twin River Loop	•		•		•
36. South Twin River Overlook	•	•	•	•	•
37. Jett Canyon Trail					•
38. Toms Canyon Trail					•
39. Peavine Canyon Trail					•
40. Cow Canyon Trail					•

	BEST PHOTOS	FAMILY FRIENDLY	WATER FEATURES	DOG FRIENDLY	FINDING SOLITUDE
CENTRAL NEVADA (CONTINUED)					
41. Mount Jefferson	•				•
42. Meadow Creek Trail			•		•
43. Moores Creek Trail			•		•
44. Morgan Creek Trail	•		•		•
45. Mosquito Creek Trail	•		•		•
46. North Mosquito Creek Trail	•		•		•
47. South Mosquito Creek Trail	•		•		•
48. Cottonwood Creek/ Barley Creek Trail	•	•	•	•	•
49. Green Monster Trail					•
50. Clear Lake Trail	•		•		•
EASTERN NEVADA					
51. Smith Creek	•				•
52. Hendrys Creek	•		•		•
53. Big Canyon	•	•		•	•
54. Osceola Tunnel					•
55. Strawberry Creek and Osceola Ditch	•	•			
56. Osceola Ditch Interpretive Trail		•			
57. Lehman Creek			•		
58. Bald Mountain	•		•		•
59. Wheeler Peak	•				
60. Alpine Lakes	•	•	•		
61. Bristlecone-Glacier Trail	•				
62. Mountain View Nature Trail		•			

	BEST PHOTOS	FAMILY FRIENDLY	WATER FEATURES	DOG FRIENDLY	FINDING SOLITUDE
EASTERN NEVADA (CONTINUED)					
63. Lehman Cave		●			
64. Baker and Johnson Lakes	●		●		
65. Timber Creek and South Fork Baker Creek	●		●		
66. Pole Canyon					●
67. Can Young Canyon					●
68. Johnson Lake	●		●		
69. Dead Lake			●		●
70. Snake Creek		●	●		
71. South Fork Big Wash					●
72. Lexington Arch		●			
SOUTHERN NEVADA					
73. Cathedral Gorge	●	●		●	
74. Mouses Tank		●			
75. White Domes	●			●	
76. Charleston Peak National Scenic Trail	●				
77. Joe May Canyon	●				●
78. Moenkopi Trail	●	●		●	
79. Calico Tanks	●	●	●		
80. Turtlehead Mountain	●				●
81. Keystone Thrust		●		●	
82. White Rock Hills		●		●	
83. White Rock Spring		●	●	●	
84. White Rock Spring to Willow Spring		●	●	●	

	BEST PHOTOS	FAMILY FRIENDLY	WATER FEATURES	DOG FRIENDLY	FINDING SOLITUDE
SOUTHERN NEVADA (CONTINUED)					
85. Lost Creek Loop		●		●	
86. Willow Spring Loop		●		●	
87. La Madre Spring					●
88. Top of the Escarpment	●				●
89. Bridge Mountain	●				●
90. Ice Box Canyon	●	●	●	●	
91. Pine Creek Canyon	●	●	●	●	
92. Oak Creek Canyon			●	●	
93. First Creek Canyon	●		●	●	
94. Spirit Peak	●				●

BEFORE YOU HIT THE TRAIL

The Silver State has a wild and diverse backcountry with a rich contrast between valley and mountain. Nevada offers not only desert salt flats shimmering in the sun but also cool mountain streams cascading down rocky slopes, shady redrock canyons, dramatic alpine peaks, young quaking aspen trees whispering in the wind, and gnarled ancient bristlecone pines silently enduring the millennia.

A Nevada hike can vary from an easy stroll on an interpretive nature trail to a strenuous multiday backpack trip. Hikes of both extremes as well as intermediate walks are represented here. This book is an invitation to escape from the human-made world and discover a world where nature still dominates and time runs on a far slower scale—a place where the foot traveler can feel at home.

HIKING IN NEVADA

This book contains a cross section of the hiking and backpacking available in Nevada. I've tried to include the widest possible variety of hiking, not only to benefit you, the reader, but also to publicize areas of the state in which hiking is threatened by noncompatible uses. Little-known and less-traveled hikes are represented, as well as more popular areas. Relevant natural and human history of the area is included with many of the hike descriptions. But no book can cover all the magnificent hiking to be found in Nevada, so you should regard this FalconGuide as a starting point for your own explorations of this varied and starkly beautiful region of the American West.

GEOLOGY AND GEOGRAPHY

Nearly all of Nevada lies within the portion of the American West known as the Great Basin: a vast area that also includes parts of California, Oregon, Idaho, Wyoming, and Utah. Within the Great Basin all mountain drainage flows into closed valleys, or basins, and none of the creeks, rivers, and intermittent streams reach the sea. More than 160 parallel mountain ranges, all trending north–south, drain into some ninety valleys. The majority of these isolated mountains are in Nevada. While a few valleys do contain lakes, most are floored with salt pans (also known as playas), created when streams from the mountains evaporate, leaving behind a crust of white minerals.

Elevation in Nevada ranges from just 300 feet to more than 13,000 feet above sea level. The average elevation is approximately 5,500 feet. The lowest valleys and mountains are in the southern and western part of the state, with elevations increasing toward the north and east. The Snake Range is the loftiest mountain range in the state, culminating in the 13,063-foot glacier-carved summit of Wheeler Peak. The title of highest summit,

More creek-sized than river-sized, the South Twin River brings the musical sound of a mountain stream to its canyon in the Toiyabe Range (Hike 36).

however, is reserved for 13,140-foot Boundary Peak, an outlying summit of the 14,000-foot White Mountains, most of which are in California.

Millions of years ago during the formation of the North American continent, the area that is now Nevada was stretched from east to west by crustal forces. Numerous north-tending fractures, or faults, formed as the rocks broke under the strain. Some of the resulting blocks sank to form the valleys, while others rose to form the mountains. As the faulting continues to lower the basins and raise the mountains, erosion, mainly from water, is wearing down the mountains and filling the valleys. The topography we see today reflects the fact that the faulting is still active enough to keep the mountains from being worn down to a flat plain.

More recently, as these events go, a colder and wetter climate caused snow to accumulate in the higher ranges and form glaciers. The last of these glacial periods ended about 10,000 years ago, but it left its mark on the topography in the form of steep, glacially carved mountain peaks and classic U-shaped mountain valleys. As the climate warmed and the glaciers receded, the massive flow of meltwater collected in huge lakes rivaling the Great Lakes in size. In many parts of Nevada, the ancient shorelines of these lakes are clearly visible as wave-cut terraces along the lower mountain slopes.

During the cooler glacial climate, extensive forests covered the valleys and bordered the lakes, and much of Nevada's landscape looked like the shores of present-day Lake Tahoe. As the last ice age gradually ended, the warming climate caused plants and animals to migrate up the mountainsides, following the upward movement of their preferred environment. Today, only the highest mountain elevations are forested, and the valleys are deserts.

NATURAL HISTORY

Most wet weather reaches Nevada from the west and northwest, in the form of Pacific winter storms. Much of the moisture from these storms falls on the high Sierra Nevada and Cascade Mountains before reaching Nevada. Because of orographic lifting, the moisture that is left tends to fall on the mountains rather than the valleys. Annual precipitation, mostly in the form of snow, varies from 5 inches in the driest valleys to 18 inches in the higher eastern Nevada ranges. Temperatures range from –40 to 115 degrees Fahrenheit. The valleys and lower mountain ranges are too hot for enjoyable hiking in the summer, and the highest ranges are too cold in the winter. The best hiking seasons are spring and fall, but there is plenty of high-elevation mountain country to explore during the summer. Winter is the season to hike the southern and western deserts.

This great variation of climate within the state makes life interesting for the native plants and animals as well. Most plants and many animals are adapted to a limited range of temperature and moisture, and so different communities are found at various elevations in the valleys and mountains.

Valleys in central and western Nevada feature tough desert shrubs: shadscale, bud sage, greasewood, and saltbush. Lower valleys in southern Nevada are covered with creosote bush, mesquite, and the striking Joshua tree, while the higher valleys are dominated by sagebrush. This shrub-grassland covers nine-tenths of the state. The most common animal is the jackrabbit, but coyotes, gophers, red foxes, and western badgers may also be found. Antelope and wild horses favor the open valleys, while mule deer range from desert to mountain depending on the season. Generally the reptiles prefer the deserts; these include rattlesnakes as well as a variety of nonpoisonous snakes, such as king snakes, along with numerous varieties of lizards.

You'll find forests along the crests of many of the mountain ranges, the mix of trees varying with elevation and location. Some of the valley animals can be found here as well, plus forest animals such as raccoons, porcupines, skunks, squirrels, and chipmunks. Along Nevada's western border the trees of the nearby Sierra Nevada dominate, with ponderosa, Jeffrey, and sugar pines constituting the forest from about 5,500 to 7,500 feet. Above, red fir, western white pine, and lodgepole pine become common up to about 9,000 feet. A subalpine forest of whitebark pine, lodgepole pine, and mountain hemlock continues to timberline at about 10,500 feet. Above this elevation is arctic tundra.

The central and southwestern ranges have the unique Great Basin forest zones, with dwarf piñon pines and juniper trees between about 7,500 and 8,500 feet. Above and extending to about 10,000 feet are mainly shrubs such as mountain mahogany and sagebrush. The subalpine forest reaches 11,500 feet and consists of limber pine and bristlecone pine. The gnarled, tough bristlecones are the oldest living trees on earth, reaching more than 4,000 years.

Eastern Nevada ranges have a Rocky Mountain forest sequence, with the lowest zone being piñon-juniper, topped by ponderosa pine, then Douglas fir and white fir. The subalpine forest consists of subalpine fir, Engelmann spruce, limber pine, and bristlecone pine. Elk and bighorn sheep generally prefer the rugged mountain slopes to the desert valleys.

Throughout the state, mountain streams are bordered by aspen, alder, chokecherry, cottonwood, water birch, and willow. These locations are favored by beavers as well as many bird species. Rainbow trout have been introduced to many streams throughout the state. Surprisingly, waterfowl are common along the desert lakes and marshes, and the rarity of desert water makes this habitat all the more precious.

HUMAN HISTORY

Numerous archaeological sites scattered across Nevada are critical to understanding the story of early humans in this state. These sites are protected by federal and state law—if they are disturbed, whether by construction, off-road vehicles, vandals and pot hunters, or well-meaning hikers, another piece of the story is gone forever.

It's generally believed that the first humans arrived in Nevada around 13,000 years ago, crossing from Siberia to Alaska via a land bridge exposed by the lower sea levels of the glacial period. New discoveries, however, suggest that humans may have arrived in North America much earlier. Whenever they appeared here, early people took advantage of the easy living provided by the great glacial lakes, catching fish as well as hunting the native American horse and camel. Others appeared to specialize in hunting mammoths. Most lived in caves or crude shelters, but toward the end of the prehistoric period, around

Phlox grows in a low mat above timberline.

AD 1000, a pueblo culture of well-organized communities developed. Some of these sites contained well over one hundred houses.

After about AD 1100 the more advanced communities were abandoned, for unknown reasons. Some of the people may have migrated elsewhere, and some probably became the ancestors of the tribes discovered by Europeans.

Four major Native American groups occupied Nevada, with the Southern Paiutes in southern Nevada probably being the first tribe encountered by Europeans. The North-ern Paiutes occupied the western third of the state; the Western Shoshones, the eastern half. A smaller group, the Washoes, ranged along the eastern Sierra Nevada.

By the time Europeans arrived in Nevada, the climate had become drier and warmer, which made it more difficult for the natives to wrest a living from the land. Most of the Native Americans were hunter-gatherers, migrating constantly to take advantage of the seasons. Recreation time was most likely limited to harvest gatherings or communal hunts.

Probably the first European to enter Nevada was Father Francisco Garces, part of a larger Spanish expedition seeking a more direct route from Santa Fe to Monterrey, California, in 1776. But the Great Basin was still unnamed and largely unexplored when competition between British and American fur trappers heated up in 1826. Jedediah Smith led an expedition across the southern tip of Nevada to California, then crossed the central part of the state from west to east. Another trapper, Peter S. Ogden, entered north-ern Nevada in 1828 and worked his way south and east to Utah. Further explorations

Colorful quaking aspen contrasting
with the gray-green sage slopes

by Ogden opened up a route along the Humboldt River across the northern third of Nevada, a route later used by wagon trains of immigrants headed for the Pacific coast.

The earliest immigrants were trespassing on Mexican soil, but by 1850 Nevada was part of the American territory of Utah. Discovery of gold in California caused the tiny trickle of immigrants to become a flood. Most of the parties used the Humboldt River route, still a major travel corridor used by I-80 and the Union Pacific Railroad to cross Nevada.

Inevitably, trading posts sprang up along the immigrant trails, while others stayed behind to try their hand at ranching and mining. By 1860, when Nevada became a territory, significant deposits of gold and silver had been discovered in the Virginia City area—the Comstock Lode. This caused rapid population growth, and Nevada became a state just 4 years later, in 1864. In comparison, neighboring Arizona Territory did not become a state until 1912.

Ranching has probably been the most stable element of Nevada's economy throughout the state's history, and it is a way of life that is cherished by many of the state's residents. Although there is no doubt that mineral exploration and extraction has contributed more to the state economy, the boom-and-bust cycle of mining has made life difficult for many Nevada communities over the decades.

Since the end of World War II, gambling, tourism, and retirement communities have supplanted mining as the major source of income. Las Vegas is now one of the fastest-growing cities in the nation, and many of the newcomers value Nevada's backcountry not for its minerals or rangeland, but for itself. Many Nevadans and Americans from other states see the undeveloped portions of Nevada as precious areas to be protected and enjoyed in their natural state. The creation of Great Basin National Park, Nevada's first national park, was initially opposed by locals but won support as it became obvious how much visiting tourists contribute to the state's economy.

HIKING TECHNIQUES AND ETHICS: LEAVE NOTHING BUT FOOTPRINTS

Although the Native Americans and the early explorers and settlers lived off the land out of necessity, the modern hiker and backpacker finds maximum freedom in being virtually independent of the land. Carrying food, shelter, and warmth in a reasonably light pack, the walker needs only water and a level place to sleep. This lightweight camping style means a camp can be established or broken in a matter of minutes rather than hours, leaving little trace of the hiker's presence. The ability to "leave nothing but footprints" could hardly have come at a better time. The shrinking American wilderness is under increasing pressure as a steadily growing population discovers the joy and serenity to be found in the outdoors. In the 19th century a small population of miners easily destroyed much of Nevada's mountain forests. Today those same mountains can provide recreation for a much larger population—*if* each person treats the countryside with respect.

While walking, stay on established human or animal trails if available, and avoid cutting switchbacks. Members of a large party traveling cross-country should spread out rather than creating a new trail by walking single-file. These practices minimize soil erosion. In the Great Basin the soil is often protected by a crusty surface composed of lichen and moss, which if undisturbed slows the processes of soil erosion.

Very few hikers deliberately litter, and much of what we see along the trail is accidental or the result of ignorance. Orange peels, for example, take a long time to decompose in the dry climate. Individual hikers can easily put an end to the litter problem by packing out a bit of someone else's litter at the end of each hike.

When making camp, look for sites that are "hard," such as sand, gravel, or hard dirt. With good sleeping pads, even solid rock slabs make comfortable campsites. Soft campsites, such as meadow grass or pine needles, recover slowly in this arid climate, and must be used with great care to avoid destroying the ground cover. Rather than constructing a level bed or tent site, look for a natural one. Avoid having to dig drainage ditches by choosing a slightly elevated or sloping site where rainwater will run away from your shelter. In heavily used areas, use an existing campsite rather than starting a new one. One of the major reasons people avoid used campsites is the litter and campfire rings left by old-style "heavy" campers. If time and load permit, clean up a messy campsite and leave a pleasant surprise for the next party. Ashes can be buried, blackened rocks scattered, and trash packed out if loads are light.

Although many hikers enjoy the freedom and relaxation of cooking meals on a backpacker's stove, for others a campfire is an essential part of the experience. In some situations campfires should not be built, such as in heavily used areas, near timberline where wood is scarce, and where prohibited by regulation. Never burn bristlecone pine or any other wood found near timberline—this wood may be thousands of years old, and even small pieces can yield climate data and other critical scientific information. In summer the fire danger may be extreme, and no fire should ever be built on a windy day. In places where it is reasonable to have a campfire, use an established campfire ring if at all possible. Otherwise look for a site in gravel, sand, or bare soil. Then dig a shallow pit, heaping the dirt around the edges to form a wind- and fire-break. Do not use stones, which become permanently blackened and may explode from the heat of the fire. Collect deadwood from the ground, or from the lower parts of trees by breaking it off by hand—never use an ax or a saw. Keep your fire small, both to avoid using large amounts of wood and to keep the amount of ashes small. Never burn trash in a fire; aluminum packaging does not burn at all, and even paper rarely burns completely. The usual result is a fire ring half full of trash, which the next camper avoids in favor of building yet another fire ring. There is no excuse for not carrying out your trash, whether day hiking, car camping, or backpacking. You carried it in—you can carry it out.

When you're ready to leave camp, make certain the fire is cold by mixing in water or dirt and stirring until there is no obvious smoke or heat. **Then check with your bare hand.** If you can't put your hand in the ashes, **your fire is NOT out**. Last, cover the fire pit with the dirt from the original pit, and scatter any remaining wood. After a short time, your fire site will again look natural.

If lightweight food is carried (modern supermarkets are full of convenient items that make ideal backpacking food) and carefully repacked to eliminate excess packaging, the trash resulting from even a week or more in the backcountry can easily be carried out.

Stunning sunsets and hundred-mile views are a common reward for hiking the ranges of Nevada.

Avoid burying food, because animals will find it by smell shortly after you leave, dig it up—and leave most of it uneaten.

Wilderness sanitation is a vital skill, yet few people know how to relieve themselves away from facilities. In some areas naturally occurring diseases such as giardiasis are being aggravated by poor human sanitation. Fortunately the rules are simple. If facilities are available, use them. Their presence means that the human population of the area is too large for the natural disposal systems of the soil. In the backcountry select a site at least 100 yards from intermittent streams, live streams, lakes, and springs, then dig a small cat-hole about 6 inches into the organic layer of the soil. Some people carry a small plastic trowel for this purpose. Avoid barren, sandy soil if possible. When finished, fill the hole, covering any toilet paper. Some areas require that all used toilet paper be packed out. Never burn toilet paper—many wildfires have been started by this practice.

OUR ARCHAEOLOGICAL AND HISTORICAL HERITAGE

In the backcountry you will encounter artifacts of various ages. Some of these structures, tools, and other artifacts date from before European discovery of the Americas. Others were built by early settlers and explorers. All are valuable links with our history and prehistory. Yet increasingly this evidence of early civilization is being destroyed by vandals. Federal and state laws have been passed to protect such antiquities, but ultimately the responsibility must lie with the users of the backcountry. Keep in mind that the

relationships among artifacts in a site are often more important than the artifacts them-selves. Petroglyphs and pictographs (rock drawings) have lasted thousands of years but are easily destroyed by thoughtless people.

MAKING IT A SAFE TRIP

Contrary to the impressions of city folk, wild country is not inherently dangerous. Nature is indifferent to hikers, in the sense that there are neither malevolent nor ben-eficial forces. We must be self-reliant, but there is no need to be paranoid. Once we develop confidence in our techniques, abilities, and equipment, then operating in the backcountry becomes a welcome relief from the complex tangle of civilized living. Wilderness decisions are usually important but also basic in nature. While out there, things that seemed important in civilization lose some of their urgency. In other words, we gain a sense of perspective.

Many wilderness accidents are caused by individuals or parties pushing too hard. Set reasonable goals, allowing for delays from weather, deteriorated trails, unexpectedly rough country, and dry springs. Travel at the rate of the slowest member of your party. Be flexible enough to eliminate part of a hike if it appears that your original plans are too ambitious.

A few plants are hazardous to the touch, such as poison ivy and stinging nettle. Spiny plants like cactus are easy to avoid. Never eat any plant, unless you know what you are doing. Many common plants, especially mushrooms, are deadly.

Animals will leave you alone unless molested or provoked. Never feed wild animals—they rapidly get used to the handouts and then will vigorously defend their new food source. Around camp, problems with rodents can be avoided by hanging your food from rocks or trees. Even the toughest pack can be wrecked by a determined mouse or squirrel that has all night in which to work. Heavily used campsites present the worst problems, but in Nevada there's not much reason to camp in heavily used areas!

Rattlesnakes cause concern but can easily be avoided. They usually warn off intruders by rattling well before you reach striking range. Since rattlesnakes can strike no farther than half their body length, avoid placing your hands and feet in areas you cannot see, and walk several feet away from rock overhangs and shady ledges. Snakes prefer surfaces at about 80 degrees Fahrenheit, so during hot weather they prefer the shade of bushes or rock over-hangs, while in cool weather they'll be found sunning themselves on open ground.

WATER

Water is the most important consideration in planning a desert hike. On day hikes make certain you carry enough. In hot weather, as much as 2 gallons per person per day may be required. On desert backpack trips, you must plan the route and itinerary around water sources. It is convenient but not always possible to be near a spring or stream for lunch stops and at camps. Collapsible water bottles of various sizes, as well as hydration systems, are available and make it possible to carry large amounts of water without filling up your pack with empty bottles. Collapsible containers allow you to carry water for a dry lunch

Storm over the Schell Creek Range

or even a dry camp. Dry-camping technique opens up almost an infinite number of pristine, beautiful campsites. However, plan to pass at least one reliable water source per day, unless the weather is cool and you are experienced in dry camping.

Springs and streams shown on maps are often unreliable. The best way to determine the reliability of desert water sources is through experience in the area, either yours or that of a trusted friend. Allowance must be made for springs and streams that may be dry—do not depend on any single water source. Be aware of reliable water sources that are off your route. Known water sources are listed in each hike description; there may be more, but I have attempted to err on the side of caution.

Very few backcountry water sources are safe to drink—and it's impossible to tell in the field. Contamination has resulted from wild and domestic animals as well as the increasing human population. Infections from contaminated water are uncomfortable and can be disabling. Giardiasis, a severe gastrointestinal infection, has been receiving more attention in recent years. The latest evidence, however, indicates that humans have probably shouldered more than our share of responsibility, as the cysts that cause giardiasis are spread by all mammals. Nevertheless, there is no doubt that poor backcountry sanitation has contributed to the problem.

Purify all backcountry water before drinking or cooking with it. Iodine water purification tablets, available from outdoor shops, are very effective, though some people don't like the taste. You can buy neutralizer tablets that remove the iodine taste after the iodine has had time to do its work. Read and carefully follow the directions on the bottle. Note that the tablets must be kept dry to retain their effectiveness. Also, iodine does not kill cryptosporidia. Newer halogen-based purifying agents are available that kill all known dangerous organisms, although they are expensive and time-consuming to use.

Water filters are popular because they remove the bacteria and contaminants that affect taste, but are slow, heavy, and don't remove viruses. A few filters are rated as purifiers; these usually have active elements that kill viruses.

The surest method of purifying water is to bring it to a rolling boil. Boiling kills all pathogens at any altitude, but uses time and fuel, and leaves you with a hot, flat-tasting drink. You can aerate the water to restore the taste and speed the cooling process by pouring it from pot to pot.

WEATHER

Nevada has an intermountain climate. The dry, clear air allows strong radiational cooling during the night so that temperatures often drop 50 degrees Fahrenheit by sunrise. Even the hottest areas generally have cool nights. Temperatures also drop about 5 degrees Fahrenheit for each 1,000-foot rise in elevation, so mountaintops are usually much cooler than lower slopes.

As mentioned earlier, Nevada receives most of its precipitation as snow, generally during the winter months. However, snow may fall at any time of year on the higher mountains. Be prepared by bringing more warm clothing than you think you will need. During the cooler season, consider synthetic garments made of polypropylene or polyester fibers. These fibers retain their insulating ability when wet better than any natural fiber, including wool. Avoid continuous exposure to chilling weather, which may subtly lower body temperature and cause sudden collapse from hypothermia, a life-threatening condition. Cool winds, especially with rain, are the most dangerous, because the heat loss is insidious. Hypothermia may be completely prevented by wearing enough clothing and wind protection to avoid chilling, and by eating and drinking regularly to keep the body fueled.

Spring, summer, and fall are generally dry, though summer thunderstorms may develop, especially in southern and eastern Nevada. Since much hiking is in the mountains, lightning can present a hazard. Less obvious are the hazards associated with sudden heavy rain, which include flash flooding and rapid temperature drops. Keep in mind that the mountains are eroded mostly during spring runoff and flash floods. Avoid camping in streambeds and dry washes.

In hot weather, water is vital. Ensure that you have a reliable supply, and drink enough to satisfy your thirst—and then some. Remember, if it gets too heavy in your pack, you can always drink it. Your body will use it efficiently.

Protection from the heat and the sun is important. Most people find a lightweight sun hat vital for desert hiking. During hot weather, plan hikes in the higher, cooler mountains instead of the low desert, or hike early in the day to avoid the afternoon heat. Summer backpack trips can be planned to take advantage of the long days by hiking from first light to midmorning, taking a long, shady lunch break, and then finishing the day's walk in early evening when it cools off. At dusk keep an eye out for rattlesnakes, which are active in the evening during hot weather.

HOW TO USE THIS GUIDE

Each hike in this book has a number and name. Some trails have more than one common name, and some hikes use more than one trail to complete a loop or otherwise create a more interesting route. Other hikes are cross-country, without a trail at all. In each case I've attempted to name the hike for the best-known trail or feature.

THE HIKES

Why Go?: This section briefly describes what makes this hike worth your time.

Start: This is the approximate distance to the nearest town or city, which is normally the starting point for the "Finding the trailhead" description.

Distance: This is the total distance of the hike. It includes the return mileage on an out-and-back or lollipop hike; for loop and shuttle hikes, it's a one-way distance. A lollipop is a hike with both an out-and-back section and a loop, and a shuttle (rare in this book) is a one-way hike that requires you to drive a vehicle to the final trailhead or make other arrangements to be picked up.

Hiking time: This is an average hiking time in hours for day hikes, and in days for backpack trips. It is based on the total distance, the elevation gain, the condition of the trail, and the difficulty of cross-country hiking, if any. Fit, fast hikers will be able to do the hikes in less time, while inexperienced or out-of-shape hikers may need considerably more.

Difficulty: All hikes are rated as easy, moderate, or strenuous. Although this is necessarily a highly subjective rating, nearly anyone who can walk should be able to do an easy hike, which can be completed in a few hours. Moderate hikes are longer—up to a full day—and may involve several hundred feet or more of elevation gain; cross-country hiking might be a factor as well. Experienced hikers will have no problems but beginners should hike with someone more experienced, and will have more fun if they are in reasonable shape. Strenuous hikes are very long, requiring a full day of hiking by fit hikers, or several days in the case of backpack trips. The hiking will probably involve cross-country or faint, rough trails that demand good map-and-compass skills, and rough terrain may require some rock scrambling. Only fit, experienced hikers should tackle these hikes.

Trail surface: Most Nevada trails are rocky, so you should expect that. Other trail surface conditions, if known, are described here, including hikes on old roads or paved trails, along with cross-country trekking.

Water: For backpackers, known water sources are described here. Most desert springs and creeks should be considered seasonal, and you should never depend on a single source of water. All water should be purified before being used to drink or cook. Day hikers should carry all the water they'll need.

Seasons: A general description of the best seasons for the hike, taking into account such things as winter weather and snow, as well as hot summer weather.

Other trail users: This is a list of the other trail users you might encounter, primarily equestrians and mountain bikers.

Canine compatibility: Many people like to hike with their furry friends, so this section mentions whether dogs are allowed, and restrictions, if any. All areas that are open to dogs require that they be under control, either by verbal command or on a leash. If your dog barks or runs up to other hikers, even in a friendly way, then it is not under control and must be kept on a leash. This is just common courtesy to other hikers, some of whom may have had bad experiences with dogs.

Land status: The agency managing the land, and the name of the management unit, if any.

Nearest town: This is the nearest town or city for resupply, lodging, restaurants, and other necessities. Keep in mind that many Nevada trailheads are extremely remote and there are no trailhead services or points of supply.

Fees and permits: This section describes and fees and permits that are required, as well as unusual rules and regulations.

USGS topo map: Here you'll find a list of the USGS 7.5-minute series topographic maps covering each hike (except for very short nature trails).

Other maps: This section includes specialized maps that may be useful, such as government national forest, wilderness, and privately produced maps.

Trail contacts: This section lists the contact information for the agency responsible for managing the land that the hike traverses. It's a good idea to call or e-mail the land management agency before your hike to check on road and trail conditions. Where possible, the contact information includes the mailing and street address, phone number, and website. E-mail addresses are not included because they often change; check the agency's website for an e-mail address, generally found under a "Contact" link. Sometimes online addresses change as well, but you can usually find land management units on the internet with a search engine.

Finding the trailhead: This description takes you from an obvious reference point that can be located on a standard highway map, usually the nearest town or city, to the trailhead. Mileages were measured using digital mapping software.

What to See: Here's the meat of the hike—a detailed description of the trail or route and the features and attractions along the way. I describe the route using landmarks as well as trail signs, when possible, because trail signs can be missing. And I sometimes leave out features of the hike, to preserve your sense of discovery and exploration. Whenever I can I add background on the natural and historical features of the hike. For even more of such information, you'll find a list of outdoor and conservation organizations, as well as relevant books, in the appendix.

Miles and Directions: This listing shows key points (such as trail intersections or turning points on a cross-country hike) by miles and tenths. You should be able to find the route with these details alone. (Note that simple hikes with few or no landmarks do not have a Miles and Directions section.) The mileages in this book do not necessarily agree with distances found on trail signs, agency mileages, and other descriptions, because trail miles are measured by a variety of methods and personnel. All mileages in this book were carefully measured using digital topographic mapping software for accuracy and consistency.

Options: If the hike has significant options, such as side hikes, shortcuts, or extensions, you'll find the description here. Minor side hikes are described in the main hike description or listed in the Miles and Directions.

FINDING AND USING MAPS

Most hikes in this book are accompanied by a map showing the access roads and the specific trail or route mentioned in the hike description. The maps in this book depict a detailed close-up of an area. These maps are intended as general guides. More detailed maps are listed in the maps category and are referred to in the description of each hike. They will be useful or even essential.

Topographic maps published by the US Geological Survey are usually the best for hiking. These maps are published in sheets, or quadrangles, covering relatively small areas, and are also available on smartphone and tablet apps, as well as trail GPS receivers. Topography is shown in detail by means of contour lines, as well as human-made features such as trails, roads, buildings, and so on. This information is very accurate at the date of publication, shown on the lower right corner of each map. Unfortunately the sheer number of maps (it takes several thousand to cover a single western state) makes updating a slow process, so often trail and road information is outdated. Many outdoor shops and some engineering and blueprint shops carry USGS maps. They are also available directly from the Geological Survey.

Other useful maps are published by the USDA Forest Service and the US Bureau of Land Management. These maps cover a larger area and are updated more often, though the topography is sometimes not shown. They are best used in conjunction with detailed topographic maps. These maps are usually available from the office listed under the heading in each hike description, from some outdoor shops, and from the regional or state offices of the land management agencies.

If you're using maps on your smartphone, tablet, or trail GPS receiver, I strongly recommend that you take a printed map as well. Electronic devices can always fail, and you will not be able to get maps on your phone or tablet in areas without cell phone coverage unless you download them in advance.

For more information, see "Maps and Mapping/GPS Apps" at the end of this book.

Looking east from the slopes of Paradise Peak

NORTHWESTERN NEVADA

THIS REGION CONSISTS OF THE PORTION OF NEVADA from approximately the town of Winnemucca north to the Oregon border and west to California. If Nevada is a sea of sage with mountains rising above like giant waves frozen in stone, then northwestern Nevada is a planet of sage. Sage covers the 4,000- to 5,000-foot valley floors and ranges to the top of the 9,000- to 10,000-foot mountain ranges. Relatively few trees break the sweep of sage from valley to summit. Here and there you'll find sparse stands of piñon pine and juniper, scraggly mountain mahogany, and patches of quaking aspen huddling in protected, lee slopes, but that's about all. The lone exception is the Pine Forest Range, a unique 9,000-foot range that harbors a relict Sierra Nevada forest, a survivor of the cooler and wetter climate of the last ice age when trees now found in California's Sierra Nevada ranged into the Nevada mountains.

1. DESERT TRAIL: HIGH ROCK CANYON SECTION

WHY GO?
A multiday backpack trip along a major section of the proposed National Scenic Desert Trail through the historic High Rock Canyon area.

THE RUNDOWN

Start: 53 miles southwest of Denio
Distance: 34.8-mile shuttle
Hiking time: 3 to 5 days
Difficulty: Strenuous
Trail surface: Cross-country hiking, two-track dirt roads
Water: Stevens Camp
Seasons: Spring and fall
Other trail users: Equestrians, motor vehicles
Canine compatibility: Dogs allowed under control
Land status: Bureau of Land Management
Nearest towns: Gerlach and Cedarville, CA

Fees and permits: None
USGS topo map: High Rock Lake, Mahogany Mtn, Yellow Hills East, Yellow Hills West, and Badger Mtn SE
Other maps: Desert Trail Association: *Desert Trail Guide,* High Rock Canyon Section
Trail contacts: Desert Trail Association, PO Box 34, Madras, OR 97741; no phone. Bureau of Land Management, Winnemucca District Office, 5100 West Winnemucca Blvd., Winnemucca, NV 89445; (775) 623-1500; www.blm.gov.

FINDING THE TRAILHEAD

From Denio Junction, the High Rock Lake (southern) trailhead can be reached by following NV 140 southwest 9 miles, then turning south onto graveled Road 34A (High Rock Lake Road). Continue about 30 miles through the Summit Lake Reservation. Continue another 14 miles south-southwest to High Rock Lake.
Trailhead GPS: N41 35.54 / W119 18.267

From Cedarville, California, the High Rock Lake (southern) trailhead can be reached by following CA 299 east-northeast for 10 miles to the Nevada border, then continuing on the graveled road for about 11 miles to Road 34. Follow the gravel road southeast about 43 miles to Road 34A (High Rock Lake Road). Turn northeast onto Road 34A and continue approximately 13 miles to High Rock Lake.

From Gerlach, the southern trailhead can be reached by following Road 34 north approximately 34 miles. This road is maintained. Exit Road 34 to the northeast onto Road 34A (High Rock Lake Road) and continue approximately 13 miles to High Rock Lake.

From Denio Junction, the Cottonwood Creek (northern) trailhead can be reached by following NV 140 west about 34 miles. Turn southwest onto the dirt road (not maintained) for about 5 miles, then turn south onto Road 8A. Continue on the dirt road about 8 miles to the Summit Lake sign and turnoff. Follow it southeast approximately 12 miles, then turn southwest at the fork in the road. Continue about 2 miles to Cottonwood Canyon on the southern boundary of the Sheldon National Wildlife Refuge.

From Cedarville, California, reach the Cottonwood Creek (northern) trailhead by following CA 299 east-northeast 10 miles to the Nevada border. Continue east on maintained Road 8A for 43 miles, then turn onto the dirt Summit Lake Road. Continue 12 miles, then turn southwest at the fork in the road and continue 2 miles to Cottonwood Canyon on the southern boundary of the Sheldon National Wildlife Refuge. **Trailhead GPS:** N41 18.126 / W119 17.396

WHAT TO SEE

The Desert Trail is not a constructed trail or clearly defined path. Usually it is a corridor without specific borders through which you may pass, choosing your own route. Avoid leaving a beaten path to minimize your impact on fragile soils and vegetation. The trail in High Rock Canyon follows a road, while the northern part of the trail follows both roads and Cottonwood Creek. You must have the USGS topographic maps and a compass to do this hike.

This description follows the Desert Trail south to north. From High Rock Lake, hike northwest on the road about a mile to a gate with a sign: "Black Rock Desert—High Rock Canyon Emigrant Trails National Conservation Area—High Rock Canyon." Proceed northwest up the canyon along the dirt road. After a short distance you enter the spectacular High Rock Canyon. About 4.5 miles from the entrance gate, Mahogany Canyon opens to the west. This canyon makes an interesting side hike. The main trail continues up High Rock Canyon. After about a mile, Pole Canyon opens to the north.

The great horned owl is a resident of this area. © ISTOCK.COM/KOJIHIRANO

Yellow Rock Canyon enters from the west 9.5 miles from the gate, offering another possible side hike. About 3 miles farther up High Rock Canyon, Grassy Canyon enters from the west, providing yet another side hike.

Continue up High Rock Canyon another 3 miles. Here the main trail follows a dirt road east out of High Rock Canyon. If desired, you can hike about 4 miles up High Rock Canyon to Stevens Camp, which has water. This side trip adds about 8 miles to the total hike.

Continuing on the main trail, hike east 2.5 miles on the dirt road to its end at Bernards Corrals. The trail enters the East Fork of High Rock Canyon Wilderness Area.

From Bernards Corrals, the route is mostly along Cottonwood Creek. If it is dry, it may be easier to hike in the sandy creekbed. About 2.5 miles from the Corrals, the creek turns generally northeast. Continue about 3 miles to the point where Cottonwood Creek turns north and joins a jeep road, skirting the east side of the Yellow Hills. Numerous other creekbeds join Cottonwood Creek, so it may be advisable to use a compass and the USGS topographic map along this section of the trail.

Hike north on the road for a little more than 2 miles, staying east of a knoll. Here you leave the road to rejoin Cottonwood Creek. Follow the creek northeast about 2 miles until you come to three forks of Cottonwood Creek. Now hike east about 0.25 mile to a dirt road. This is to avoid the private land in Shoestring Valley. It is a good idea to consult the USGS topographic map in this section. There should be a fork in the road near the point where you first reach it. Take the right fork northeast about 1.5 miles to another road, which runs east to west. Cross this road then, staying on the approximately 5,700-foot contour, and hike northwest about 0.5 mile to Wildcat Gorge. This is a spectacular gorge where a large cave offers shade. The cave is also an example of vandalism to an archaeological site.

The road parallels Wildcat Gorge, so you can avoid it if you prefer. The hiking distance is about the same.

Follow Wildcat Gorge northeast about 2.5 miles until you reach a road that heads north. Follow the road for about 4 miles as it turns northwest and rejoins Cottonwood Canyon at the southern boundary of the Sheldon National Wildlife Refuge. This is the northern trailhead. About a mile northwest of here, there is a spring where camping is allowed. This would be an excellent spot to end your hike.

High Rock Canyon was the route of the Applegate Trail, a major immigrant trail connecting California and Oregon with the eastern states. The route was discovered by an Oregon party led by Jesse and Lindsay Applegate in 1846. Their intent was to find an alternative to the already established Oregon Trail that would bypass both the dangerous Columbia River and threats from the British. Many people expected war to break out between the United States and Great Britain over the bitterly disputed Oregon Territory, and the American settlers were looking for a route not subject to control by the British Hudson's Bay Company forts along the Oregon Trail. The Applegate Trail was used sporadically at first due to Indian troubles, but by 1849 it was well established. It remained the main route into and out of southern Oregon throughout the 1860s, until modern roads and railroads appeared.

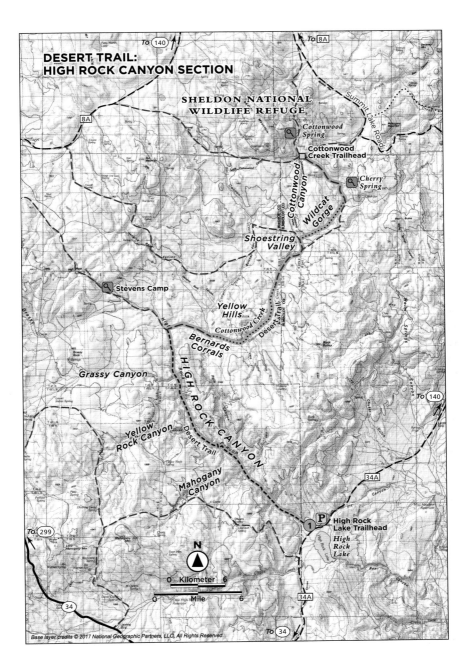

The sheer rock walls of High Rock Canyon—as high as 800 feet in places—comprise numerous volcanic lava flows, starting about 10 to 25 million years ago. More recent volcanic activity and the effects of erosion have carved the lava into awesome gorges. The upper layer of dark basaltic rocks is from the final lava flow. The underlying distinct red band is a layer of fine soil that was baked by the intense heat as the molten lava moved across the earth. Beige bands beneath the red zone are volcanic ash deposits.

High Rock Canyon has been protected from grazing since 1984 in order to protect one of the last major examples of a native desert ryegrass ecosystem. The Great Basin wild rye, tall sagebrush, and rice grass are prevalent. Willows are coming back along the riparian (streamside) zone, and erosion is decreasing.

Mule deer live in the canyons year-round, while antelope spend the winters on the neighboring tablelands and benches. Golden eagles, prairie falcons, diverse species of hawks, and great horned owls make their nests on the steep canyon walls. Because birds of prey are so sensitive to the presence of humans during the spring and summer nesting period, care must be taken to minimize disturbance of these majestic inhabitants. A raptor may leave its nest when humans are in the area, not returning until the visitor has left. A long absence from the nest could result in death for the eggs or newborn.

The Bureau of Land Management also manages the tablelands adjacent to the canyon to maintain about a hundred wild horses.

—Desert Trail Association

MILES AND DIRECTIONS

0.0 High Rock Lake trailhead.

4.9 Mahogany Canyon on left.

9.5 Yellow Rock Canyon on left.

12.4 Grassy Canyon on left.

15.2 Turn right (east) on road, leaving High Rock Canyon. (**Option:** Take side hike northwest 4.2 miles to Stevens Camp.)

17.9 Bernards Corrals; drop east into Cottonwood Creek and hike upstream (east).

22.6 Follow road right out of Cottonwood Creek, heading north.

24.1 Road rejoins Cottonwood Creek; continue north.

25.8 Leave Cottonwood Creek to east and hike to road junction.

26.1 Cross north–south road and head northeast on road.

26.6 Turn left (north) at junction. (**Option:** Stay right to avoid hike through Wildcat Gorge.)

27.2 Leave road to right and hike east down Wildcat Gorge.

31.0 Meet bypass road and head north, then northwest.

34.8 Cottonwood Creek trailhead.

2. DESERT TRAIL: SHELDON NATIONAL WILDLIFE REFUGE SECTION

WHY GO?

A multiday hike along the remote Desert Trail. Unlike other national trails, the Desert Trail is not a constructed or clearly defined path but rather a corridor through which you may pass, choosing your own specific route. Avoid leaving a beaten path by minimizing your impact on soils and vegetation. The trail follows roads and also goes cross-country. Stay on the described route to avoid private land. USGS topographic maps are essential.

THE RUNDOWN

Start: 10 miles west of Denio
Distance: 57.2-mile shuttle
Hiking time: 5 to 6 days
Difficulty: Strenuous
Trail surface: Cross-country
Water: None—water should be cached by vehicle in advance
Seasons: Spring and fall
Other trail users: Equestrians
Canine compatibility: Dogs must be on leashes in Sheldon National Wildlife Refuge.
Land status: Sheldon National Wildlife Refuge, Bureau of Land Management
Nearest town: Denio
Fees and permits: A permit is required for backpacking.
USGS topo map: Badger Mtn SE, Denio, Bog Hot Spring, Alder Creek Ranch, McGee Mtn, Virgin Valley, Rock Spring Table, and Van Horn Basin
Other maps: Desert Trail Association: *Desert Trail Guide,* Sheldon National Wildlife Refuge Section
Trail contacts: Desert Trail Association, PO Box 34, Madras, OR 97741; no phone. Bureau of Land Management, Winnemucca District Office, 5100 West Winnemucca Blvd., Winnemucca, NV 89445; (775) 623-1500; www.blm.gov. US Fish and Wildlife Service, Sheldon-Hart Mountain Refuge Complex, PO Box 111, 20995 Rabbit Hill Rd., Lakeview, OR 97630; (541) 947-3315; www.fws .gov/refuge/Hart_Mountain/About _the_Complex.html.

FINDING THE TRAILHEAD

From Denio Junction, the Cottonwood Creek (southern) trailhead can be reached by following NV 140 west about 34 miles. Turn southwest onto the dirt road (not maintained) for about 5 miles, then turn south onto Road 8A. Continue on the dirt road about 8 miles to the Summit Lake sign and turnoff. Follow it southeast approximately 12 miles, then turn southwest at the fork in the road. Continue about 2 miles to Cottonwood Canyon on the southern boundary of the Sheldon National Wildlife Refuge.

From Cedarville, California, reach the Cottonwood Creek (southern) trailhead by following CA 299 east-northeast 10 miles to the Nevada border. Continue east on maintained Road 8A for approximately 43 miles, then turn onto the dirt Summit Lake Road. Continue 12 miles, then turn southwest at the fork in the road and continue 2 miles to Cottonwood Canyon on the southern boundary of the Sheldon National Wildlife Refuge. **Trailhead GPS:** N41 35.54 / W119 18.267

From Denio Junction, the Denio Basin (northern) trailhead can be reached by following NV 140 west 3 miles, then turning sharply northeast on a graveled road. Turn again, almost immediately, to the northwest on a dirt road. If the ground is wet, this road requires a four-wheel-drive vehicle. Continue about 7 miles north toward Denio Basin to the trailhead.

From Lakeview, Oregon, reach the Denio Basin (northern) trailhead by driving 5 miles north, then turning east onto OR 140. Continue eastward for approximately 93 miles. About 3 miles west-southwest of Denio Junction, turn sharply northeast on a graveled road. Turn again, almost immediately, to the northwest on a dirt road. If the ground is wet, this road requires a four-wheel-drive vehicle. Continue about 7 miles north toward Denio Basin to the trailhead. **Trailhead GPS:** Coordinates not available.

WHAT TO SEE

This description follows the Desert Trail from south to north. The trail begins at the southern boundary of the Sheldon National Wildlife Refuge near Cottonwood Canyon. You may wish to camp and begin your hike about 1.5 miles to the north at Cottonwood Spring or at one of the two camping areas about 0.2 mile north of the boundary fence. You must have the USGS topographic maps and a compass to do this hike.

From the refuge boundary, hike 0.25 mile north and follow the dirt road northeast and east about 2 miles to Bateman Spring. Continue past Bateman Spring on the road for less than a mile, then leave the road and choose your route up to the saddle north of Mahogany Mountain. Continue northeast, then east, and choose the safest route down from the saddle—about 2 miles. Hike east, staying between the steep walls of the canyon, and continue on toward Alkali Flat.

You may want to take the extended trail and camp at Perry Spring. If so, hike southeast about 1 mile along the jeep road to Perry Spring.

Return to the trail across Alkali Flat, hike east, and carefully work your way up onto Wild Horse Pasture, where you will join a jeep trail for about 1 mile. Leave the jeep trail and hike northeast up the slope to Rock Spring Table. Continue northeast across the relatively flat terrain for approximately 3 miles and descend to East Rock Spring Campground.

Leave the campground and hike northeast on the road for about 11 miles. Stay on the road in a northerly direction for another 8 miles to Virgin Valley Campground. Leave the campground and hike northeast along the rim overlooking the spectacular Virgin Creek and Thousand Creek Gorge.

From the rim overlooking Thousand Creek Gorge, descend to the east–northeast and hike about 3 miles to NV 140. Cross the highway and numerous creekbeds, usually dry, then climb up the talus slope of Railroad Point. Watch for snakes and loose boulders. The

The escarpment at Thousand Creek Gorge, Desert Trail

view from the top is well worth the short climb. Hike north–northeast along the flat terrain and choose a safe place to descend near Black Ridge.

Hike northeast approximately 6 miles to the eastern boundary of Sheldon National Wildlife Refuge. The remainder of the hike is on Bureau of Land Management land. Continue northeast for about 0.5 mile until you join a road. Hike north–northeast on the road for 3 to 4 miles to Mustang Spring and a water tank. Leave the road and hike about 1.25 miles northeast. You are now in Oregon.

Hike north about 0.4 mile, then east and northeast around the shoulder of the ridge until you join a jeep road. Follow the road northwest for about 2 miles to the trailhead at Denio Basin.

Sheldon National Wildlife Refuge was set aside in 1931 for the conservation of the American pronghorn antelope. It is currently managed by the US Fish and Wildlife Service as a representative area of high-desert habitat for optimum populations of all native plants and wildlife. The name of the refuge honors Charles Sheldon, who developed the wildlife refuge concept, with others, early in the 20th century.

Vegetation and habitat types include big and low sagebrush areas, and mountain mahogany and bitterbrush in the mountains above 6,000 feet. Other important habitat types include alkaline lakes, marshes, grassy spring-fed meadows, greasewood flats, juniper-covered uplands, and aspen stands in the more secluded canyons.

Bird populations vary greatly in numbers and species according to seasons. Heavy migrations of waterfowl and waterbirds visit the Sheldon Refuge during the spring and fall, with some remaining through the breeding season. During the summer months a wide variety of smaller birds and birds of prey are present. The spring-fed riparian areas

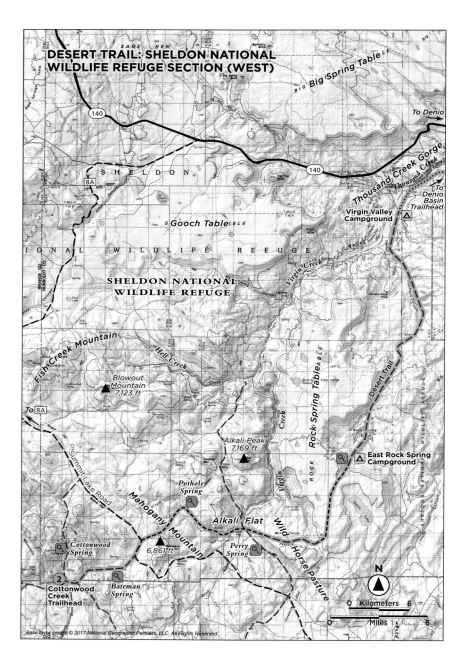

DESERT TRAIL: SHELDON NATIONAL
WILDLIFE REFUGE SECTION (WEST)

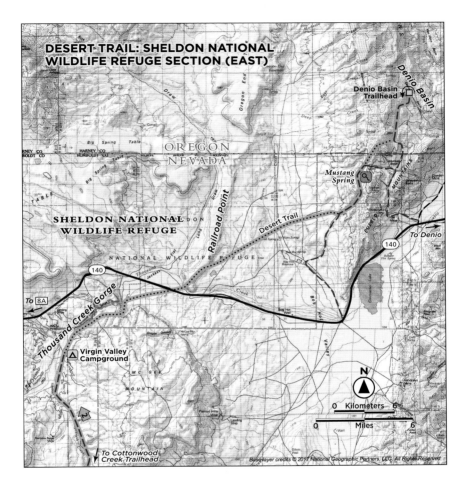

and the rock cliffs attract the summer bird populations. May to October are the best months to observe the greatest variety of birdlife on the refuge. While hiking, you may see the bald eagle or the peregrine falcon, both endangered species.

Big Springs Table, a short distance north and west of the Desert Trail, provides a wintering area for up to 3,500 pronghorn antelope, which migrate to the area from as far away as Hart Mountain National Antelope Refuge, 40 miles to the north.

—Desert Trail Association

Sagebrush covers much of the valleys and mountains.
© ISTOCK.COM/FTLAUDGIRL

MILES AND DIRECTIONS

0.0 Cottonwood Creek (southern) trailhead.

2.8 Bateman Spring; follow road northeast.

4.5 Leave road and hike east-northeast to saddle on Mahogany Mountain.

5.6 Saddle on Mahogany Mountain; descend northeast toward Pothole Spring, then turn southeast along Virgin Creek toward Alkali Flat.

10.7 Alkali Flat (*Option:* Take side hike 2.4 miles southeast to Perry Spring); climb east to rim of Wild Horse Pasture.

12.2 Join jeep trail on Wild Horse Pasture and follow it southeast.

14.5 Leave jeep trail and hike northeast onto Rock Spring Table.

15.1 Turn north and follow Sagebrush Creek, then descend to East Rock Spring Campground.

18.8 East Rock Spring Campground; hike northeast and north on the road along Sagebrush Creek.

33.6 Virgin Valley Campground; follow road north-northeast to mouth of Thousand Creek Gorge, then climb to south rim of gorge and follow it east.

37.2 Heading northeast, descend the escarpment at the mouth of Thousand Creek Gorge, then continue northeast—crossing NV 140—to Railroad Point.

40.8 Climb Railroad Point and hike northeast to Black Ridge, then descend east slopes and hike northeast.

49.5 Join jeep trail in western foothills of Pueblo Mountains and follow it north.

57.2 Denio Basin (north) trailhead.

3. BLUE LAKES

WHY GO?

This is a lovely day hike to a unique series of small glacial lakes.

THE RUNDOWN

Start: 67 miles north of Winnemucca
Distance: 1.4-mile out and back
Hiking time: About 2 hours
Difficulty: Easy
Trail surface: Old road
Water: Blue Lakes
Seasons: Summer through fall
Other trail users: Equestrians
Canine compatibility: Dogs allowed under control

Land status: Bureau of Land Management
Nearest town: Winnemucca
Fees and permits: None
USGS topo map: Duffer Peak
Trail contacts: Bureau of Land Management, Winnemucca District Office, 5100 West Winnemucca Blvd., Winnemucca, NV 89445; (775) 623-1500; www.blm.gov

FINDING THE TRAILHEAD

From Winnemucca, drive 30 miles north on US 95, and then 65.5 miles northwest on NV 140. At Denio Junction, turn right to stay on NV 140 and drive 10.1 miles. Turn left onto a maintained dirt road signed "Knott Creek." Drive south and southwest 9.5 miles, and then turn left onto an unsigned, maintained dirt road. Follow this road 8.7 miles to Onion Valley Reservoir and a junction. Turn left and drive 0.9 mile to a junction signed "Blue Lakes." Turn right and drive 1.6 miles to the end of the road to reach the Blue Lakes trailhead. **Trailhead GPS:** N41 41.241 / W118 43.279

WHAT TO SEE

The trail winds through groves of aspen and around a terminal moraine left by the ancient glacier and proceeds to Blue Lakes, a series of clear, cold lakes set in a mountain cirque. Fed by a spring and by snowmelt, the five interconnected lakes are surrounded by a mixture of willow, aspen, pine, and mountain mahogany. A spur of Duffer Peak forms part of the scenic backdrop. The view from the trail yields vast panoramas that extend into California and Oregon. The lakes support a cold-water fishery for trout.

Glacial moraines are distinguished from ordinary talus by the fact that they are composed of unsorted material. Glaciers collect massive amounts of rock and dirt as they slowly move down the mountain valleys, gouging their beds like giant bulldozers. Even more debris falls on the glacier from above. As the ice reaches lower elevations, it melts and drops its load of dirt, pebbles, rocks, and boulders in a jumbled, unsorted heap. This feature is clearly visible in the Blue Lakes moraines. In contrast, talus slopes form when rocks weather and fall from cliffs. Larger rocks roll farther before stopping, while small

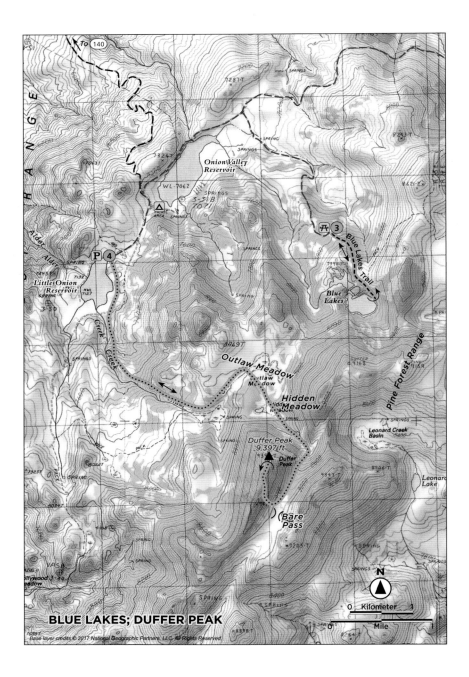

To 140

Onion Valley Reservoir

Alder Creek

Little Onion Reservoir

Blue Lakes Trail

Blue Lakes

Outlaw Meadow

Hidden Meadow

Pine Forest Range

Leonard Creek Basin

Duffer Peak 9,397 ft

Duffer Peak

Leonard Range

Leonard Lake

Bare Pass

N

0 Kilometer 1

0 Mile 1

BLUE LAKES; DUFFER PEAK

Base layer credits © 2017 National Geographic Partners, LLC. All Rights Reserved.

Blue Lakes,
Pine Forest Range

stones and pebbles tend to come to rest near the top of the slope. Likewise, rocks, sand, and silt carried by water in streams, rivers, and floods tend to be sorted by size as they are deposited, since the carrying power of moving water decreases rapidly as the speed of the water decreases.

—Bureau of Land Management and Bruce Grubbs

4. DUFFER PEAK

WHY GO?

Enjoy this cross-country day hike to the highest peak in the Pine Forest Range.

THE RUNDOWN

See map on page 30
Start: 68 miles north of Winnemucca
Distance: 7.6-mile out and back
Hiking time: About 5 hours
Difficulty: Moderate
Trail surface: Cross-country
Water: Alder Creek
Seasons: Summer through fall
Other trail users: None
Canine compatibility: Dogs allowed under control

Land status: Bureau of Land Management
Nearest town: Winnemucca
Fees and permits: None
USGS topo map: Duffer Peak and Knott Creek
Trail contacts: Bureau of Land Management, Winnemucca District Office, 5100 West Winnemucca Blvd., Winnemucca, NV 89445; (775) 623-1500; www.blm.gov

FINDING THE TRAILHEAD

From Winnemucca, drive 30 miles north on US 95, and then 65.5 miles northwest on NV 140. At Denio Junction, turn left to stay on NV 140 and drive 10.1 miles. Turn left onto a maintained dirt road signed "Knott Creek." Drive south and southwest 9.5 miles, and then turn left onto an unsigned, maintained dirt road. Follow this road 8.7 miles to Onion Valley Reservoir and a junction. Turn right and drive 0.7 mile, over a low pass, to the northeast side of Little Onion Reservoir and park. **Trailhead GPS:** N41 41.138 / W118 45.102

WHAT TO SEE

The cross-country route goes through an aspen grove, skirting the east edge of Little Onion Reservoir, then follows the steep drainage of Alder Creek southeast to Outlaw Meadow. Stay on the left (north) side of this series of spacious alpine meadows past a small swampy lake, then cross the creek and head for the foot of the steep north ridge of Duffer Peak, 0.5 mile south. Pass the small but scenic Hidden Meadow and continue southeast up the steep drainage northeast of the peak. As the drainage opens out into the level expanse of Bare Pass, turn right (west) and climb the steep slopes about 0.3 mile to the rugged granite ridge that forms the crown of the Pine Forest Range. Once on the ridge, turn north and follow it to the summit.

From the summit, much of the forest for which the Pine Forest Range is named is visible. Whitebark and limber pine, along with quaking aspen, are rare in northwestern Nevada, but they are abundant in this relict forest. During wetter and cooler times, when

Onion Reservoir, below Duffer Peak, Pine Forest Range

glaciers were present in a few Nevada mountains and the valleys below were covered by vast lakes, trees such as these extended over a much larger area. As the climate warmed and dried, the trees and the animals that depend on them were forced higher into the mountains. In most of northwestern Nevada, the pine forests simply disappeared, leaving only this tiny remnant.

Wildlife is relatively common because of the favorable habitat. Often seen are deer, coyote, chukar, and sage grouse, as well as waterfowl near the lakes and reservoirs. Pronghorn, bighorn sheep, bobcat, mountain lion, beaver, badger, and golden eagle are harder to spot. Also watch for birds such as the pine grosbeak and red crossbill not usually seen in this part of Nevada.

MILES AND DIRECTIONS

0.0 Little Onion Reservoir; walk east shore, then head south up Alder Creek.

1.9 Outlaw Meadow; head south.

2.4 Hidden Meadow; continue south toward east side of Duffer Peak.

3.1 Bare Pass; climb east slope of Duffer Peak.

3.8 Duffer Peak.

7.6 Return to Little Onion Reservoir.

5. BUCKSKIN MOUNTAIN

WHY GO?

This is a great day hike to a colorful peak, with excellent views of the wild and rugged northern portion of the Santa Rosa Range.

THE RUNDOWN

Start: 26 miles northeast of Orovada
Distance: 5.2-mile out and back
Hiking time: About 4 hours
Difficulty: Moderate
Trail surface: Two-track roads
Water: None
Seasons: Summer through fall
Other trail users: Vehicles, mountain bikes
Canine compatibility: Dogs allowed under control
Land status: Humboldt-Toiyabe National Forest

Nearest town: Orovada
Fees and permits: None
USGS topo map: Buckskin Mtn
Other maps: Forest Service: Humboldt-Toiyabe National Forest, Santa Rosa Ranger District
Trail contacts: Humboldt-Toiyabe National Forest, Santa Rosa Ranger District, 1200 East Winnemucca Blvd., Winnemucca, NV 89445; (775) 623-5025

FINDING THE TRAILHEAD

From Orovada, drive 14 miles north on US 95, then turn right onto FR 084 (signed "Buckskin Canyon"). Follow the graveled dirt road east approximately 12 miles through a major wildfire burn that occurred in 1992 to Windy Gap, the pass on the crest of the Santa Rosa Range. Buckskin Mountain is the striking peak north of the road, visible from the dramatic switchbacks leading to Windy Gap. Turn north onto an unmaintained road and park. **Trailhead GPS:** N41 46.006 W117 32.825

Buckskin Mountain,
Santa Rosa Range

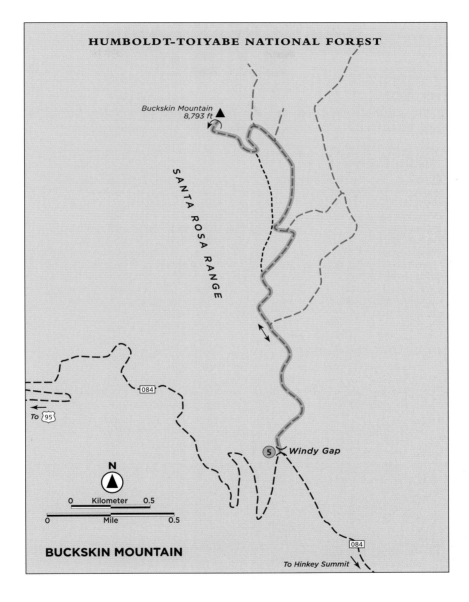

HUMBOLDT-TOIYABE NATIONAL FOREST

Buckskin Mountain
8,793 ft

SANTA ROSA RANGE

084

To 95

N

0   Kilometer   0.5
0   Mile   0.5

5   Windy Gap

BUCKSKIN MOUNTAIN

084

To Hinkey Summit

WHAT TO SEE

This is a moderate but very scenic hike along the seldom-traveled road to the summit. Stay left at the junctions. An easy alternative is to follow the main ridge crest cross-country. Large mammals that may be observed in this area are California bighorn sheep and mule deer.

6. LYE CREEK BASIN

WHY GO?

A cross-country day hike in the Granite Peak area of the Santa Rosa Range to an alpine basin with limber pine and quaking aspen.

THE RUNDOWN

Start: 14 miles north of Paradise Valley
Distance: 2.6-mile out and back
Hiking time: About 3 hours
Difficulty: Easy
Trail surface: Old road
Water: None
Seasons: Summer through fall
Other trail users: Equestrians, mountain bikes
Canine compatibility: Dogs allowed under control

Land status: Humboldt-Toiyabe National Forest
Nearest town: Paradise Valley
Fees and permits: None
USGS topo map: Hinkey Summit
Other maps: Forest Service: Humboldt-Toiyabe National Forest
Trail contacts: Humboldt-Toiyabe National Forest, Santa Rosa Ranger District, 1200 East Winnemucca Blvd., Winnemucca, NV 89445; (775) 623-5025

FINDING THE TRAILHEAD

From Paradise Valley, drive north on paved FR 792. After 4 miles, the pavement ends; continue straight ahead on the dirt road (FR 084) another 12 miles to Hinkey Summit, the pass at the head of Indian Creek. Continue north then turn left onto FR 087 to Lye Creek Campground. **Trailhead GPS:** N41 41.115 / W117 33.641

Lye Creek Basin, Santa Rosa Range

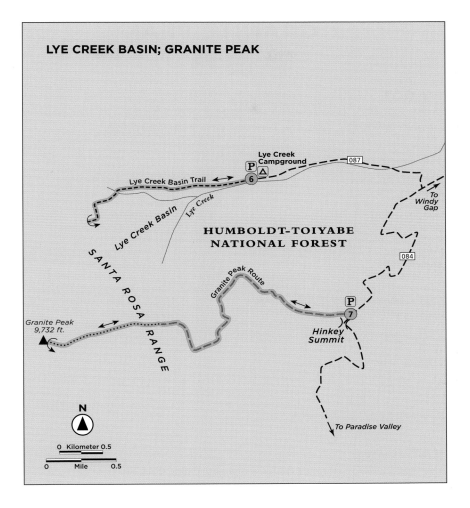

LYE CREEK BASIN; GRANITE PEAK

Lye Creek Campground

Lye Creek Basin Trail

087

To Windy Gap

084

Lye Creek Basin

Lye Creek

HUMBOLDT-TOIYABE NATIONAL FOREST

Granite Peak Route

S A N T A   R O S A   R A N G E

Granite Peak 9,732 ft.

Hinkey Summit

To Paradise Valley

N

0   Kilometer   0.5

0   Mile   0.5

WHAT TO SEE

Walk up the jeep road west of Lye Creek into the aspen-filled basin of Lye Creek. Snowbanks continue to melt into the hot days of late August, nurturing the last flowers of summer. Cross-country hiking on game trails will bring you to small wet meadows, jumbled granite boulders, and finally a magnificent limber pine.

During the short, crisp days of fall, brilliant red, orange, gold, and yellow aspen leaves drift silently to the ground. It is at this time of year that mule deer bucks come out of their hiding places and can be seen with a watchful eye. Soon winter snows will put the land to sleep and you will have to wait for a new spring to awaken the buttercups and shooting stars.

—USDA Forest Service

7. GRANITE PEAK

WHY GO?

A cross-country day hike to a rugged granite peak in the southern Santa Rosa Range, and the highest point in the range.

THE RUNDOWN

See map on page 37
Start: 13 miles north of Paradise Valley
Distance: 5.8-mile out and back
Hiking time: About 5 hours
Difficulty: Moderate
Trail surface: Old road, cross-country
Water: None
Seasons: Summer through fall
Other trail users: None
Canine compatibility: Dogs allowed under control

Land status: Humboldt-Toiyabe National Forest
Nearest town: Paradise Valley
Fees and permits: None
USGS topo map: Hinkey Summit
Other maps: Forest Service: Humboldt-Toiyabe National Forest, Santa Rosa Ranger District
Trail contacts: Humboldt-Toiyabe National Forest, Santa Rosa Ranger District, 1200 East Winnemucca Blvd., Winnemucca, NV 89445; (775) 623-5025

FINDING THE TRAILHEAD

From Paradise Valley, drive north on paved Hinkey Summit Road. After 4 miles, the pavement ends; continue straight ahead on the dirt road (FR 084) another 12 miles to Hinkey Summit, the pass at the head of Indian Creek. **Trailhead GPS:** N41 40.229 / W117 32.831

WHAT TO SEE

Granite Peak is visible to the west from the trailhead. Follow a seldom-used dirt road toward the summit, climbing gradually, and passing through several meadows and stands of aspen.

The road ends in a broad sage saddle at a fence line. Follow the fence left (west) over a rocky section, then continue up a steep slope with excellent views of Lye Creek Basin to the north. As the slope moderates, the summit again becomes visible. Contour around the head of a steep gully to reach the broad sage saddle below the summit. Now scramble up and left to the summit.

From this airy peak, you are likely to see a golden eagle soaring on thermals as it hunts for prey. Below you in the aspen, northern goshawks and Cooper's hawks defend nesting territories. Rarely, you may see tufts of grass drying on the rocky talus slopes, left there by the elusive pika while laying in its winter food supply. Look sharp when the pika gives its short, shrill warning whistle and you may see one of the small rodents ducking out of sight in the rocks.

Granite Peak, Santa Rosa Range

Even on a hot summer day, the thin mountain air is chilly. While enjoying a warm granite seat, check out the views. To the northwest, the faulted eastern face of Steens Mountain rises above the Alvord Desert in Oregon. Southeast, the Ruby Mountains still hold patches of last winter's snow. Lofty Mount Tobin is due south, and, to the west, the rugged Jackson Mountains. Humanity and its works seem to fade to insignificance in the face of such vastness.

—Bruce Grubbs and USDA Forest Service

Sage below Granite Peak,
Santa Rosa Range

MILES AND DIRECTIONS

0.0 Hinkey Summit; follow jeep road west.

2.1 End of jeep road; climb peak via east ridge then southeast face.

2.9 Granite Peak.

5.8 Return to Hinkey Summit.

8. REBEL CREEK TRAIL

WHY GO?

A day hike in the Santa Rosa Range featuring access to Santa Rosa–Paradise Peak Wilderness, with granite basin-and-range topography and aspen groves.

THE RUNDOWN

Start: 3 miles north of Orovada
Distance: 10.8-mile out and back
Hiking time: About 6 hours
Difficulty: Strenuous
Trail surface: Dirt and rocks
Water: Rebel Creek is not recommended for drinking.
Seasons: Summer through fall
Other trail users: Equestrians
Canine compatibility: Dogs allowed under control
Land status: Humboldt-Toiyabe National Forest

Nearest town: Orovada
Fees and permits: None
USGS topo map: Santa Rosa Peak
Other maps: Forest Service: Humboldt-Toiyabe National Forest, Santa Rosa Ranger District
Trail contacts: Humboldt-Toiyabe National Forest, Santa Rosa Ranger District, 1200 East Winnemucca Blvd., Winnemucca, NV 89445; (775) 623-5025

FINDING THE TRAILHEAD

Drive 3 miles north of Orovada on US 95, and turn right onto Rebel Creek Road. Continue 3 miles east on the dirt road, bypassing the ranch to the right (south). The road ends at the mouth of the canyon. **Trailhead GPS:** N41 36.458 / W117 45.065

WHAT TO SEE

Note: There may be issues with access across private land for this hike. Check with the US Forest Service before planning a hike in this area.

The foot trail is maintained and stays on the north side of the creek. After a stiff climb, the trail crosses the creek and then fades out in an aspen grove well below the main crest. It is possible to continue cross-country through the sage and aspen to the crest of the Santa Rosa Range.

Cheatgrass, an introduced annual, and native grasses along with sagebrush cover the lower drainage. Willows and cottonwoods shade the stream, which supports brook and rainbow trout. Chukar are common game birds found in this environment. In the spring buttercups, bluebells, and yellow bells bloom first, followed by lupines, skyrockets, and sunflowers, which bloom until late July. Rattlesnakes can be found in this warmer climate also.

Santa Rosa Range
ZACK SHEPPARD,
WIKIMEDIA COMMONS

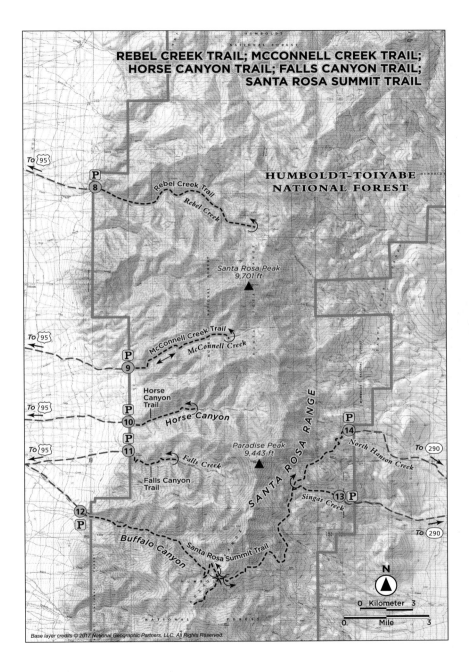

REBEL CREEK TRAIL; McCONNELL CREEK TRAIL;
HORSE CANYON TRAIL; FALLS CANYON TRAIL;
SANTA ROSA SUMMIT TRAIL

HUMBOLDT-TOIYABE
NATIONAL FOREST

Rebel Creek Trail

Rebel Creek

Santa Rosa Peak
9,701 ft

McConnell Creek Trail

McConnell Creek

Horse
Canyon
Trail

Horse Canyon

Paradise Peak
9,443 ft

SANTA ROSA RANGE

North Hanson Creek

Falls Creek

Falls Canyon
Trail

Singas Creek

Buffalo Canyon

Santa Rosa Summit Trail

To 95

To 95

To 95

To 95

To 290

To 290

N

Kilometer

Mile

Base layer credits © 2017 National Geographic Partners, LLC. All Rights Reserved.

Chukar is a common bird in the area.
© ISTOCK.COM/HSTIVER

In the higher country mountain mahogany, aspen, serviceberry, and snowberry are common. Yellow violet, monkshood, and red columbine are found in the shade of aspen groves. Mountain and western bluebirds can be seen along with many raptors. Mule deer make their summer home in the high basins and draws.

The geology changes from phyllite to granite as you move to the high country. Phyllite is a fine-grained, greenish gray metamorphic rock similiar to slate but often having a wavy surface and a luster due to small flecks of embedded mica. Granite, in contrast, is a light-colored metamorphic rock with a coarse, granular structure. Santa Rosa Peak at 9,701 feet is the dominant feature of the basin. The nearly vertical rim is crescent shaped with windswept limber pine growing at the tree line. This peak lends its name to the nearby Santa Rosa–Paradise Peak Wilderness.

In the Rebel Creek drainage, the effects of heavy use by domestic stock, mainly cattle, are evident. At best the sage rangeland can support only small numbers of cattle, and the animals naturally congregate near water sources. They form strong competition for grazing wildlife.

—USDA Forest Service and Bruce Grubbs

MILES AND DIRECTIONS

0.0   Rebel Creek trailhead.

3.3   Trail crosses creek.

5.4   Aspen grove.

10.8   Return to Rebel Creek trailhead.

9. MCCONNELL CREEK TRAIL

WHY GO?

A short day hike in the Santa Rosa Range featuring access to Santa Rosa–Paradise Peak Wilderness and granite-phyllite geology, with open views of Santa Rosa Peak.

THE RUNDOWN

See map on page 43
Start: 40 miles north of Winnemucca
Distance: 6.2-mile out and back
Hiking time: About 4 hours
Difficulty: Strenuous
Trail surface: Dirt and rocks
Water: None
Seasons: Summer through fall
Other trail users: Equestrians
Canine compatibility: Dogs allowed under control
Land status: Humboldt-Toiyabe National Forest

Nearest town: Winnemucca
Fees and permits: None
USGS topo map: Santa Rosa Peak
Other maps: Forest Service: Humboldt-Toiyabe National Forest, Santa Rosa Ranger District
Trail contacts: Humboldt-Toiyabe National Forest, Santa Rosa Ranger District, 1200 East Winnemucca Blvd., Winnemucca, NV 89445; (775) 623-5025

FINDING THE TRAILHEAD

Drive 40 miles north of Winnemucca on US 95, and turn right onto McConnell Creek Road. Continue 3 miles east of the highway. The trailhead is 100 yards inside the Forest Service boundary fence on the northeast side of the creek.
Trailhead GPS: N41 32.159 / W117 43.864

WHAT TO SEE

Minimal trail maintenance is done at the beginning of the season. The upper basin is wide with a view of Santa Rosa Peak, the striking granite peak that dominates the southern part of the range.

Phyllite outcrops and grassy hillsides greet you in the lower portion of the drainage. Access to the creek is difficult due to a deeply cut channel, but brook trout can be caught if you're persistent. A sharp eye might catch a glimpse of the California bighorn sheep that inhabit the area to the north. The lack of trees gives an open feeling to the lower canyon.

The geology changes midway up the canyon to granite ridges and soil made up of decomposed granite. Golden eagles soar on the air currents, and small lizards watch from their sunny perches on the rocks. Aspen, mountain mahogany, and snowberry begin to fill the draws and slopes. Willows grow along the drainages. As you enter McConnell Basin, there is a stunning view of the steep and rocky west slope of Santa Rosa Peak.

—USDA Forest Service

10. **HORSE CANYON TRAIL**

WHY GO?

A short day hike in the Santa Rosa Range offering access to Santa Rosa–Paradise Peak Wilderness and basalt-granite geology.

THE RUNDOWN

See map on page 43
Start: 38 miles north of Winnemucca
Distance: 3.8-mile out and back
Hiking time: About 3 hours
Difficulty: Moderate
Trail surface: Dirt and rocks
Water: Horse Creek; not recommended for drinking
Seasons: Summer through fall
Other trail users: Equestrians
Canine compatibility: Dogs allowed under control

Land status: Humboldt-Toiyabe National Forest
Nearest town: Winnemucca
Fees and permits: None
USGS topo map: Santa Rosa Peak
Other maps: Forest Service: Humboldt-Toiyabe National Forest, Santa Rosa Ranger District
Trail contacts: Humboldt-Toiyabe National Forest, Santa Rosa Ranger District, 1200 East Winnemucca Blvd., Winnemucca, NV 89445; (775) 623-5025

FINDING THE TRAILHEAD

Drive 38 miles north of Winnemucca on US 95, and turn right onto Horse Canyon Road (signed). Vehicles with high clearance are recommended to reach this trailhead, which is 3.5 miles east of the highway. The actual trailhead is 150 yards southeast inside the Forest Service boundary fence. From here, the trail follows the creek, becoming a cattle trail near the end. **Trailhead GPS:** N41 30.807 / W117 43.887

WHAT TO SEE

Record snow accumulated on the Santa Rosa Mountains in the winter of 1983–84. In late May a sudden change of temperature from freezing to more than 90 degrees Fahrenheit caused rapid snowmelt. The ground became saturated with water and the creeks rose. Within 24 hours of the abrupt temperature change, mudslides containing massive amounts of debris and torrents of water gutted several streams. Damage caused by that hundred-year flood event is still evident today in the form of steeply cut banks, mudslide scars, and high-water debris. The skeletal remains of aspen and old cottonwood trees are now home to birds and small animals.

Eastern slopes of the Santa Rosa Range
JASON HOLLINGER, WIKIMEDIA COMMONS

The granite-rimmed skyline rings the basin. While sitting under a mountain mahogany in the cool breeze, you can view a wide variety of vegetation. Quaking aspen, alder, and limber pine occur on the north-facing slopes, which hold snow longer. Mountain mahogany, serviceberry, snowberry, and sagebrush occur on the sun-dried south-facing slopes. House wrens, red-shafted flickers, and mountain chickadees call from the trees. Inconspicuous Jacob's ladder, penstemon, and clarkia flowers grow among the rocks.
—USDA Forest Service

MILES AND DIRECTIONS

0.0 Horse Creek trailhead.

1.9 Trail fades out.

3.8 Return to Horse Creek trailhead.

11. FALLS CANYON TRAIL

WHY GO?

A short day hike in the Santa Rosa Range featuring access to the Santa Rosa–Paradise Peak Wilderness and a waterfall.

THE RUNDOWN

See map on page 43
Start: 38 miles north of Winnemucca
Distance: 3.2-mile out and back
Hiking time: About 2 hours
Difficulty: Moderate
Trail surface: Dirt and rocks
Water: Falls Creek is not recommended for drinking
Seasons: Summer through fall
Other trail users: Equestrians
Canine compatibility: Dogs allowed under control
Land status: Humboldt-Toiyabe National Forest

Nearest town: Winnemucca
Fees and permits: None
USGS topo map: Santa Rosa Peak and Five Fingers
Other maps: Forest Service: Humboldt-Toiyabe National Forest, Santa Rosa Ranger District
Trail contacts: Humboldt-Toiyabe National Forest, Santa Rosa Ranger District, 1200 East Winnemucca Blvd., Winnemucca, NV 89445; (775) 623-5025

FINDING THE TRAILHEAD

Drive 37 miles north of Winnemucca on US 95, and turn right onto Falls Canyon Road (signed). Vehicles with high clearance are recommended to reach this trailhead, which is 3.5 miles east of the highway. The actual trailhead is 100 yards northeast inside the Forest Service boundary fence. **Trailhead GPS:** N41 30.81 / W117 43.891

WHAT TO SEE

Generally this trail stays along the creek until you get into the upper basin. Minimal trail maintenance is done at the beginning of the season.

Just after entering the canyon, you'll come to the waterfall that gives the canyon its name. It is small, but when the water is flowing wildly during the spring snowmelt or is frozen in hanging needles of ice in the winter, it can be a beautiful sight. The vertical walls of phyllite to the south at the canyon entrance are awe-inspiring. Granite features take over a short distance up the canyon. A lone limber pine grows out of a fissure in a single granite boulder in the sagebrush basin. Robins love the chokecherries in the fall when the fruit is ripe. Elderberries can be picked and made into jelly, syrup, and wine.

Occurring in fairly widespread stands in the Santa Rosa Range, the quaking aspen is North America's most widely distributed tree. It grows throughout the western mountains at elevations between the pine belt and the spruce-fir belt. In the Santa Rosa Range

Quaking aspen showcasing their brilliant yellow fall leaves.
© ISTOCK.COM/TENLEY THOMPSON

where the alpine forests are conspicuously absent, aspen is the major tree, sharing the slopes with a few limber pine. In fall the leaves turn a brilliant yellow with patches of orange and red, brightening entire mountainsides. The name *quaking aspen* refers to the fact that the leaves, attached by thin flat stems, tremble in the lightest breeze.

—USDA Forest Service and Bruce Grubbs

12. SANTA ROSA SUMMIT TRAIL: BUFFALO CANYON

WHY GO?
A day hike in the Santa Rosa Range giving access to the Santa Rosa–Paradise Peak Wilderness as well as panoramic views.

THE RUNDOWN

See map on page 43
Start: 35 miles north of Winnemucca
Distance: 9.6-mile out and back
Hiking time: About 7 hours
Difficulty: Strenuous
Trail surface: Dirt and rocks
Water: Avoid drinking from streams and springs because of *Giardia lamblia*
Seasons: Summer through fall
Other trail users: Equestrians
Canine compatibility: Dogs allowed under control

Land status: Humboldt-Toiyabe National Forest
Nearest town: Winnemucca
Fees and permits: None
USGS topo map: Five Fingers, Paradise Peak, Hinkey Summit
Other maps: Forest Service: Humboldt-Toiyabe National Forest, Santa Rosa Ranger District
Trail contacts: Humboldt-Toiyabe National Forest, Santa Rosa Ranger District, 1200 East Winnemucca Blvd., Winnemucca, NV 89445; (775) 623-5025

FINDING THE TRAILHEAD
From Winnemucca, drive 35 miles north on US 95, then turn right at the Buffalo Canyon Road sign. Follow the dirt road 2 miles. The trailhead is northwest of the Forest Service boundary fence. **Trailhead GPS:** N41 28.575 / W117 45.093

WHAT TO SEE
The first half of the trail to the crest was constructed in 1986 and passes through sagebrush, various grasses, willows, and cottonwoods. The upper half is older and more primitive and passes among snowberry, serviceberry, mahogany, and aspen. A steep climb to the crest completes the last 0.5 mile. The trail crosses Buffalo Canyon Creek several times during its journey to the summit at 8,000 feet. Passage in the lower part of the drainage is via a trail constructed around phyllite outcrops and narrow benches. The harsh weather conditions of the mountain country have molded the channel of Buffalo Creek. Severe thunderstorms are hazardous to both the environment and humans. Be prepared for sudden changes in the weather.

Mountain lions are known to travel throughout the drainage. Mule deer can be seen browsing on the snowberry and aspen saplings in the high basins. The fall colors of the

Mountain lions are known to travel throughout the drainage. © ISTOCK.COM/ FERNANDOQUEUEDO

aspen and snowberry are brilliant gold, orange, yellow, and red. Rabbitbrush and sage-brush are late bloomers with yellow flowers.

The view to the east from the summit of Buffalo Canyon includes Paradise Valley, dotted with ranches and farms, and the Snowstorm and Independence Mountains of Elko County. The Jackson and Pine Forest Ranges are to the west. A trail south along the crest affords more panoramic views.

—USDA Forest Service

MILES AND DIRECTIONS

0.0 Buffalo Canyon trailhead.

3.8 Trail leaves canyon bottom for final climb to crest.

4.8 Santa Rosa crest and end of hike.

9.6 Return to Buffalo Canyon trailhead.

13. SANTA ROSA SUMMIT TRAIL: SINGAS CREEK

WHY GO?

A day hike in the Santa Rosa Range featuring Singas trailhead with ample parking, a major access point for the Santa Rosa–Paradise Peak Wilderness.

THE RUNDOWN

See map on page 43
Start: 42 miles northeast of Winnemucca
Distance: 12.2-mile out and back
Hiking time: About 8 hours
Difficulty: Strenuous
Trail surface: Old road, dirt and rocks
Water: Avoid drinking perennial streams due to *Giardia lamblia*
Seasons: Summer through fall
Other trail users: Equestrians
Canine compatibility: Dogs allowed under control

Land status: Humboldt-Toiyabe National Forest
Nearest town: Winnemucca
Fees and permits: None
USGS topo map: Five Fingers and Paradise Valley
Other maps: Forest Service: Humboldt-Toiyabe National Forest, Santa Rosa Ranger District
Trail contacts: Humboldt-Toiyabe National Forest, Santa Rosa Ranger District, 1200 East Winnemucca Blvd., Winnemucca, NV 89445; (775) 623-5025

FINDING THE TRAILHEAD

From Winnemucca, go 22 miles north on US 95, then turn right onto NV 290 and continue 17 miles to the signed Singas Creek Road. Turn left and drive 5 miles to the parking area (a high-clearance vehicle is necessary).
Trailhead GPS: N41 29.039 / W117 37.597

WHAT TO SEE

From the parking area, it is a steep 0.5-mile climb along an old road to the Santa Rosa Summit Trail, which goes south and north from Singas Basin. This hike covers the trail to the saddle at the head of Buffalo Canyon. After the initial climb, the trail ascends south across the hillside toward a saddle, then descends slightly as it crosses the head of Morey Creek. After contouring through the head of Abel Creek, the Summit Trail climbs southwest over a point on the ridge south of Abel Creek. A final steep climb across the slope to the west brings the trail to the main crest of the Santa Rosa Range at the head of Buffalo Canyon.

Hidden from view by foothills, the Singas Creek Basin is filed with aspen, peaks with steep granite faces, and streams fed by the spring snowmelt. Views are spectacular from

Singas Creek
JASON HOLLINGER,
WIKIMEDIA COMMONS

either direction on the Summit Trail. Marmots, large alpine rodents, chirp a warning before disappearing into their rock dens. Patience may be rewarded when a curious marmot pops his head back out to get a look at the intruder. You may see a downy woodpecker, which nests in cavities. House wrens and Wilson's warblers flit among the willows and aspen trees. Early morning and late evening are the mule deer's favorite time for browsing. Tall flowering bluebell, larkspur, and jewelflower can be found. The fragile blue flax and hardy mountain iris favor wet meadows.

—USDA Forest Service and Bruce Grubbs

MILES AND DIRECTIONS

0.0 Singas Creek trailhead.

1.5 Santa Rosa Summit Trail; turn left (south).

6.1 Santa Rosa crest and end of hike.

12.2 Return to Singas Creek trailhead.

14. SANTA ROSA SUMMIT TRAIL: NORTH HANSON CREEK

WHY GO?

A day hike in the Santa Rosa Range, providing the closest vehicle access to the Summit Trail, plus access to the Santa Rosa–Paradise Peak Wilderness.

THE RUNDOWN

See map on page 43
Start: 44 miles northeast of Winnemucca
Distance: 5.8-mile out and back
Hiking time: About 4 hours
Difficulty: Moderate
Trail surface: Dirt and rocks
Water: Avoid drinking perennial streams due to *Giardia lamblia*
Seasons: Summer through fall
Other trail users: Equestrians
Canine compatibility: Dogs allowed under control

Land status: Humboldt-Toiyabe National Forest
Nearest town: Winnemucca
Fees and permits: None
USGS topo map: Mullinix Creek and Paradise Valley
Other maps: Forest Service: Humboldt-Toiyabe National Forest, Santa Rosa Ranger District
Trail contacts: Humboldt-Toiyabe National Forest, Santa Rosa Ranger District, 1200 East Winnemucca Blvd., Winnemucca, NV 89445; (775) 623-5025

FINDING THE TRAILHEAD

From Winnemucca, go 22 miles north on US 95, then turn right onto NV 290 and continue 18 miles to Paradise Valley. Turn left (west) at the main intersection and drive 1.5 miles to the end of the road. Turn left (south) and continue for 0.5 mile. Now turn right (west) onto the dirt road that follows the fence line. Continue up the foothills until you reach a fork in the road. Here you cross the creek and continue northwest up into the basin. The trail is just west of the parking area. A high-clearance vehicle should be used to reach this trail. **Trailhead GPS:** N41 30.608 / W117 37.313

WHAT TO SEE

The Santa Rosa Summit Trail goes both south and north from the trailhead; this hike describes the section to the south. The trail climbs the hillside to the southwest, then passes through a saddle after about 0.5 mile and climbs gradually along the sage-covered hillside. Another short steep section leads through a saddle at 7,000 feet; then the Summit Trail drops to Singas Creek. It is approximately 0.5 mile to Singas Creek Road, visible below.

Blue Forget-me-nots dot this trail.
© ISTOCK.COM/LIOR2

Limber pines dot the granite basins high above the trail. The North Hanson and Lamance drainages meld together to form one large basin. Willow, aspen, snowberry, and blue forget-me-not greet the hiker. Red-tailed hawks perch in aspen, and the noisy raven is common.

—USDA Forest Service and Bruce Grubbs

MILES AND DIRECTIONS

0.0 North Hanson Creek trailhead; go southwest on the Summit Trail.

0.5 Saddle; continue south.

1.6 Second saddle; continue south.

2.9 Junction with Singas Creek Trail and end of hike.

5.8 Return to North Hanson Creek trailhead.

15. WATER CANYON

WHY GO?

A day hike in the Sonoma Range offering outstanding views of the historic Humboldt River Valley.

THE RUNDOWN

Start: 5 miles south of Winnemucca
Distance: 8.1-mile loop
Hiking time: About 6 hours
Difficulty: Strenuous
Trail surface: Old roads, cross-country
Water: None
Seasons: Summer through fall
Other trail users: None
Canine compatibility: Dogs allowed under control

Land status: Bureau of Land Management
Nearest town: Winnemucca
Fees and permits: None
USGS topo map: Winnemucca East, Sonoma Canyon, Adelaide, and Pole Creek
Trail contacts: Bureau of Land Management, Winnemucca District Office, 5100 West Winnemucca Blvd., Winnemucca, NV 89445; (775) 623-1500; www.blm.gov

FINDING THE TRAILHEAD

From downtown Winnemucca at the junction of business I-80 and US 95, drive east 1 block, then turn right onto South Bridge Street and continue about 1 mile to the end of the street. Turn right, then go left at the edge of town on the dirt Water Canyon Road. Continue about 5 miles to the end of the road and picnic area, located in an aspen grove. **Trailhead GPS:** N40 55.259 / W117 39.202

WHAT TO SEE

On the left a jeep road switchbacks steeply up the slope. Either walk up the road or go directly up the slope to the right of it. Both routes lead to the top of the ridge northeast of Water Canyon. Follow the jeep road and the ridge southeast around the head of Water Canyon to the high point about 3 miles north of Sonoma Peak.

From this high point, it is possible to take a side hike south to Sonoma Peak, the highest summit in the Sonoma Range.

To continue the main loop, hike cross-country along the ridge west and northwest above Water Canyon, then drop down the ridge north to reach the creek about a mile upstream of the parking area. An old road leads down the creek to the parking area.

During the walk along the high ridges, a large portion of the Humboldt River Valley is visible. The Humboldt is Nevada's longest river but never reaches the sea, in keeping with the character of the Great Basin. It rises near the town of Wells in northeastern Nevada and crosses northern Nevada to the west and then south to finally disappear in

Water Canyon, Sonoma Range

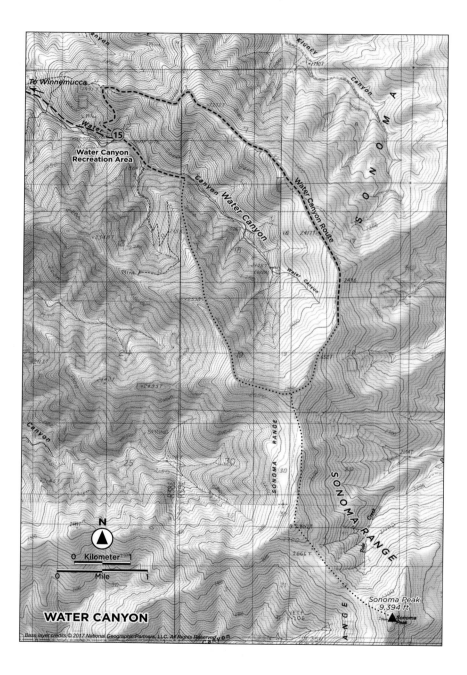

WATER CANYON

the alkaline flats of the Humboldt Sink. Although it covers only 280 airline miles, it has a very low gradient and meanders so much that the river channel is actually 1,000 miles long. The Humboldt River was a major immigrant trail during the settling of California and Oregon; the ill-fated Donner Party passed this way.

MILES AND DIRECTIONS

0.0 End of Water Canyon Road; hike north to top of ridge.

0.7 Ridgetop; turn southeast and follow ridge.

5.0 High point of hike at head of Water Canyon (*Option:* An out-and-back hike south to Sonoma Peak adds 4.8 miles to the hike.) Continue main loop by hiking west and then north along ridge.

6.1 Descend north into Water Canyon.

7.4 Turn left and descend Water Canyon.

8.1 Return to end of Water Canyon Road.

16. STAR PEAK

WHY GO?

This day hike to the highest peak in the East Humboldt Range offers expansive views of northwestern Nevada.

THE RUNDOWN

Start: 56 miles northwest of Winnemucca
Distance: 10.6-mile out and back
Hiking time: About 8 hours
Difficulty: Strenuous
Trail surface: Old roads, cross-country
Water: None
Seasons: Summer through fall
Other trail users: None
Canine compatibility: Dogs allowed under control

Land status: Bureau of Land Management
Nearest town: Winnemucca
Fees and permits: None
USGS topo map: Star Peak
Trail contacts: Bureau of Land Management, Winnemucca District Office, 5100 West Winnemucca Blvd., Winnemucca, NV 89445; (775) 623-1500; www.blm.gov

FINDING THE TRAILHEAD

From Winnemucca, drive approximately 46 miles west on I-80 and exit at the Humboldt interchange. Follow the dirt road south along the east side of the freeway approximately 4.5 miles, then turn east toward Star Peak (the highest point in the East Humboldt Range) and drive 3 miles into Eldorado Canyon. After crossing the creek several times, the road veers left and climbs steeply out of the creek. Park here. **Trailhead GPS:** N40 31.031 / W118 13.201

WHAT TO SEE

It is a steep hike up the road through the juniper forest, but the reward is an ever-expanding view. After about 1.5 miles, the road follows the ridgetop east and climbs less steeply. About 3 miles from Eldorado Creek, the road turns left (north) along the slopes of Star Peak. Continue north along the road until it reaches the summit ridge, then leave the road and walk cross-country south up the ridge to Star Peak. There are 100-mile views in all directions, and the views of the Humboldt River Valley and Rye Patch Reservoir are especially fine.

The pygmy forest of juniper trees on the lower slopes of the Humboldt Range is almost startling to the hiker who has spent time in the ranges of northwestern Nevada. There are few trees on most of the ranges from the vicinity of Winnemucca northward and westward—the exceptions being a few junipers on the lower slopes and a few aspens on the higher. In comparison, ranges with similar elevations in eastern Nevada support varied forests. Probably the lack of trees is caused by the Sierra Nevada and Cascade

Star Peak, Humboldt Range

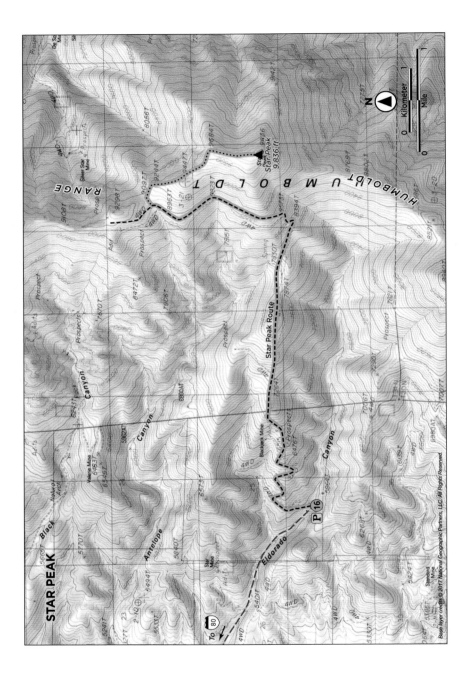

**A juniper tree gnarled and
shaped by the wind.**
© ISTOCK.COM/UNDERWORLD111

Mountains to the west, which intercept much of the moisture from winter storms. Also, little moisture in the form of summer thunderstorms reaches northwestern Nevada. Farther to the southeast, closer to the source of tropical moisture, there are more summer rains and more trees on the mountains.

MILES AND DIRECTIONS

0.0 Trailhead at Eldorado Creek.

1.5 Road reaches west ridge of Star Peak.

3.0 Road turns left (north) along west slopes of Star Peak.

4.2 Saddle on main ridge north of Star Peak; leave road and hike south, cross-country.

5.3 Star Peak.

10.6 Return to trailhead at Eldorado Creek.

Storm over Robinson Lake,
Ruby Mountains (Hike 18)

NORTHEASTERN NEVADA

INCLUDING THE PORTION OF NEVADA FROM approximately Elko north to the Idaho border and east to Utah, northeastern Nevada has the state's most alpine mountain ranges, notably the Jarbidge, East Humboldt, and Ruby Mountains. Erosion by glaciers during several glacial periods is evident in all these mountains. Probably the most striking glacial feature is Lamoille Canyon in the Ruby Mountains, a 10-mile-long U-shaped valley carved by a vanished river of ice. Unlike the ranges in central and northwestern Nevada, these eastern ranges are well forested, primarily with trees associated with the Rocky Mountains.

17. MATTERHORN LOOP

📷 🏕

WHY GO?

A very long trail and cross-country day hike or 2-day backpack trip over the major peaks of the Jarbidge Crest featuring spectacular views of much of the Jarbidge Mountains.

THE RUNDOWN

Start: 105 miles north of Elko
Distance: 15.5-mile lollipop
Hiking time: About 10 hours, or 2 days
Difficulty: Strenuous
Trail surface: Old roads, dirt trail, cross-country
Water: Upper Jarbidge River, Jarbidge Lake
Seasons: Summer through fall
Other trail users: Equestrians on trails
Canine compatibility: Terrain not suitable for dogs

Land status: Humboldt-Toiyabe National Forest
Nearest town: Elko
Fees and permits: None
USGS topo map: Jarbidge South and Gods Pocket Peak
Other maps: Forest Service: Humboldt-Toiyabe National Forest, Jarbidge Ranger District
Trail contacts: Humboldt-Toiyabe National Forest, Mountain City–Ruby Mountains–Jarbidge Ranger District, P2035 Last Chance Rd., Elko, NV 89801; (775) 738-5171; www.fs.fed.us/r4/htnf

FINDING THE TRAILHEAD

The Jarbidge Mountains in extreme northeastern Nevada are located in Nevada's first wilderness area. Remote and time-consuming to reach, they are well worth the effort. From Twin Falls, Idaho, go south on US 93 for approximately 28 miles to Rogerson, Idaho. Take the signed turnoff for Jarbidge and follow this road 70 miles (the first 50 miles are paved, the rest unpaved) to the trailhead at the end of the road at Snowslide Gulch. **Trailhead GPS:** N41 48.971 / W117 24.725

From Elko, go north on NV 225 for 73 miles to the signed turnoff (CR 748) for Jarbidge. Twenty-six miles after leaving the pavement, turn right and continue 0.8 mile to Pine Creek Campground.

WHAT TO SEE

The Jarbidge River Trail starts out as an old road and becomes a foot trail as it climbs up the canyon. The forest is open, and there are excellent views. Partway up, an old trail is visible as it branches to the right into an area of avalanche debris. The amount of destruction caused by snow avalanches can be awesome. In remote areas such as this, they are only a hazard to backcountry travelers, but in developed areas such as ski resorts or mining camps they can be very destructive. Several mining camps in the western mountains of the United States were destroyed by avalanches in the 19th century. Avalanches tend

Jarbidge Peak, Square Top, and
Matterhorn Peak, Jarbidge Mountains

to recur on the same slopes, so the location of avalanche paths can be mapped by exam-
ining the growth pattern of trees. Often an avalanche path will have a central area that's
bare of all but grass and low brush. This indicates that avalanches occur often enough to
keep trees from growing—at least every few years and possibly every year. On the fringes
of the avalanche path, there may be a uniform growth of short, young trees. The age of
these trees shows the time, possibly 50 years, that has elapsed since the last avalanche large
enough to sweep the entire path. Less obvious may be the possibility that the much older
trees to either side of the young trees may also be uniform in age, even though they are
200 or more years old. This means that periodic oversize avalanches also occur, though
perhaps only every 200 to 300 years.

There is good camping in the vicinity of Jarbidge Lake (really a pond). Switchbacks
lead up to the crest south of the lake, where a signed trail descends south into the Marys
River country. Continue up more switchbacks to the pass between Marys River Peak
and Cougar Peak.

The strenuous and difficult crest traverse begins by crossing Cougar Peak, which is
relatively easy. To the north the ridge is narrow, with a 250-foot cliff and limber pines
crowding the narrow crest. The Matterhorn looks steep but is easy to climb when dry (it
would be dangerous if the route was snow covered). Of course the views are excellent
in all directions, and the view down the precipitous north face is dizzying. North of the

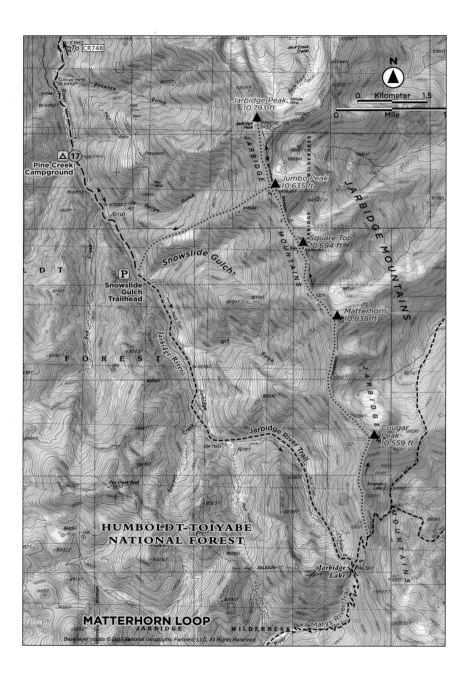

Matterhorn the ridge becomes easier. There is some limited camping in the saddles, but the only water source is snow, if available. It is possible to continue north to Jarbidge Peak, the last high peak in the range, which has fine views north into Idaho.

Return to the trailhead by descending the steep west ridge of Jumbo Peak. This route is straightforward until about 1,000 feet above the trailhead. Here a flat terminates in steep cliffs, which can be bypassed by dropping south into Snowslide Gulch. The worst of the brush can be avoided by means of deer trails.

MILES AND DIRECTIONS

0.0   Trailhead at Pine Creek Campground

1.5   Snowslide Gulch.

5.7   Jarbidge Lake.

5.8   Marys River Trail; stay left.

6.3   Trail crosses crest; leave trail and hike north, cross-country.

7.7   Cougar Peak.

9.0   Matterhorn.

9.9   Square Top.

10.6 Jumbo Peak.

11.4 Jarbidge Peak; turn around and hike back to Jumbo Peak.

12.1 Jumbo Peak; descend west ridge.

14.0 Snowslide Gulch.

15.5 Trailhead at Pine Creek Campground.

18. SOLDIER CREEK

WHY GO?

A long day hike into a less used section of the Ruby Mountains.

THE RUNDOWN

Start: 43 miles east of Elko
Distance: 12.4-mile out and back
Hiking time: About 8 hours
Difficulty: Strenuous
Trail surface: Dirt and rocks
Water: Soldier Creek
Seasons: Summer through fall
Other trail users: Equestrians
Canine compatibility: Dogs allowed under control
Land status: Humboldt-Toiyabe National Forest

Nearest town: Elko
Fees and permits: None
USGS topo map: Soldier Peak and Verdi Peak
Other maps: Forest Service: Ruby Mountains Wilderness
Trail contacts: Humboldt-Toiyabe National Forest, Mountain City–Ruby Mountains–Jarbidge Ranger District P2035 Last Chance Rd., Elko, NV 89801; (775) 738-5171; www.fs.fed.us/r4/htnf

FINDING THE TRAILHEAD

From Elko at the junction of I-80 and NV 225, drive 20.5 miles east on I-80, then exit at NV 229. Drive southeast 10.8 miles, and then turn right onto Lamoille Road, which is graded dirt. Continue 7.5 miles, and then turn left onto the unsigned Soldier Creek Road. Drive 4.2 miles to the Soldier Creek trailhead.
Trailhead GPS: N40 46.493 / W115 18.803

Ruby Valley from the Ruby Mountains

WHAT TO SEE

Follow the rough road across the creek, and upstream along the north side of Soldier Creek through open sage flats. After a mile, the road ends at the wilderness boundary; a foot trail continues climbing steeply along and above the boisterous creek. Views are limited in the deep canyon bottom, but the trail finally emerges into an open sage valley and turns sharply south, directly below Soldier Peak.

The trail, popular with hunters and horse parties, now meanders south, climbing gradually to the headwaters of Soldier Creek through sage and stands of ancient limber pine and quaking aspen. There are great views of the main crest of the Ruby Mountains above to the west, all along this section.

Soldier Lakes, consisting of several small ponds and a larger lake, mark the head of Soldier Creek, which, even though it is east of the highest crest of the range, drains to the west side. The trail continues over a broad pass and into the headwaters of Robinson

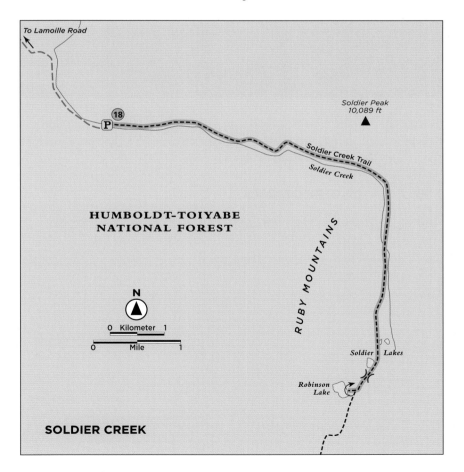

Bristlecone pines,
Ruby Mountains

Lake, which drains to the east. Watch for a spur trail turning right, and take this 0.1 mile to Robinson Lake, your destination on this hike—a truly wild-feeling place surrounded by the ice-carved crags of the Ruby Mountains.

MILES AND DIRECTIONS

0.0 Soldier Creek trailhead.

1.0 End of jeep road.

3.3 Trail emerges from canyon and turns south.

5.4 Soldier Lakes.

6.1 Turn right onto unmarked spur trail to Robinson Lake.

6.2 Robinson Lake.

12.4 Return to Soldier Creek trailhead.

19. **ISLAND LAKE**

WHY GO?

A spectacular hike to a glacial lake perched high on the side of Lamoille Canyon in the Ruby Mountains.

THE RUNDOWN

See map on pages 75–77
Start: 42 miles southeast of Elko
Distance: 2.8-mile out and back
Hiking time: About 2 hours
Difficulty: Moderate
Trail surface: Dirt and rocks
Water: Island Lake
Seasons: Summer through fall
Other trail users: Equestrians
Canine compatibility: Dogs allowed under control
Land status: Humboldt-Toiyabe National Forest

Nearest town: Elko
Fees and permits: None
USGS topo map: Ruby Dome
Other maps: Forest Service: Ruby Mountains Wilderness
Trail contacts: Humboldt-Toiyabe National Forest, Mountain City–Ruby Mountains–Jarbidge Ranger District, P2035 Last Chance Rd., Elko, NV 89801; (775) 738-5171; www.fs.fed.us/r4/htnf

FINDING THE TRAILHEAD

From Elko, drive south on NV 227. Just before the hamlet of Lamoille, turn right onto Lamoille Canyon Road. Continue to the Lamoille trailhead at the end of the road. **Trailhead GPS:** N40 36.276 / W115 22.569

DEHYDRATION

Have you ever hiked in hot weather and had a roaring headache and felt fatigued after only a few miles? More than likely you were dehydrated. Symptoms of dehydration include fatigue, headache, and decreased coordination and judgment. When you are hiking, your body's rate of fluid loss depends on the outside temperature, humidity, altitude, and your activity level. On average, a hiker walking in warm weather will lose four liters of fluid a day. That fluid loss is easily replaced by normal consumption of liquids and food. However, if a hiker is walking briskly in hot, dry weather and hauling a heavy pack, he or she can lose one to three liters of water an hour. It's important to always carry plenty of water and to stop often and drink fluids regularly, even if you aren't thirsty.

Island Lake, Ruby Mountains

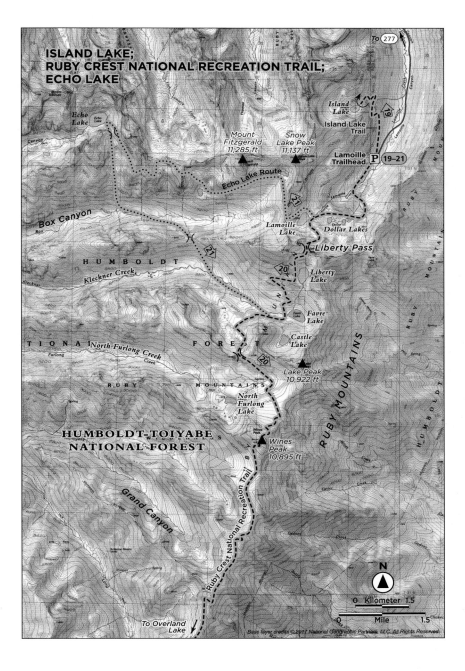

ISLAND LAKE;
RUBY CREST NATIONAL RECREATION TRAIL;
ECHO LAKE

To 277

Island Lake

Island Lake Trail

Echo Lake

Mount Fitzgerald 11,285 ft

Snow Lake Peak 11,137 ft

Lamoille Trailhead P 19–21

Echo Lake Route

Box Canyon

Lamoille Lake

Dollar Lakes

Liberty Pass

Liberty Lake

HUMBOLDT

Kleckner Creek

Favre Lake

Castle Lake

Lake Peak 10,922 ft

RUBY MOUNTAINS

FOREST

TIONA

North Furlong Creek

RUBY MOUNTAINS

North Furlong Lake

HUMBOLDT-TOIYABE
NATIONAL FOREST

Wines Peak 10,895 ft

Ruby Crest National Recreation Trail

Grand Canyon

To Overland Lake

N

0 Kilometer 1.5

0 Mile 1.5

Base layer credits © 2017 National Geographic Partners, LLC. All Rights Reserved.

WHAT TO SEE

The Island Lake Trail starts from the north end of the trailhead parking area, and climbs north up the west slopes of Lamoille Canyon. This open slope gives you a great view of the head of Lamoille Canyon to the south. After the trail crosses Island Creek, it ascends west in a few switchbacks, passing through isolated stands of trees, before ending at the edge of aptly named Island Lake. This small alpine lake is a classic cirque lake, or alpine tarn, left behind when the glacier that created the surrounding bowl-shaped canyon melted away.

Cirques such as this one form near the head of glaciers, where, during the last glacial period about 10,000 years ago, snow accumulated faster than it melted. As the snow piled up in the glacier's accumulation zone and the ice began to flow down the valley, it scooped out a depression in its bed, much the way a waterfall creates a deep plunge pool at its base. When the ice melted, a cold, clear lake filled the depression.

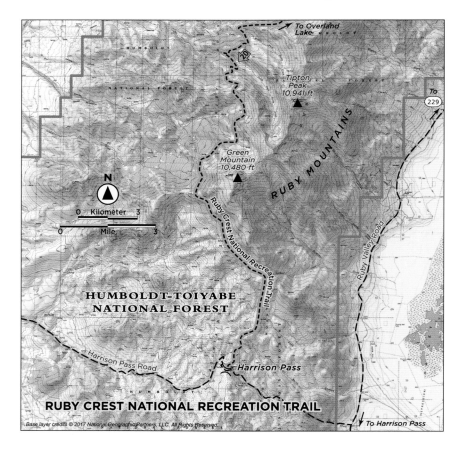

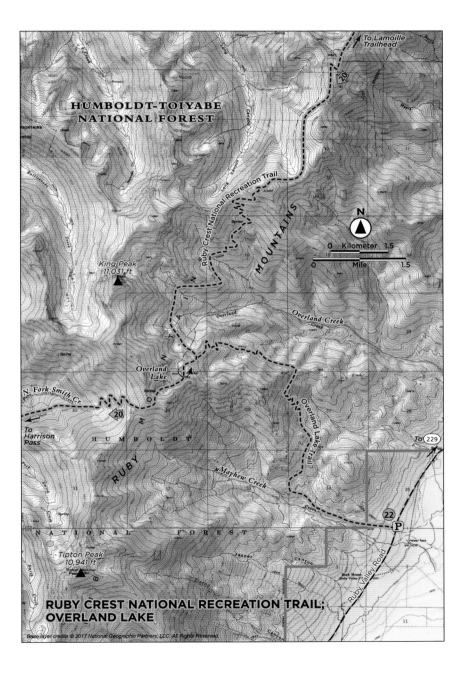

RUBY CREST NATIONAL RECREATION TRAIL;
OVERLAND LAKE

Base layer credits © 2017 National Geographic Partners, LLC. All Rights Reserved.

20. **RUBY CREST NATIONAL RECREATION TRAIL**

WHY GO?

A 4-day backpack trip in the Ruby Mountains along the crest of Nevada's most alpine range featuring classic alpine scenery, glacial valleys, cirques, and mountain lakes and streams.

THE RUNDOWN

See map on pages 75–77
Start: 42 miles southeast of Elko
Distance: 33.1-mile shuttle
Hiking time: About 4 days
Difficulty: Strenuous
Trail surface: Dirt and rocks
Water: Lamoille Lake, Liberty Lake, North Furlong Creek, Overton Lake
Seasons: Late summer through fall
Other trail users: Equestrians
Canine compatibility: Dogs allowed under control
Land status: Humboldt-Toiyabe National Forest

Nearest town: Elko
Fees and permits: None
USGS topo map: Ruby Valley School, Ruby Dome, Green Mountain, Franklin Lake NW, Franklin Lake SW, and Harrison Pass
Other maps: Forest Service: Ruby Mountains Wilderness
Trail contacts: Humboldt-Toiyabe National Forest, Mountain City–Ruby Mountains–Jarbidge Ranger District, P2035 Last Chance Rd., Elko, NV 89801; (775) 738-5171; www.fs.fed.us/r4/htnf

FINDING THE TRAILHEAD

From Elko, drive south on NV 228 and turn left onto NV 277. Just before the hamlet of Lamoille, turn right onto Lamoille Canyon Road. Continue to the Lamoille trailhead at the end of the road. **Trailhead GPS:** N40 36.276 / W115 22.569

If you hike the complete Ruby Crest Trail one way, you should leave a vehicle at Harrison Pass, which is reached from Elko via NV 228. Continue past Jiggs on the good dirt road to a junction. Turn left (east) onto the signed Harrison Pass Road and continue to Harrison Pass. **Trailhead GPS:** N40 19.52 / W115 30.664

WHAT TO SEE

Lamoille Canyon displays the classic U-shaped profile of a glacier-carved alpine valley. Forest Service interpretive displays along the road point out the distinctive features of the canyon. Numerous avalanche paths descend the steep walls; some years the road is blocked by a tangled mixture of trees and rock-hard snow brought down by the avalanches. The Ruby Mountains are the most alpine of all Nevada ranges, with rugged granite peaks and crystal lakes.

Lamoille Canyon from the Ruby Crest National Recreation Trail

From the Lamoille trailhead, the trail climbs past Lamoille Lake over Liberty Pass, then descends past Liberty Lake to Favre Lake. After passing the turnoff to North Furlong Lake—the last of the series of glacial lakes—the trail reaches its highest point at Wines Peak. To the south of the peak, the trail follows the general crest until it drops into the Overland Creek drainage and contours to Overland Lake. Above the lake, the trail climbs steeply over the crest to the North Fork Smith Creek. Now the trail stays well west of the crest as it crosses the heads of the canyons, only regaining the crest about 2 miles north of Harrison Pass.

The northern section of the Ruby Mountains contains more glacial lakes than any other range in Nevada. These lakes are the main reason the mountains look so much like the Alps. The lakes formed after the glaciers melted and runoff water filled the depressions left behind. Glaciers tend to form depressions in their beds in two ways: by bulldozing rocks into a dam (known as a terminal moraine), or by carving out basins in the bedrock (called grinding down at the heel).

Lamoille Lake, Ruby Crest National
Recreation Trail, Ruby Mountains

Liberty Pass, Ruby Crest National Recreation Trail, Ruby Mountains

MILES AND DIRECTIONS

0.0 Lamoille trailhead.

1.7 Lamoille Lake.

2.4 Liberty Pass.

2.9 Liberty Lake.

4.1 Favre Lake.

5.5 Unnamed pass.

7.3 Wines Peak, the high point of the trail.

16.8 Overland Lake Trail; turn right to stay on Ruby Crest Trail.

17.1 Overland Lake.

33.1 Harrison Pass.

21. ECHO LAKE

WHY GO?

A 2- or 3-day cross-country and trail backpack trip through a rugged but scenic, less traveled area of the popular Ruby Mountains.

THE RUNDOWN

See map on pages 75–77
Start: 42 miles south of Elko
Distance: 14.6-mile loop
Hiking time: 2 to 3 days
Difficulty: Strenuous
Trail surface: Cross-country
Water: Dollar, Lamoille, Echo, Favre, and Liberty Lakes; Box, Kleckner, and Lamoille Creeks
Seasons: Summer through fall
Other trail users: None
Canine compatibility: Dogs allowed under control

Land status: Humboldt-Toiyabe National Forest
Nearest town: Elko
Fees and permits: None
USGS topo map: Ruby Valley School and Ruby Dome
Other maps: Forest Service: Ruby Mountains
Trail contacts: Humboldt-Toiyabe National Forest, Mountain City–Ruby Mountains–Jarbidge Ranger District, P2035 Last Chance Rd., Elko, NV 89801; (775) 738-5171; www.fs.fed.us/r4/htnf

FINDING THE TRAILHEAD

From Elko, drive south on NV 228 and turn left onto NV 277. Just before the hamlet of Lamoille, turn right onto the paved Lamoille Canyon Road (signed). Continue to the parking loop at the end of the road. **Trailhead GPS:** N40 36.276 / W115 22.569

WHAT TO SEE

Follow the Ruby Crest Trail to Lamoille Lake, then leave the trail and—skirting the lake on either side—climb to the saddle at the head of Box Canyon. Now contour to the right around the head of Box Canyon and generally work east to the saddle south of Echo Lake. This traverse is strenuous, but the fine views and the two small unnamed hanging lakes are worth it. It is probably easier to descend into Box Canyon and climb up the side drainage to the saddle south of Echo Lake. From this saddle, drop down to the lake; there are campsites in the trees near the outlet.

From Echo Lake, climb back to the saddle south of the lake, then descend the scenic hanging valley to the south into Box Canyon. There are good campsites in aspen stands along the broad valley floor. About 1 mile east of the point where you first reach Box Creek, climb south over a saddle then contour east to the head of Kleckner Creek. Some sections of the traverse are rough.

Liberty Lake, Ruby Mountains

Both Kleckner and Box Canyons are very scenic, with grassy north slopes, pine-forested south slopes, and aspen glades on the canyon floors. At the west end of Favre Lake, rejoin the Ruby Crest Trail.

Follow the trail east and north around Favre Lake and up to Liberty Lake, over Liberty Pass, and past Lamoille Lake to the trailhead.

Glacial features such as horn-shaped peaks, cirques, hanging valleys, and U-shaped valleys dominate the scenery on this rugged loop. Cirques are the birthplace of glaciers, which start to form when more snow falls than melts each year. After many layers of snow are deposited, the weight compresses the lower layers into ice, which begins to flow slowly downhill. At the heads of the valleys, the ice eats away at all three slopes. The melting of the glacier exposes the classic bowl-shaped valley head, often containing one or more deep lakes. The mountain summits, their flanks worn away by the ice in the valleys, present sheer faces and knife-edge ridges. As the ice progresses down the valleys, it carves away at the sides, converting the V-shaped valley created by water to a U shape. Side glaciers contribute ice to the main glacier just as creeks contribute water to a river. The main glacier lowers its bed much faster than its tributaries, so that when the ice melts, hanging valleys are formed with floors much higher than the main valley. The ice also leaves behind such telltale signs as moraines and polished rock slabs with scratches showing the direction that the ice moved.

MILES AND DIRECTIONS

0.0 Lamoille trailhead.

1.7 Leave trail and hike cross-country west, around Lamoille Lake and up to pass west of lake.

2.1 Pass; contour north along west slope at head of Box Canyon.

2.8 Cross outlet of nameless lake and descend gradually across south slopes of Mount Fitzgerald, heading for another unnamed lake.

3.8 Pass unnamed lake on east, then climb northwest up talus slope to ridge south of Peak 10528. Head west across ridge crest, then contour west and northwest to a pass overlooking Echo Lake.

6.0 Pass; descend northwest directly to Echo Lake.

6.2 Echo Lake; retrace steps up to unnamed pass southeast of lake.

6.4 From pass, descend south to floor of Box Canyon.

7.6 Hike east up Box Canyon until you can see the way up to pass between Box and Kleckner Canyons; diagonal east up south slopes of Box Canyon to pass.

8.7 Unnamed pass; descend southeast to floor of Kleckner Canyon.

9.2 Kleckner Canyon; hike east up canyon and join Ruby Crest Trail just west of Favre Lake.

10.2 Ruby Crest Trail; turn left and hike north to return to trailhead.

14.6 Return to Lamoille trailhead.

Leading up to the Ruby Mountains.
© ISTOCK.COM/ TRAILRUNNER925

22. OVERLAND LAKE

WHY GO?

A long day hike or overnight backpack trip to an isolated alpine lake in the Ruby Mountains. This loop has superb scenery and great views of the Ruby Valley.

THE RUNDOWN

See map on page 77
Start: 60 miles southeast of Elko
Distance: 11.8-mile out and back
Hiking time: About 8 hours, or 2 days
Difficulty: Strenuous
Trail surface: Dirt and rocks
Water: Overland Lake
Seasons: Summer through fall
Other trail users: Equestrians
Canine compatibility: Dogs allowed under control

Land status: Humboldt-Toiyabe National Forest
Nearest town: Elko
Fees and permits: None
USGS topo map: Franklin Lake NW
Other maps: Forest Service: Ruby Mountains Wilderness
Trail contacts: Humboldt-Toiyabe National Forest, Mountain City–Ruby Mountains–Jarbidge Ranger District, P2035 Last Chance Rd., Elko, NV 89801; (775) 738-5171; www.fs.fed.us/r4/htnf

FINDING THE TRAILHEAD

Access to the spectacular east side of the Ruby Mountains is difficult due to the private land along the foothills. Overland Lake is an exception, being reachable by Forest Service trail.

From Elko, drive east on I-80 for 20 miles, then turn right (southeast) onto NV 229 and continue over Secret Pass. The paved road continues south along the east side of the range for several miles, then abruptly turns northeast at a junction. Continue south on the dirt Ruby Valley Road approximately 17 miles, parking at the jeep trail shown on the USGS topographic map just north of Mayhew Creek, about a mile north of Rock House. **Trailhead GPS:** N40 25.872 / W115 24.305

WHAT TO SEE

Do not follow the jeep trail. The Overland Lake Trail follows the fence, crosses the small drainage, and again follows the fence. This section is confused by numerous cattle trails. At the section corner where the USGS topographic map shows the elevation 6,278, another trail comes through a gate from the left (south). Above this point, the trail is more distinct. Stay on the trail approximately 1 mile, where the trail turns sharply right (north) and climbs away from Mayhew Creek. The trail climbs steadily, crossing a ridge into an unnamed basin, then switchbacks steeply up the head of this basin. At the top of the switchbacks, the Overland Lake Trail again heads north, soon crossing a ridge into the

Overland Creek drainage. Here the trail turns west and climbs to meet the Ruby Crest National Recreation Trail on a small ridge at the 9,200-foot contour.

Turn left onto the Ruby Crest Trail and follow it up the ridge to Overland Lake. This lake, the southernmost alpine lake in the Ruby Mountains (unless you count the small unnamed lake a few hundred yards up the cirque to the southwest), is set in a classic glacial cirque snuggled against the crest of the range.

MILES AND DIRECTIONS

0.0   Overland Lake trailhead.

1.5   Trail turns north, away from Mayhew Creek.

3.6   Trail crosses ridge into Overland Creek drainage.

5.6   Ruby Crest Trail; turn left.

5.9   Overland Lake.

11.8   Return to Overland Lake trailhead.

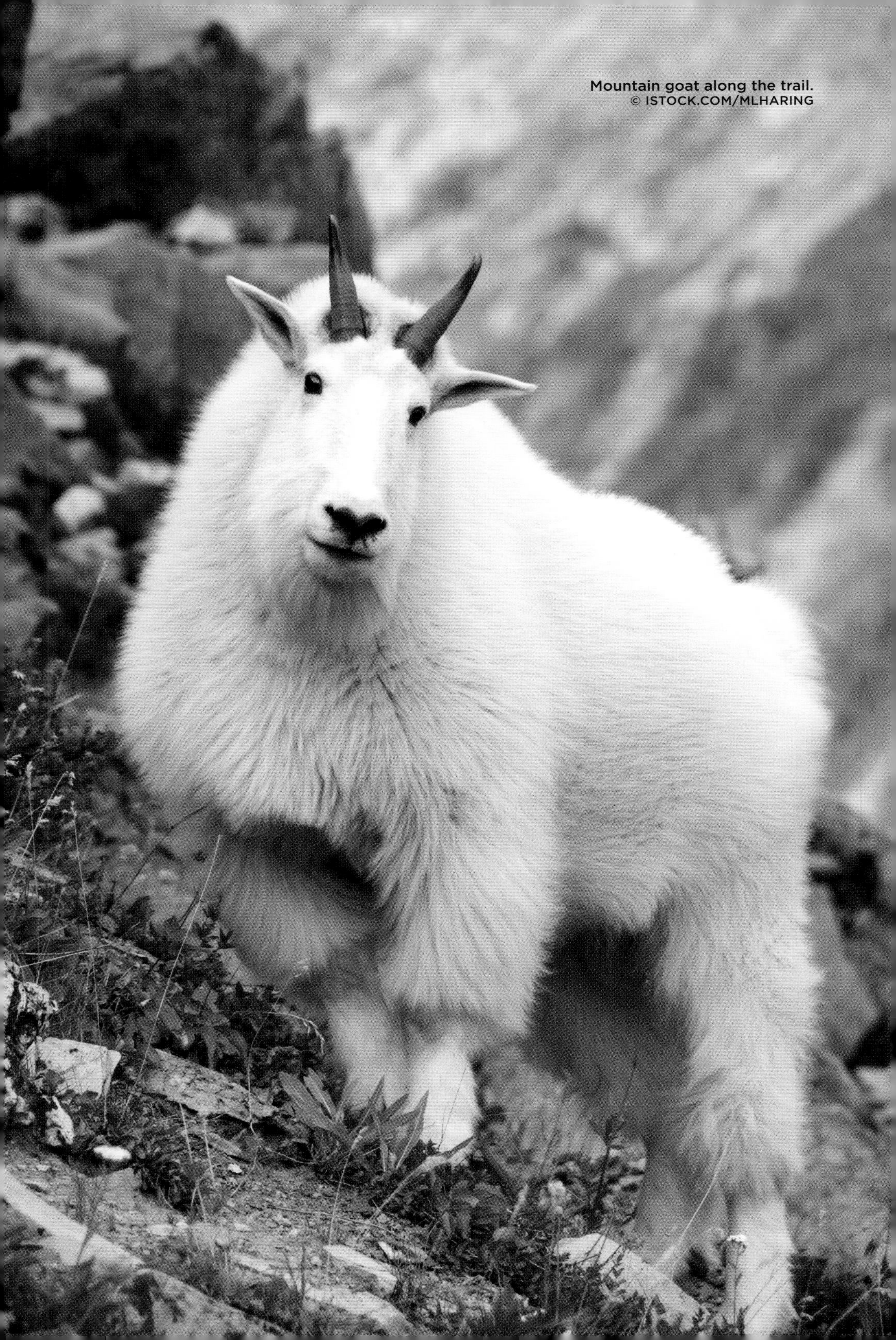

Mountain goat along the trail.

Petroglyphs, Grimes Point
Trail (Hike 29)

WESTERN NEVADA

MOST OF THE HIKING IN WESTERN NEVADA centers on the Carson Range, a parallel offshoot of the Sierra Nevada Range on the east side of Lake Tahoe. Like the main Sierra, the Carson Range is alpine in character, composed of light-colored granite that beautifully contrasts with the extensive forest cover found on the intermediate slopes, below the highest peaks. Because of its proximity to Reno and its suburbs, the Carson Range is popular. The far-lower desert ranges to the east offer more solitude for the desert hiker willing to do a bit of exploration.

23. HOBART CREEK RESERVOIR

WHY GO?

A day hike or overnight backpack trip to a historic water system in the Carson Range.

THE RUNDOWN

Start: 21 miles west of Carson City
Distance: 12.4-mile out and back
Hiking time: About 4 hours
Difficulty: Strenuous
Trail surface: Dirt and rocks
Water: Franktown Creek designated campsite
Seasons: Summer through fall
Other trail users: Equestrians
Canine compatibility: Dogs allowed on a leash
Land status: State park
Nearest town: Carson City

Fees and permits: None. Camping is permitted only in the two designated sites in the backcountry.
USGS topo map: Marlette Lake and Carson City
Other maps: Forest Service: Humboldt-Toiyabe National Forest, Carson Ranger District
Trail contacts: Nevada Division of State Parks, 901 S. Stewart St., 5th Floor, Suite 5005, Carson City, NV 89701-5248; (775) 684-2770; http://parks.nv.gov

FINDING THE TRAILHEAD

From Carson City, drive south on US 395 for 3 miles, then turn west onto US 50. Continue 10 miles, then turn north onto NV 28. The trailhead is at Hidden Beach, 8 miles from US 50. Parking is very limited. **Trailhead GPS:** N39 13.791 / W119 55.892

Marlette Lake.
© NEVADA DEPARTMENT OF CONSERVATION AND NATURAL RESOURCES/FLICKR

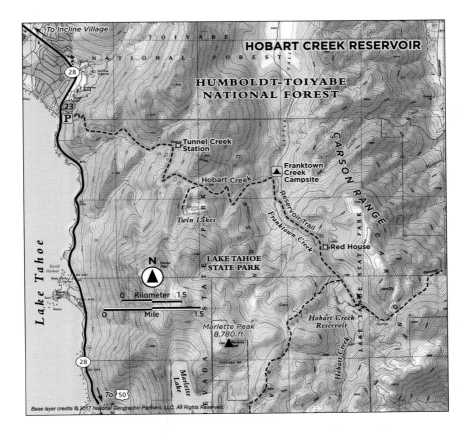

WHAT TO SEE

This trail climbs from the shore of Lake Tahoe a little over 1.5 miles to Tunnel Creek Station, a maintenance station on the Marlette water system. This water system transported lumber as well as valuable water to Virginia City during the mining period. Flume lines originating at Marlette Lake and Mill Creek carried water and wood to the western portal of this 4,000-foot tunnel through the Carson Range. At the eastern portal, the flumes then connected to the Hobart Creek water system. Some of the flume lines are still visible.

The trail continues over an 8,000-foot pass, where short side trails lead to Twin Lakes. The main trail continues about 1 mile down to Franktown Creek, a designated campsite, then on for another mile to Red House, which was occupied by the Marlette water system flume tenders. This was the site of the first diversion dam on Hobart Creek, a project that marked the beginning of the use of Sierra Nevada water for the Virginia City mines—a revolutionary engineering feat for the times. The original Red House was built in 1887 but washed away in a 1907 flood. The present building dates to about 1910 and was used until the late 1950s.

Continuing up Hobart Creek, the trail reaches Hobart Creek Reservoir in about another mile. The dam was constructed in 1887 to add extra capability to the Marlette water system. It is now the sole water source for Virginia City, Silver City, and Gold Hill. It also supplies parts of Carson City and Lakeview. It is popular for fishing although strictly regulated (only artificial lures can be used).

—Nevada Division of Parks

MILES AND DIRECTIONS

0.0 Hobart Creek Reservoir trailhead.

1.9 Tunnel Creek Station.

2.6 Pass. (***Option:*** From the pass, you can hike 0.5 mile south to Twin Lakes, a pair of seasonal lakes. This side hike adds 1 mile to the trip.)

4.2 Franktown Creek; designated campsite.

5.3 Red House.

6.2 Hobart Creek Reservoir.

12.4 Return to Hobart Creek Reservoir trailhead.

24. SPOONER LAKE

WHY GO?
A day hike around Spooner Lake in the Carson Range.

THE RUNDOWN
Start: 13 miles west of Carson City
Distance: 1.8-mile loop
Hiking time: About 1 hour
Difficulty: Easy
Trail surface: Dirt
Water: None
Seasons: Summer through fall
Other trail users: None
Canine compatibility: Dogs allowed on a leash
Land status: State park

Nearest town: Carson City
Fees and permits: None
USGS topo map: Glenbrook
Other maps: Forest Service: Humboldt-Toiyabe National Forest, Carson Ranger District
Trail contacts: Nevada Division of State Parks, 901 S. Stewart St., 5th Floor, Suite 5005, Carson City, NV 89701-5248; (775) 684-2770; http://parks.nv.gov

FINDING THE TRAILHEAD

From Carson City, drive south on US 395 for 3 miles, then turn west onto US 50. Continue 10 miles, then turn north onto NV 28. Leave your vehicle at the state park. **Trailhead GPS:** N39 6.408 / W119 54.801

Spooner Meadow, near Spooner Lake
(PUBLIC DOMAIN)

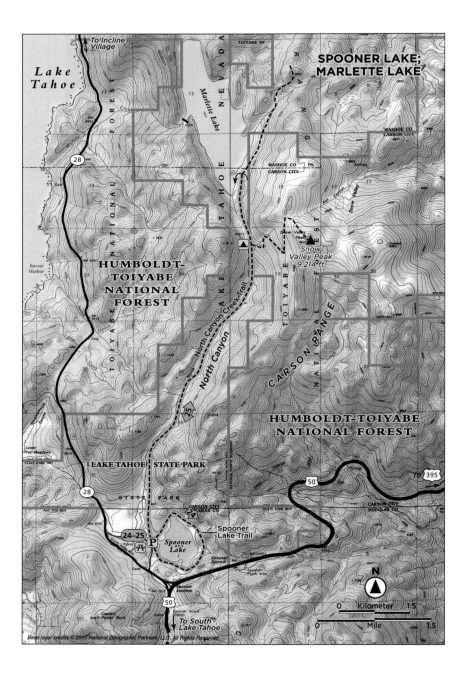

WHAT TO SEE

This is an easy but scenic loop around the shore of Spooner Lake. It passes through open stands of Jeffrey pine and provides opportunities for viewing wildlife. The northeast side of the lake, where there are aspen groves along the shore, is an especially good area for birds.

The Spooner Lake area was a transitory camp for the Washoe Indians and their predecessors as much as 7,000 years ago. As they migrated from the Carson and Eagle Valleys to Lake Tahoe each summer, these people would use the Spooner area as a rest camp.

Starting in the 1870s, Spooner became a collection point for wood being transported from Glenbrook Bay to the Comstock Mines at Virginia City. A small dam built in the 1850s created a millpond for use by the loggers. The present dam was built in about 1929 for irrigation.

—Nevada Division of Parks and Bruce Grubbs

25. MARLETTE LAKE

WHY GO?

A day hike or overnight backpack trip to Marlette Lake in the Carson Range.

THE RUNDOWN

See map on page 94
Start: 13 miles west of Carson City
Distance: 8.8-mile out and back
Hiking time: About 6 hours, or 2 days
Difficulty: Moderate
Trail surface: Dirt and rocks
Water: North Canyon Creek
Seasons: Summer through fall
Other trail users: Equestrians
Canine compatibility: Dogs allowed on a leash
Land status: State park

Nearest town: Carson City
Fees and permits: None
USGS topo map: Marlette Lake and Glenbrook
Other maps: Forest Service: Humboldt-Toiyabe National Forest, Carson Ranger District
Trail contacts: Nevada Division of State Parks, 901 S. Stewart St., 5th Floor, Suite 5005, Carson City, NV 89701-5248; (775) 684-2770; http://parks.nv.gov

FINDING THE TRAILHEAD

From Carson City, drive south on US 395 for 3 miles, then turn west onto US 50. Continue 10 miles, then turn north onto NV 28. Leave your vehicle at the state park. **Trailhead GPS:** N39 6.408 / W119 54.801

WHAT TO SEE

The North Canyon Trail generally follows North Canyon Creek for about 5 miles to Marlette Lake, a human-made reservoir. There is designated camping near the turnoff to 9,214-foot Snow Valley Peak, 4 miles from the trailhead.

Marlette Lake was constructed as the centerpiece of the elaborate water system supplying 25,000 to 40,000 people at Virginia City and Carson City. The chimney standing on the southeastern shore of the lake was once part of the watermaster's house, occupied until the late 1950s. The dam was originally built in 1873 to aid in fluming wood to Spooner Summit and then on to Carson City. It has since undergone several reconstructions and is now 52 feet high. The lake water is still used as a backup supply for Virginia City and Carson City. It is also used by the Nevada Department of Wildlife as a breeding area for cutthroat trout and is closed to fishing.

Take a 1.4-mile side trip to Snow Valley Peak. A watershed rehabilitation project developed by the USDA Forest Service is visible on the eastern slope. The area was decimated first by logging and then by 40 years of overgrazing by sheep.

A sign leading hikers to Marlette Lake.
© NEVADA DEPARTMENT OF CONSERVATION
AND NATURAL RESOURCES/FLICKR

It is possible to continue about 3 miles to the Hobart Creek Reservoir Trail, and then hike another 6 miles to the Hidden Beach trailhead.

—Nevada Division of Parks

MILES AND DIRECTIONS

0.0 Spooner Lake trailhead.

3.6 Trail to Snow Valley Peak; stay left. (*Option:* The Snow Valley Peak side trail adds 2.8 miles to this hike.)

4.4 Marlette Lake.

8.8 Return to Spooner Lake trailhead.

26. JONES CREEK/ WHITES CREEK TRAIL

WHY GO?
A day hike in the Carson Range featuring outstanding views.

THE RUNDOWN

Start: 10 miles southwest of Reno
Distance: 10.1-mile lollipop
Hiking time: About 7 hours
Difficulty: Strenuous
Trail surface: Dirt and rocks
Water: Jones and Whites Creek
Seasons: Summer through fall
Other trail users: Equestrians
Canine compatibility: Dogs allowed under control
Land status: Humboldt-Toiyabe National Forest
Nearest town: Reno

Fees and permits: None
USGS topo map: Mount Rose, Mount Rose NW, Mount Rose NE, and Washoe City
Other maps: Forest Service: Humboldt Toiyabe National Forest, Carson Ranger District
Trail contacts: Humboldt-Toiyabe National Forest, Carson Ranger District, 1536 South Carson St., Carson City, NV 89701; (775) 882-2766; www.fs.fed.us/r4/htnf

FINDING THE TRAILHEAD

From Reno, drive 8 miles south on US 395, then turn right (west) onto NV 431. Continue 4 miles west to Galena Creek Park. The trailhead is located at the north picnic area. **Trailhead GPS:** N39 21.203 / W119 51.461

WHAT TO SEE

The trail follows a jeep road for about 0.5 mile, then crosses Jones Creek. At the trail junction, turn right (east) to start the loop trail, which then heads in a northerly direction. Climbing gradually through stands of Jeffrey pine and mountain mahogany, the trail enters Whites Canyon and then turns sharply west. Continue on the old road approximately 1.5 miles. After entering the Mount Rose Wilderness, the trail turns right (leaving the old road), crosses Whites Creek, and heads west. At about the halfway point, the trail leaves Whites Canyon to the southeast and climbs onto an 8,000-foot ridge with excellent views. About a mile farther on, a spur trail leads west about 0.6 mile to a small lake, locally called Church's Pond. James East Church was a professor at the University of Nevada–Reno who established the first winter snow survey in the world. He devised his system on Mount Rose early in the 20th century. Snow surveys are used to predict the amount of spring runoff that will fill the reservoirs supplying water to lowland farms and cities.

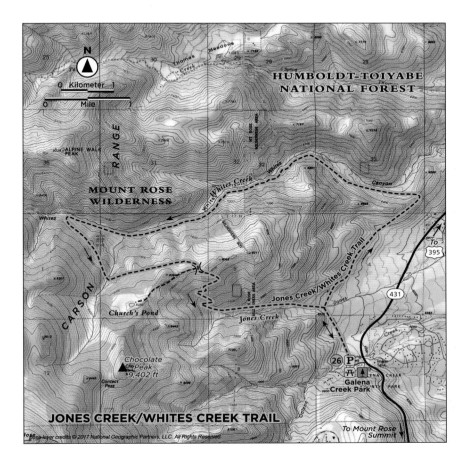

JONES CREEK/WHITES CREEK TRAIL

The main trail continues east, switchbacking down to Jones Creek to complete the loop. At the trail junction turn right (southeast) and follow the trail 0.5 mile to the trailhead.

The mountain mahogany found here is common throughout most of Nevada's mountain ranges. Not related to the tropical mahogany used for cabinetmaking, mountain mahogany is a 15- to 30-foot evergreen tree with narrow, shiny, dark green leathery leaves. It may have received its name from its dark reddish-brown mahogany-colored heartwood. Native Americans made a red dye from its roots.

—USDA Forest Service and Bruce Grubbs

Mule deer are popular in the area. © ISTOCK.COM/ PHOTOGRAPHYBYJHWILLIAMS

MILES AND DIRECTIONS

0.0   Galena Creek Park trailhead.

0.5   Trail junction; turn right to start loop.

2.0   Cross pass and enter Whites Creek Canyon; trail turns west and climbs canyon.

4.1   End of old road at wilderness boundary.

5.7   Trail turns sharply southeast and climbs to pass.

7.5   Pass and side trail to Church's Pond. (**Option:** The side trip to Church's Pond adds 1.2 miles to this hike.)

9.5   Finish loop at Whites Creek Trail; turn right to return.

10.1   Return to Galena Creek Park trailhead.

27. **MOUNT ROSE**

📷

WHY GO?

A day hike in the Carson Range offering spectacular views of the Lake Tahoe region of the Sierra Nevada.

THE RUNDOWN

Start: 15 miles southwest of Reno
Distance: 11.2-mile out and back
Hiking time: About 8 hours
Difficulty: Strenuous
Trail surface: Dirt and rocks
Water: Several small creeks
Seasons: Summer through fall
Other trail users: Equestrians
Canine compatibility: Dogs allowed under control
Land status: Humboldt-Toiyabe National Forest

Nearest town: Reno
Fees and permits: Self-register at trailhead
USGS topo map: Mount Rose
Other maps: Forest Service: Humboldt-Toiyabe National Forest, Carson Ranger District
Trail contacts: Humboldt-Toiyabe National Forest, Carson Ranger District, 1536 South Carson St., Carson City, NV 89701; (775) 882-2766; www.fs.fed.us/r4/htnf

FINDING THE TRAILHEAD

From Reno, drive 8 miles south on US 395, then turn right (west) onto NV 431 and drive 14.5 miles. The unsigned trailhead is at the maintenance station building on the right (north) just beyond Mount Rose Summit. This is also the Upper Ophir Creek trailhead. **Trailhead GPS:** N39 18.605 / W119 54.095

WHAT TO SEE

Hikers should beware of the strong winds that rake the mountain above timberline on most afternoons. Most of the trail is somewhat protected in the forest, but the last mile is exposed. Be sure to bring adequate wind gear.

The Mount Rose Trail initially follows an old dirt road, which is closed to vehicles. After a couple of miles of gradual ascent, the trail turns right, leaving the road, and crosses a saddle into the headwaters basin of Galena Creek. For about a mile the trail descends, following an old road. Then it crosses the creek and starts to climb steeply up the canyon below Mount Rose. At the saddle at the head of the canyon, the trail turns right at a signed junction. Here it enters the Mount Rose Wilderness. Now the trail generally follows the ridge to the summit, switchbacking occasionally. This section is steep but not as steep as the canyon below the saddle.

The 360-degree view from the summit includes Lake Tahoe, the Great Basin ranges to the east, and Reno to the north.

A small alpine pond along the Mount Rose Trail

The beautiful and famous Lake Tahoe is one of the highest large lakes in the world, but it is only a small remnant of the great Lake Lahontan system that covered many of the valleys in northwestern Nevada during the last glacial period. Looking at the dry desert valleys with their alkaline sinks and scanty vegetation, it is hard to believe that the view eastward was as green and forested 10,000 years ago as the view to the west is now.
—USDA Forest Service and Bruce Grubbs

MILES AND DIRECTIONS

0.0 Mount Rose/Upper Ophir Creek trailhead.

2.4 Saddle.

3.2 Cross Galena Creek and start final ascent.

4.2 Saddle and trail junction; turn right.

5.6 Mount Rose.

11.2 Return to Mount Rose/Upper Ophir Creek trailhead.

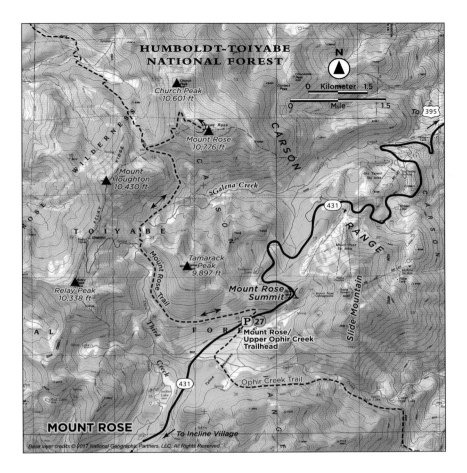

28. OPHIR CREEK TRAIL

WHY GO?
A day hike in the Carson Range near Lake Tahoe featuring the remnants of a massive landslide.

THE RUNDOWN

Start: 2 miles southwest of Washoe City
Distance: 6.6-mile shuttle
Hiking time: About 5 hours
Difficulty: Strenuous
Trail surface: Dirt and rocks
Water: None
Seasons: Summer through fall
Other trail users: Equestrians
Canine compatibility: Dogs allowed under control
Land status: Humboldt-Toiyabe National Forest

Nearest town: Washoe City
Fees and permits: None
USGS topo map: Washoe City and Mount Rose
Other maps: Forest Service: Humboldt-Toiyabe National Forest, Carson Ranger District
Trail contacts: Humboldt-Toiyabe National Forest, Carson Ranger District, 1536 South Carson St., Carson City, NV 89701; (775) 882-2766; www.fs.fed.us/r4/htnf

FINDING THE TRAILHEAD
To reach the lower (east) trailhead from Reno, drive south on US 395 and turn right onto NV 429 1 mile south of Washoe City. After 0.5 mile turn right into Davis Creek County Park. **Trailhead GPS:** N39 17.713 / W119 49.889

To reach the upper (west) trailhead from Reno, drive 8 miles south on US 395, then turn right (west) onto NV 431 and drive 14.5 miles. The unsigned trailhead is at the maintenance station building on the right (north) just beyond Mount Rose Summit. **Trailhead GPS:** N39 18.605 / W119 54.095

WHAT TO SEE
This hike is a difficult and strenuous climb up the Ophir Creek drainage to the remains of Upper and Lower Price Lakes, which were destroyed when part of Slide Mountain fell into them in 1983. The resulting mud and water accumulation rushed down the Ophir Creek drainage and created a massive movement of earth that was deposited at Washoe Lake. It also removed part of the trail. Three miles from the western end, the trail turns into a jeep road that's open to hiking only. The last 3 miles also parallel scenic Tahoe Meadows, and the trail ends at NV 431. There is a new trailhead 0.5 mile to the east along the highway. This trailhead is shared with the Mount Rose Trail.

The tall pines featuring three long needles per bundle commonly found in the Carson Range and Sierra Nevada are Jeffrey pine. These beautiful trees closely resemble the

Lupine is a common alpine flower throughout Nevada's mountains.

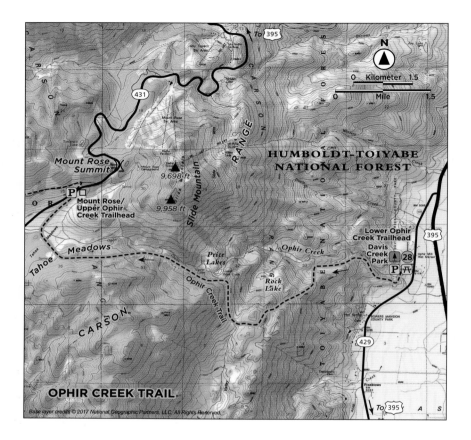

OPHIR CREEK TRAIL

Base layer credits © 2017 National Geographic Partners, LLC. All Rights Reserved.

ponderosa pine found in eastern and southern Nevada ranges, but are distinguished by the lighter color of their needles and by the unique strong smell of vanilla or lemon given off by crushed needles or twigs.

—USDA Forest Service and Bruce Grubbs

MILES AND DIRECTIONS

- **0.0** Lower Ophir Creek trailhead (east).
- **2.8** Trail passes through a saddle.
- **5.7** Tahoe Meadows.
- **6.6** Upper Ophir Creek/Mount Rose trailhead (west).

29. GRIMES POINT ARCHAEOLOGICAL AREA

WHY GO?

A day hike on an interpretive trail featuring numerous prehistoric petroglyphs, pictographs, rock shelters, and caves.

THE RUNDOWN

Start: 10 miles east of Fallon
Distance: 1.0-mile loop
Hiking time: About 1 hour
Difficulty: Easy
Trail surface: Rocky volcanic
Water: None
Seasons: Year-round
Other trail users: None
Canine compatibility: Dogs not allowed

Land status: Bureau of Land Management
Nearest town: Fallon
Fees and permits: None
USGS topo map: Grimes Point
Trail contacts: Bureau of Land Management, Carson City District, 5665 Morgan Mill Rd., Carson City, NV 89701; (775) 885-6000; www .blm.gov

FINDING THE TRAILHEAD

The signed Grimes Point Archaeological Site is located on US 50 approximately 10 miles east of Fallon. Turn left (north) onto the maintained gravel road. To reach the Petroglyph Trail, turn right just after leaving the highway and park at the signed trailhead. To reach the Hidden Cave Trail, continue 1.5 miles north on the gravel road from the highway, then turn right into the signed trailhead. **Trailhead GPS:** N39 24.092 / W118 38.848

WHAT TO SEE

Grimes Point Archaeological Area offers two trails. The easy Petroglyph Trail is a short trail through a petroglyph boulder field. The longer Hidden Cave Trail provides access to petroglyphs, rock shelters, and geological features. Interpretive leaflets are available at the trailhead. Hidden Cave, a major archaeological site, was used prehistorically by hunter-gatherers as a cache or storage site. The cave was occupied between 3,400 and 4,000 years ago. Free public tours of the cave begin in Fallon at 9:30 a.m. on the second and fourth Saturday of each month. The trails are open to the public all year.

In the Grimes Point area, it is possible to see a series of horizontal lines or terraces along the hillsides. These are wave terraces cut into the slopes by the waters of ancient Lake Lahontan, which reached depths of 700 feet. Although Grimes Point is presently a desert, about 10,000 years ago it was a rich lakeshore, teeming with life. Given those conditions, it is not surprising that the ancient people spent a lot of time here.

—Bureau of Land Management and Bruce Grubbs

30. **SAND SPRINGS DESERT STUDY AREA**

WHY GO?

An interpretive day hike through a sand dune area featuring a historic Pony Express station.

THE RUNDOWN

Start: 23 miles southeast of Fallon
Distance: 0.5-mile loop
Hiking time: About 1 hour
Difficulty: Easy
Trail surface: Sand
Water: None
Seasons: Year-round
Other trail users: None
Canine compatibility: Dogs not allowed

Land status: Bureau of Land Management
Nearest town: Fallon
Fees and permits: None
USGS topo map: Fourmile Flat
Trail contacts: Bureau of Land Management, Carson City District, 5665 Morgan Mill Rd., Carson City, NV 89701; (775) 885-6000; www .blm.gov

FINDING THE TRAILHEAD

From Fallon, drive east approximately 23 miles east on US 50. **Trailhead GPS:** N39 16.487 / W118 24.776

WHAT TO SEE

The Sand Springs Desert Study Area is located in a 50-acre area closed to off-road vehicles just south of Sand Mountain. Sand Mountain is approximately 3.5 miles long, 1 mile wide, and rises about 600 feet above the valley floor, making it the largest single dune in the Great Basin. The interpretive trail is accessible by dirt road approximately 1.5 miles north of US 50. You can learn about the unique sand dune environment and view a Pony Express station along with other historic features.

Although many people unfamiliar with it think of the American desert as a vast area of sand dunes, the Sand Springs area is typical of sand dune areas in the Southwest. A particular combination of circumstances must combine before dunes are formed. There must be a supply of sand, prevailing winds tending to push the sand in the same direction, and a topographic feature acting as a trap to contain the sand. Here the surrounding mountains capture the windblown grains.

Little is left of the Sand Springs Pony Express Station. FAMARTIN

It can be especially rewarding to explore the dunes at sunrise. The slanting sunlight emphasizes the texture of the surface and clearly shows the tracks and activities of animals active on the sand during the cool night hours.

—Bureau of Land Management and Bruce Grubbs

WATER

You need at least two quarts of water a day to function efficiently. Add heat and taxing terrain and you can bump that figure up to one gallon. That's simply a base to work from—your metabolism and your level of conditioning can raise or lower that amount. Unless you know your level, assume that you need one gallon of water a day. Now, where do you plan on getting the water? Certainly not on this trail! The easiest solution is to bring water with you. Besides, even if natural water sources existed here, they can be loaded with intestinal disturbers, such as bacteria, viruses, and fertilizers. *Giardia lamblia*, the most common of these disturbers, is a protozoan parasite that lives part of its life cycle as a cyst in water sources. The parasite spreads when mammals defecate in water sources. Once ingested, *Giardia* can induce cramping, diarrhea, vomiting, and fatigue within two days to two weeks after ingestion. If you believe you've contracted giardiasis, see a doctor immediately, as it is treatable with prescription drugs. If you're hiking too far to bring all the water you'll need, carry a lightweight water filter so you can get water from streams and lakes.

Summit Canyon is an east side access to the Toiyabe Crest National Recreation Trail (Hike 33).

CENTRAL NEVADA

ARGUABLY, THE BASIN-AND-RANGE TOPOGRAPHY that dominates Nevada's landscape reaches its maximum expression in the long, high ranges that stretch across the central portion of the state. The Toiyabe Range is more than 75 miles long, and the Monitor Range stretches out over 100 miles. The summits reach elevations well above 11,000 feet, yet these mountains have a unique Nevada flavor. Isolated from moisture sources such as the Pacific Ocean and Gulf of Mexico, the mountains support only sparse stands of mountain mahogany, bristlecone pine, and the occasional patch of aspen, yet there are a surprising number of springs and permanent streams. Since these ranges are about as far from major population centers as it's possible to be in the United States outside Alaska, overcrowding is not a problem. Even on the most popular trails, such as the Toiyabe Crest National Recreation Trail, you can hike for days without seeing anyone.

31. COLD SPRINGS PONY EXPRESS STATION

WHY GO?
A day hike to a Pony Express station with scenic views of the Desatoya Mountains.

THE RUNDOWN

Start: 51 miles west of Austin
Distance: 3.0-mile out and back
Hiking time: About 2 hours
Difficulty: Easy
Trail surface: Dirt
Water: None
Seasons: Fall through spring
Other trail users: None
Canine compatibility: Dogs not allowed

Land status: Bureau of Land Management
Nearest town: Austin
Fees and permits: None
USGS topo map: Cold Springs
Trail contacts: Carson City Field Office, 5665 Morgan Mill Rd., Carson City, NV 89701; (775) 885-6000; www.blm.gov

FINDING THE TRAILHEAD

From Austin, go 51 miles west on US 50 to the Pony Express interpretive sign.
Trailhead GPS: N39 23.543 / W117 51.128

WHAT TO SEE
The Cold Springs Trail begins near US 50 at an interpretive display that describes the Pony Express. In 1860 and 1861 the Pony Express delivered mail by horseback from

Ruins of the Cold Springs Pony Express Station

Missouri to California. This trail provides access to a well-preserved Pony Express station. Other historic sites in the vicinity include an Overland Stage and a Transcontinental Telegraph station.

The Pony Express operated for only a year and a half but became famous for the speed and dangers of its service. Mail, at the rate of $5 per half ounce, was carried nearly 2,000 miles from St. Joseph, Missouri, to San Francisco in 10 days by riders covering 60 to 100 miles a day at a full gallop. Stations were 25 miles apart, and the riders stopped only to change horses. The Pony Express carried important dispatches to California at the outbreak of the Civil War and is credited with keeping California in the Union. Several station men, including the Cold Springs stationmaster, and at least one rider were lost to hostile Indian attacks. Advertisements for riders looked for young men without family ties, preferably orphans, who were willing to risk death daily. Late in 1861 the first successful telegraph message was sent between the same cities, ending the need for the Pony Express. Regular mail continued to travel via the Overland Stage system.

—Bureau of Land Management and Bruce Grubbs

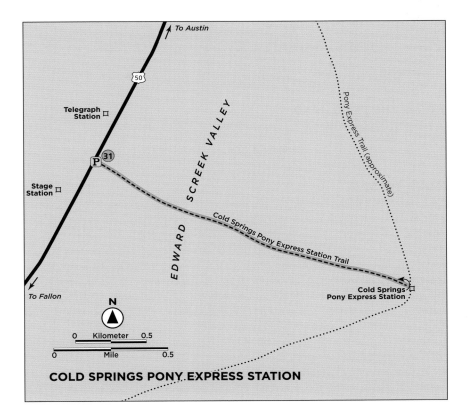

COLD SPRINGS PONY EXPRESS STATION

32. BERLIN-ICHTHYOSAUR STATE PARK

WHY GO?
A day hike in a turn-of-the-20th-century mining town.

THE RUNDOWN
Start: 23 miles northwest of Gabbs
Distance: 1.0-mile loop
Hiking time: About 2 hours
Difficulty: Easy
Trail surface: Dirt
Water: At ranger station and campground
Seasons: Late spring through fall
Other trail users: None
Canine compatibility: Dogs not allowed
Land status: State park

Nearest town: Gabbs
Fees and permits: None
USGS topo map: Ione and Grantsville
Other maps: Forest Service: Humboldt-Toiyabe National Forest, Tonopah Ranger District
Trail contacts: Nevada Division of State Parks, 901 S. Stewart St., 5th Floor, Suite 5005, Carson City, NV 89701-5248; (775) 684-2770; http://parks.nv.gov

FINDING THE TRAILHEAD

From Gabbs, drive north on NV 361 about 3 miles, then turn east onto NV 844. Continue approximately 20 miles on this maintained dirt road to Berlin-Icthyosaur State Park. **Trailhead GPS:** N38 52.549 / W117 35.368

WHAT TO SEE
A self-guided trail leads through the old town of Berlin, with extensive signs explaining the history and features. A nature trail also leads from the campground to the ichthyosaur fossil shelter.

The mining history of the area started in 1863 when a group of prospectors discovered silver in Union Canyon. The Union Mining District was formed in 1864, but the Berlin Mine wasn't established until 1895. The town of Berlin was now in its heyday, which lasted until 1911. At its peak Berlin and its suburbs included about 250 people. Many buildings from this period still remain. The Berlin Mine, a shaft mine with 3 miles of tunnels, produced approximately $849,000 of gold.

Ichthyosaurs—the name means "fish-lizards"—were a group of highly specialized marine reptiles. Fossils have been found dating back 240 million years, and the ichthyosaurs became extinct 90 million years ago. During this time they seem to have occupied the same ecological niche as toothed whales and dolphins. Ichthyosaurs ranged in length from 2 to 50 feet.

The view from Berlin-Ichthyosaur
State Park FAMARTIN

The oldest rocks in the park area are volcanic deposits of unknown age. The rocks exposed in Union Canyon are marine limestones from the Mesozoic era (245 to 65 million years ago). The ichthyosaurs lived in this ocean, and when they died their carcasses sank to the seafloor, where they were slowly covered with hundreds of feet of sediments. Later, as great continental blocks of the earth's crust collided to expand the North American continent westward, the seafloor rose and the ocean drained. About 34 million years ago, the region was buried in lava flows and ashfalls from massive volcanism. Only in recent time, geologically speaking, has faulting and uplifting created the basin-and-range topography characterizing the region today. During this process most of the volcanic rock was eroded away, exposing the marine sediments of Union Canyon.

—Nevada Division of State Parks

33. TOIYABE CREST NATIONAL RECREATION TRAIL

WHY GO?

A 6- to 7-day backpack in the Toiyabe Range along the Toiyabe Crest National Recreation Trail featuring far-ranging alpine and desert views, aspens, and alpine streams.

THE RUNDOWN

Start: 35 miles south of Austin
Distance: 60.5-mile shuttle
Hiking time: 6 to 7 days
Difficulty: Strenuous
Trail surface: Dirt and rocks
Water: Numerous creeks and springs
Seasons: Summer through fall
Other trail users: Equestrians
Canine compatibility: Dogs allowed under control
Land status: Humboldt-Toiyabe National Forest
Nearest town: Austin
Fees and permits: None

USGS topo map: Brewer Canyon, Millet Ranch, Tierney Creek, South Toiyabe Peak, Carvers NW, Arc Dome, and Bakeoven Creek
Other maps: Forest Service: Humboldt-Toiyabe National Forest, Austin Ranger District and Tonopah Ranger District
Trail contacts: Humboldt-Toiyabe National Forest, Austin-Tonopah Ranger District, PO Box 3940, 1400 S. Erie Main St., Tonopah, NV 89049-3940; (775) 482-6286; www.fs.fed .us/r4/htnf

FINDING THE TRAILHEAD

To reach the starting (northern) trailhead from Austin, drive east on US 50, then turn south onto NV 376. Approximately 27 miles from Austin, turn west onto the graded Kingston Creek Road. Park 8 miles from the highway at the head of a reservoir, opposite an abandoned ranch. There is no trailhead sign, but the Toiyabe Crest Trail is obvious switchbacking up the slope to the south. **Trailhead GPS:** N39 14.754 / W117 10.025

The trip will require a car left at the southern trailhead, South Twin River. From Tonopah, drive about 6 miles east on US 95, then turn left (north) onto NV 376 and continue for 60.5 miles. At the signed, graded Twin River Road (FR 080), turn left (west) and continue 3 miles to the signed trailhead. **Trailhead GPS:** N38 53.314 / W117 14.599

WHAT TO SEE

Since its designation as a national recreation trail, the Toiyabe Crest Trail has received more maintenance and signage, though some sections are still little used and may be difficult to find. The trail is depicted fairly accurately on USGS topographic maps, but sections of old trail confuse the route, and new roads have been constructed in some of

Backpacking the Toiyabe Crest
National Recreation Trail

Some of the Toiyabe Crest
National Recreation Trail is
faint and difficult to find.

the side canyons along the northern portion of the trail. Be sure you have the USGS topographic maps and some experience in off-trail route finding.

In early summer water is plentiful: Most drainages and springs will be flowing, and there will be snow to melt along the higher sections. Late in the summer and into fall, it may be necessary to carry more water along for the drier sections, especially at the north end of the trip.

From 7,500 feet at the trailhead, the trail climbs steeply to the crest over a distance of several miles, and reaches a flat-topped section of ridge at 10,400 feet. The trail stays along the crest until it descends into an aspen grove at the head of Washington Creek, where there is good camping.

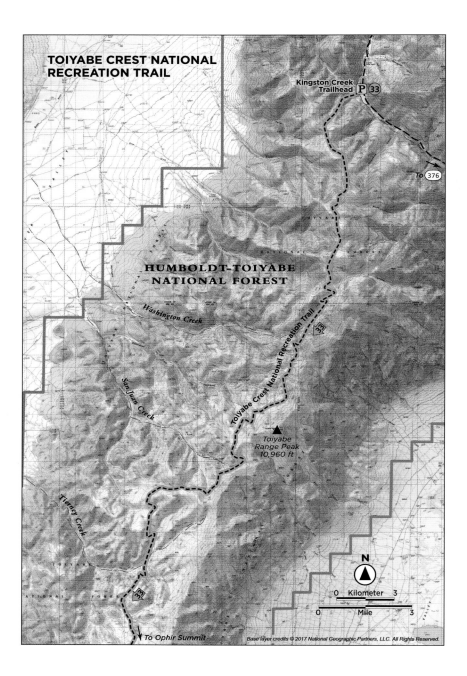

TOIYABE CREST NATIONAL
RECREATION TRAIL

Kingston Creek
Trailhead P 33

To 376

HUMBOLDT-TOIYABE
NATIONAL FOREST

Washington Creek

San Juan Creek

Toiyabe Crest National Recreation Trail

33

Toiyabe
Range Peak
10,960 ft

Tierney Creek

33

N

0   Kilometer   3

0   Mile   3

To Ophir Summit

Base layer credits © 2017 National Geographic Partners, LLC. All Rights Reserved.

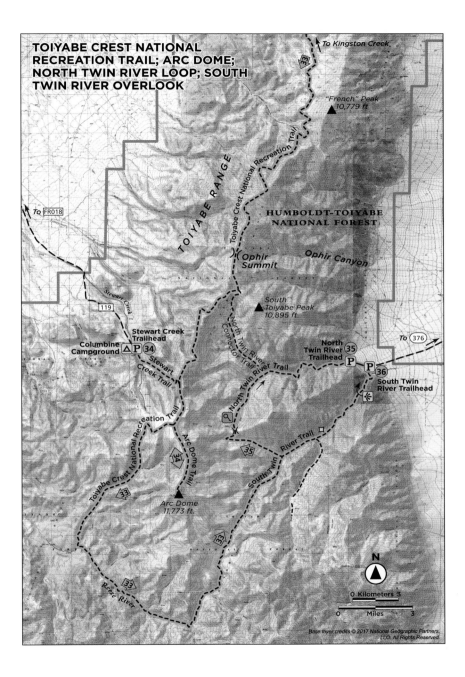

TOIYABE CREST NATIONAL RECREATION TRAIL; ARC DOME; NORTH TWIN RIVER LOOP; SOUTH TWIN RIVER OVERLOOK

To Kingston Creek

33

"French" Peak
10,779 ft

Toiyabe Crest National Recreation Trail

TOIYABE RANGE

To FR018

HUMBOLDT-TOIYABE
NATIONAL FOREST

Ophir Summit

Ophir Canyon

Stewart Creek

119

South
Toiyabe Peak
10,895 ft

North Twin River Connector Trail

Stewart Creek
Trailhead

Columbine
Campground   34

Stewart
Creek Trail

North Twin River Trail

To 376

North
Twin River
Trailhead   35

South Twin
River Trailhead   36

Toiyabe Crest National Recreation Trail

Arc Dome Trail

34

35

South Twin River Trail

33

Arc Dome
11,773 ft.

33

N

33

Reese River

0 Kilometers 3

0 Miles 3

South of Washington Creek, the trail traverses the northwest slopes of Toiyabe Range Peak. This 10,960-foot mountain is an easy climb, and the views of the desert 6,000 feet below and the adjoining ranges are well worth the effort. Boundary Peak in the White Mountains, the highest point in Nevada, is visible far to the southwest.

Continuing on the trail, there is good camping in an aspen grove on the west ridge of Toiyabe Range Peak. To the south, the trail stays on the west side of the crest as it heads the numerous forks of San Juan and Tierney Creeks. This is the faintest section of the trail and may be lost occasionally. The springs at the two heads of the south forks of Tierney Creek provides good camping.

The trail south of "French" Peak (10,779 feet) is clearer. After crossing Ophir Summit and the end of FR 017, the trail continues south toward Arc Dome. Just south of Ophir Summit, it is possible to end the trip early by turning southeast onto the North Twin River Connector Trail and descending about 7 miles to the trailhead on Twin River Road.

The Crest Trail continues along the main crest, meeting the Stewart Creek Trail, which descends to the northwest. Finally, about 1.5 miles south of the junction with the Stewart Creek Trail, the Crest Trail itself leaves the crest and descends west to Sawmill Creek.

Before leaving the crest, you might want to take the worthwhile side trip to the 11,773-foot summit of Arc Dome. This hike is 5.2 miles out and back.

The Crest Trail then follows Sawmill Creek south for about 5 miles to the Reese River, where it turns southeast upriver. In just over a mile, the Peavine Canyon Trail comes in from the south. About 4 miles farther on, the Reese River turns sharply to the northeast where the Toms Canyon Trail comes in from the south. The Crest Trail continues 4 miles to a pass at the head of the Reese River, where it meets the South Twin River Trail. Follow the South Twin River Trail down South Twin River to the trailhead.

The Toiyabe Crest Trail and its spur trails were constructed by the Civilian Conservation Corps during the 1930s. Evidence of their skilled work still survives today along the trails.

Looking south along the Toiyabe Crest

Old trail sign,
Toiyabe Range

Although the Toiyabe Range is well watered for a Nevada mountain range, it has noticeably fewer trees than the ranges farther to the east. This is probably due to the lack of summer rain. In the Southwest most summer rain comes in the form of afternoon thunderstorms, which form in warm humid air moving up from the Gulf of Mexico. Central Nevada is too far from the source of moisture to have reliable summer rains.

MILES AND DIRECTIONS

0.0 Kingston Creek trailhead.

8.5 Washington Creek.

14.1 San Juan Creek.

19.7 Tierney Creek.

27.4 Marysville Canyon.

31.3 Ophir Summit (pass at head of Ophir Canyon).

32.6 North Twin River Connector Trail descends southeast.

36.9 Stewart Creek Trail descends northwest.

38.3 Crest Trail descends southwest into Sawmill Creek. (**Option:** Take side trip to Arc Dome.)

44.6 Reese River; Crest Trail turns east upriver.

46.4 Peavine Canyon Trail joins from south.

49.3 Toms Canyon Trail joins from south.

53.0 Pass at head of Reese River and start of South Twin River Trail.

60.5 South Twin River trailhead.

34. ARC DOME

📷 🚶

WHY GO?

A long day hike to Arc Dome, which at 11,773 feet is the highest peak in the Toiyabe Range. This is the shortest route to the summit.

THE RUNDOWN

See map on page 119
Start: 80 miles northwest of Tonopah
Distance: 12.8-mile out and back
Hiking time: About 8 hours
Difficulty: Strenuous
Trail surface: Dirt and rocks
Water: None
Seasons: Summer through fall
Other trail users: Equestrians on Stewart Creek and Toiyabe Crest Trails
Canine compatibility: Dogs allowed under control
Land status: Humboldt-Toiyabe National Forest

Nearest town: Tonopah
Fees and permits: None
USGS topo map: Corral Wash, Bakeoven Creek, South Toiyabe Peak, and Arc Dome
Other maps: Forest Service: Humboldt-Toiyabe National Forest, Tonopah Ranger District
Trail contacts: Humboldt-Toiyabe National Forest, Austin-Tonopah Ranger District, PO Box 3940, 1400 S. Erie Main St., Tonopah, NV 89049-3940; (775) 482-6286; www.fs.fed.us/r4/htnf

FINDING THE TRAILHEAD

From Tonopah, drive west about 6 miles on US 95 to the Gabbs Poleline Road. Continue on Poleline Road, then turn east onto Cloverdale Road. Just past the old Cloverdale Ranch, turn east onto FR 018. Continue 30 miles to the Reese River administrative site, then turn east onto FR 119; follow this road 13 miles to its end at Columbine Campground and the signed trailhead. **Trailhead GPS:** N38 53.995 / W117 22.582

WHAT TO SEE

The Stewart Creek Trail stays on the right (south) side of the creek as it climbs steadily through quaking aspen groves. About a mile from the campground, a signed junction falsely indicates that the Stewart Creek Trail goes left. (This fork is actually a shortcut if you're heading north on the Toiyabe Crest National Recreation Trail, or over to North Twin River.) Staying to the right, continue along Stewart Creek for another mile to meet the Toiyabe Crest Trail at a signed junction. Turn right; the trail climbs into a pleasant valley floored with a broad meadow. It stays near a fence line on the north side of the valley, then crosses the creek and switchbacks up to a sage flat at 10,000 feet. The Crest Trail, an old jeep trail, now climbs gradually along a gentle sagebrush bench. Toward the south end of this bench, watch for an unsigned fork. The Crest Trail contours south; turn

Summer dryness and harsh winters make difficult growing conditions high in the Toiyabe Range.

Arc Dome, at 11,773 feet the highest summit in the Toiyabe Range, high above the South Twin River Trail

left, uphill, onto the Arc Dome Trail, which is the old jeep trail. The Arc Dome Trail climbs steeply to the southeast to reach the broad crest of the Toiyabe Range at 11,000 feet. The trail now swings east, then south as the crest gradually climbs. The impressive north ridge of Arc Dome comes into view, and the trail, now a footpath, descends about 600 feet into a saddle. The trail uses many short switchbacks to go almost directly up the north ridge to the summit.

The view is expansive, encompassing much of the Toiyabe Range and the Arc Dome Wilderness to the east and north, and, to the southwest, the White Mountains and the Sierra Nevada.

—USDA Forest Service and Bruce Grubbs

MILES AND DIRECTIONS

0.0 Stewart Creek trailhead.

2.3 Toiyabe Crest Trail; turn right (south).

3.8 Arc Dome Trail; turn left (south).

6.4 Arc Dome.

12.8 Return to Stewart Creek trailhead.

35. **NORTH TWIN RIVER LOOP**

WHY GO?
A long day hike or overnight backpack trip through a series of spectacular canyons in the Toiyabe Range.

THE RUNDOWN

See map on page 119
Start: 70 miles north of Tonopah
Distance: 13.4-mile loop
Hiking time: About 9 hours, or 2 days
Difficulty: Strenuous
Trail surface: Dirt and rocks
Water: South Twin River, North Twin River
Seasons: Summer through fall
Other trail users: Equestrians
Canine compatibility: Dogs allowed under control
Land status: Toiyabe National Forest

Nearest town: Tonopah
Fees and permits: None
USGS topo map: Carvers NW, South Toiyabe Peak, and Arc Dome
Other maps: Forest Service: Humboldt-Toiyabe National Forest, Tonopah Ranger District
Trail contacts: Humboldt-Toiyabe National Forest, Austin-Tonopah Ranger District, PO Box 3940, 1400 S. Erie Main St., Tonopah, NV 89049-3940; (775) 482-6286; www.fs.fed .us/r4/htnf

FINDING THE TRAILHEAD
From Tonopah, drive about 6 miles east on US 95, then turn left (north) onto NV 376 for 60.5 miles. At the signed Twin River Road (FR 080), turn left (west) and drive 4.1 miles to the trailhead (passing the South Twin River trailhead at 3 miles). **Trailhead GPS:** N38 53.661 / W117 15.241

WHAT TO SEE
This is a loop hike using the South Twin River and North Twin River Trails. Although it can be done in one long day, there are enough side attractions to make this a 2- or even 3-day backpack trip.

You'll be hiking this loop clockwise. To start, walk 1.0 mile down the access road to the South Twin River trailhead. Hike up the obvious but unsigned trail that climbs the slope east of the canyon. One large switchback takes you to a saddle overlooking the spectacular lower South Twin River Canyon, a gorge rivaling the Granite Gorge of the Grand Canyon. The trail contours to another pass, and an old jeep road joins from the right. This road was built to allow motorized access to a mine within the wilderness area, and is open only to the permittee. Fortunately the miner doesn't seem to be using it.

After the second saddle, the trail drops to the creek, where it stays, crossing as necessary. The somber walls tower high above, and there are places where it seems unlikely that a trail would have been built. About 3 miles from the trailhead, you'll see the ruins

Late afternoon sun highlights the rough slopes of the North Twin River canyon in the Toiyabe Range.

Old waterwheel, North Twin River, Toiyabe Range

Fall color contrasts with the craggy sage-covered slopes at the North Twin River trailhead, Toiyabe Range.

The North Twin River tumbles through an aspen grove in the Toiyabe Range.

of an old waterwheel and ore crusher on the right. Although much of the structure has collapsed, the waterwheel can still be turned by hand. Just beyond the ruin there is a fine campsite, and within a short distance, the old mine road turns left up the south fork. The South Twin River Trail, signed the "Crest Trail," continues up the main fork and becomes a foot trail.

After a steep climb through another deep, narrow canyon, the trail levels out somewhat as the canyon opens out, providing views of the high country. In 1.5 miles turn right (west) at the trail going up the north fork of the South Twin River, which is signed "North Twin River." There is limited camping at this junction.

The trail up the north fork climbs steadily along the right side of the canyon. Water is available intermittently, but other sections of the creek are dry. The trail is distinct and easy to follow, but watch for an abrupt switchback near the head of the canyon, about 2 miles from the junction. The switchback leads through a dense stand of mountain mahogany to the pass between the South and North Twin Rivers.

Dropping off the saddle to the north, the trail passes the springs shown on the USGS topographic map, which appears to be reliable. The trail stays generally west of the creek for the first mile, then descends through a stand of aspen. About 0.7 mile beyond this point, a side canyon comes in from the west, and the North Twin River Connector Trail goes left here, heading northwest to the Toiyabe Crest National Recreation Trail. Only the first 0.2 mile of this trail is shown on the USGS topographic map. Continue down the North Twin River Trail through more magnificent aspens. In 0.6 mile there is a second signed trail going left (west) to the Crest Trail, and it is not shown at all on the USGS topographic map. To the right (east) of this junction is a large campsite in the aspen forest.

The main trail stays left of the creek for nearly a mile and then climbs slightly for a nice view of the rugged lower gorge. The last 2 miles of the trail drop rapidly through the gorge, and the stream noisily follows suit. The aspens give way to narrowleaf cottonwoods, water birches, and other lower-elevation streamside growth. About 0.5 mile from the mouth of the canyon, there is a brief view of the Smokey Valley. Shortly thereafter the trail turns into a jeep road and emerges from the canyon at the trailhead.

—Bruce Grubbs and USDA Forest Service

MILES AND DIRECTIONS

0.0   North Twin River trailhead.

0.8   South Twin River trailhead.

1.2   First saddle.

3.9   South Fork Twin River; stay right on South Twin River (Crest) Trail.

5.2   North Twin River Trail; turn right.

7.6   Pass.

10.0   North Twin River Connector Trail; stay right.

13.4   North Twin River trailhead.

36. **SOUTH TWIN RIVER OVERLOOK**

WHY GO?

An easy day hike to a spectacular canyon in the Toiyabe Range.

THE RUNDOWN

See map on page 119
Start: 70 miles north of Tonopah
Distance: 0.8-mile out and back
Hiking time: About 1 hour
Difficulty: Easy
Trail surface: Dirt and rocks
Water: South Twin River at trailhead
Seasons: Summer through fall
Other trail users: Equestrians
Canine compatibility: Dogs allowed under control
Land status: Humboldt-Toiyabe National Forest

Nearest town: Tonopah
Fees and permits: None
USGS topo map: Carvers NW and Arc Dome
Other maps: Forest Service: Humboldt-Toiyabe National Forest, Tonopah Ranger District
Trail contacts: Humboldt-Toiyabe National Forest, Austin-Tonopah Ranger District, PO Box 3940, 1400 S. Erie Main St., Tonopah, NV 89049-3940; (775) 482-6286; www.fs.fed.us/r4/htnf

FINDING THE TRAILHEAD

From Tonopah, drive about 6 miles east on US 95, then turn left (north) onto NV 376 and continue for 60.5 miles. At the signed, graded Twin River Road (FR 080), turn left (west) and continue 3 miles to the signed trailhead.
Trailhead GPS: N38 53.314 / W117 14.599

WHAT TO SEE

This is an easy hike with a short, graded access road in a mountain range where most of the hikes are difficult and the access roads long. Hikers passing by on NV 376 can complete this hike in an hour or so, and get a quick idea what treats await deeper in the mountains.

The South Twin River Trail is part of the Toiyabe Crest National Recreation Trail and visible from the trailhead as it climbs the mountainside in a large switchback. (Ignore the road going into the creek.) This hike takes you up the switchback to the first saddle. From this vantage point, 500 feet above the trailhead, there is a fine view of the lower South Twin River Canyon, with its cascading mountain stream, cottonwood trees, and towering rock walls. In contrast, the vast Smokey Valley spreads out to the north, and the buttresses forming the east slopes of the Toiyabe Range march off into the distance.

The South Twin River Trail in the Toiyabe Range makes a dramatic entry into the craggy lower canyon.

37. JETT CANYON TRAIL

WHY GO?
A day hike through a dramatic canyon and bighorn sheep area in the Toiyabe Range.

THE RUNDOWN

Start: 60 miles north of Tonopah
Distance: 4.0-mile out and back
Hiking time: About 2 hours
Difficulty: Easy
Trail surface: Dirt and rocks
Water: Jett Creek
Seasons: Summer through fall
Other trail users: Equestrians
Canine compatibility: Dogs allowed under control
Land status: Humboldt-Toiyabe National Forest
Nearest town: Tonopah

Fees and permits: None
USGS topo map: Pablo Canyon Ranch, Toms Canyon, and Arc Dome
Other maps: Forest Service: Humboldt-Toiyabe National Forest, Tonopah Ranger District
Trail contacts: Humboldt-Toiyabe National Forest, Austin-Tonopah Ranger District, PO Box 3940, 1400 S. Erie Main St., Tonopah, NV 89049-3940; (775) 482-6286; www.fs.fed.us/r4/htnf

Old mines and mill sites are found throughout the Toiyabe Range.

FINDING THE TRAILHEAD

From Tonopah, drive about 6 miles east on US 95, then turn left (north) onto NV 376 and continue for 47.7 miles. At the signed Jett Canyon Road (FR 090), turn left (west), continue 5 miles to a cattle guard at the mouth of the canyon, and park on the right. The road turns into a jeep road here and is normally closed at a locked gate about 0.3 mile farther on. **Trailhead GPS:** N38 43.402 / W117 12.441

WHAT TO SEE

This is an easy walk up a deep, narrow canyon. The rugged walls are ideal bighorn sheep country, and if you're alert, you may see a band running casually across impossible-looking terrain. The trail continues about 5 miles up the canyon before ending near the head of the drainage, but stopping after 2 miles keeps this an easy hike, if you prefer. It is possible for those skilled in cross-country hiking and map reading to continue beyond the end of the trail into the Arc Dome area.

—USDA Forest Service and Bruce Grubbs

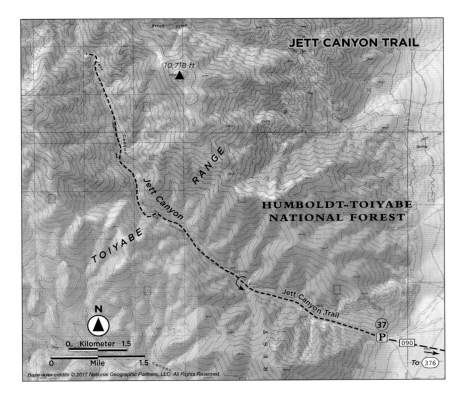

38. **TOMS CANYON TRAIL**

WHY GO?

An overnight or longer backpack trip providing access to the upper Reese River country and the Toiyabe Crest National Recreation Trail.

THE RUNDOWN

Start: 50 miles north of Tonopah
Distance: 13.0-mile out and back
Hiking time: About 8 hours
Difficulty: Strenuous
Trail surface: Dirt and rocks
Water: Toms Canyon
Seasons: Summer through fall
Other trail users: Equestrians
Canine compatibility: Dogs allowed under control
Land status: Humboldt-Toiyabe National Forest
Nearest town: Tonopah

Fees and permits: None
USGS topo map: Toms Canyon and Arc Dome
Other maps: Forest Service: Humboldt-Toiyabe National Forest, Tonopah Ranger District
Trail contacts: Humboldt-Toiyabe National Forest, Austin-Tonopah Ranger District, PO Box 3940, 1400 S. Erie Main St., Tonopah, NV 89049-3940; (775) 482-6286; www.fs.fed .us/r4/htnf

FINDING THE TRAILHEAD

From Tonopah, drive east on US 95 about 6 miles, then turn left (north) onto NV 376. Continue 34.5 miles to the signed, graded Peavine Campground turnoff on the left (FR 020), and follow it past the campground to a signed junction at 14.5 miles. Turn right and drive 0.7 mile to the trailhead. There is good camping and also water in the creek at the trailhead. **Trailhead GPS:** N38 41.232 / W117 20.084

WHAT TO SEE

The Toms Canyon Trail follows Toms Canyon, then crosses a 9,360-foot pass between Peavine and Mahogany Mountains. This pass is a good destination for a day hike. The trail continues north down Trail Creek about 2 miles to join the Toiyabe Crest National Recreation Trail. A 3-day loop trip could be completed using the Peavine Canyon Trail, and longer trips could use the Crest Trail and the North Twin River Trail.
—USDA Forest Service and Bruce Grubbs

MILES AND DIRECTIONS

0.0   Toms Canyon trailhead.

4.9   Pass.

6.5   Toiyabe Crest National Recreation Trail and turnaround point.

13.0   Return to Toms Canyon trailhead.

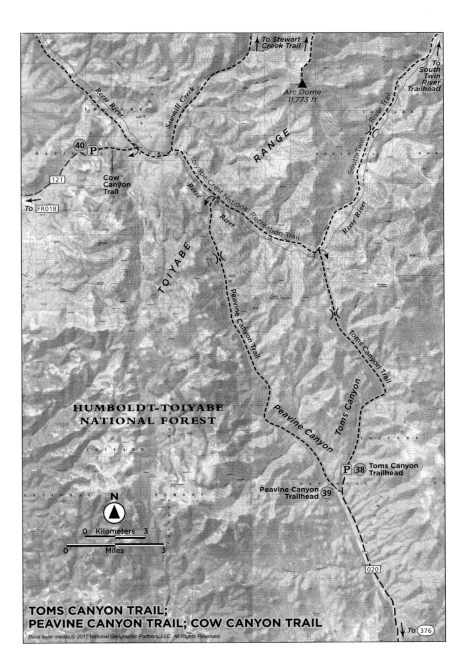

To Stewart
Creek Trail

To
South
Twin
River
Trailhead

Reese River

Sawmill Creek

Arc Dome
11,773 ft

RANGE

40 P

Cow
Canyon
Trail

Toiyabe Crest National Recreation Trail

Reese River

South Twin River Trail

121

To FR018

Reese River

TOIYABE

Peavine Canyon Trail

Toms Canyon Trail

HUMBOLDT-TOIYABE
NATIONAL FOREST

Peavine Canyon

Toms Canyon

N

Toms Canyon
Trailhead

P 38

0   Kilometers   3

Peavine Canyon
Trailhead

39

0   Miles   3

020

**TOMS CANYON TRAIL;
PEAVINE CANYON TRAIL; COW CANYON TRAIL**

To 376

39. PEAVINE CANYON TRAIL

WHY GO?

An overnight or longer backpack trip in the Toiyabe Range. This route provides access to the Arc Dome Wilderness from the south via a long but gradual trail.

THE RUNDOWN

See map on page 133
Start: 50 miles north of Tonopah
Distance: 17.6-mile out and back
Hiking time: About 10 hours
Difficulty: Strenuous
Trail surface: Dirt and rocks
Water: Peavine Canyon
Seasons: Summer through fall
Other trail users: Equestrians
Canine compatibility: Dogs allowed under control
Land status: Humboldt-Toiyabe National Forest
Nearest town: Tonopah

Fees and permits: None
USGS topo map: Toms Canyon, Farrington Canyon, and Bakeoven Creek
Other maps: Forest Service: Humboldt-Toiyabe National Forest, Tonopah Ranger District
Trail contacts: Humboldt-Toiyabe National Forest, Austin-Tonopah Ranger District, PO Box 3940, 1400 S. Erie Main St., Tonopah, NV 89049-3940; (775) 482-6286; www.fs.fed.us/r4/htnf

FINDING THE TRAILHEAD

From Tonopah, drive east on US 95 about 6 miles, then turn left (north) onto NV 376. Continue 47.7 miles to the signed, graded Peavine Campground turnoff on the left (FR 020), and follow it past the campground to a signed junction at 14.5 miles. Turn left and park. There are no campsites at the trailhead and there is limited parking. **Trailhead GPS:** N38 41.032 / W117 20.286

WHAT TO SEE

The Peavine Canyon Trail follows an old jeep trail initially. It has a much gentler gradient than most Toiyabe trails. The trail stays in Peavine Canyon to its head, crosses a pass at 8,634 feet, then gradually descends a drainage to meet the Toiyabe Crest National Recreation Trail at the Reese River. This trail is useful for access to the Crest Trail and could also be used for a 3-day backpack in a loop with the Toms Canyon Trail, with a short car shuttle or road walk between trailheads. For an overnight backpack trip, the Reese River is a logical destination.

—USDA Forest Service and Bruce Grubbs

Snow lingers until late in the summer along the high Toiyabe Range.

MILES AND DIRECTIONS

0.0 Peavine Canyon trailhead.

7.1 Pass.

8.8 Toiyabe Crest Trail at Reese River.

17.6 Return to Peavine Canyon trailhead.

40. **COW CANYON TRAIL**

WHY GO?

A day hike in the Toiyabe Range offering easy access to Arc Dome Wilderness and the Toiyabe Crest National Recreation Trail.

THE RUNDOWN

See map on page 133
Start: 50 miles northwest of Tonopah
Distance: 2.4-mile out and back
Hiking time: About 2 hours
Difficulty: Easy
Trail surface: Dirt and rocks
Water: None
Seasons: Summer through fall
Other trail users: Equestrians
Canine compatibility: Dogs allowed under control
Land status: Humboldt-Toiyabe National Forest

Nearest town: Tonopah
Fees and permits: None
USGS topo map: Bakeoven Creek
Other maps: Forest Service: Humboldt-Toiyabe National Forest, Tonopah Ranger District
Trail contacts: Humboldt-Toiyabe National Forest, Austin-Tonopah Ranger District, PO Box 3940, 1400 S. Erie Main St., Tonopah, NV 89049-3940; (775) 482-6286; www.fs.fed .us/r4/htnf

FINDING THE TRAILHEAD

From Tonopah, drive about 6 miles west on US 95 to Gabbs Poleline Road. Continue on Poleline Road approximately 30 miles, then turn east onto Cloverdale Road. Pass the old Cloverdale Ranch, then turn east onto FR 018. Continue just past Cloverdale Summit, then turn right onto FR 121; stay on this road to its end. **Trailhead GPS:** N38 48.47 / W117 26.843

WHAT TO SEE

The trail starts at an 8,000-foot saddle then drops east 1.2 miles into the Reese River Canyon. This route is a popular, short access to the Reese River country, and also connects with the Toiyabe Crest National Recreation Trail. It is possible to create a 4-day or longer loop backpack trip using the Crest Trail and the North Twin River Trail.
—USDA Forest Service and Bruce Grubbs

41. MOUNT JEFFERSON

WHY GO?

A 2- or 3-day trail and cross-country backpack trip over the top of Mount Jefferson, in the Toquima Range.

THE RUNDOWN

Start: 65 miles northeast of Tonopah
Distance: 16.8-mile loop
Hiking time: 2 or 3 days
Difficulty: Strenuous
Trail surface: Cross-country
Water: Pasco Creek, Pine Creek, and an unnamed spring on Mount Jefferson
Seasons: Summer through fall
Other trail users: Equestrians on the Pine Creek Trail
Canine compatibility: Dogs allowed under control
Land status: Humboldt-Toiyabe National Forest

Nearest town: Tonopah
Fees and permits: None
USGS topo map: Pine Creek Ranch and Mount Jefferson
Other maps: Forest Service: Humboldt-Toiyabe National Forest, Tonopah Ranger District
Trail contacts: Humboldt-Toiyabe National Forest, Austin-Tonopah Ranger District, PO Box 3940, 1400 S. Erie Main St., Tonopah, NV 89049-3940; (775) 482-6286; www.fs.fed .us/r4/htnf

---

FINDING THE TRAILHEAD

From Tonopah, drive east about 6 miles on US 6, then turn left (north) onto NV 376. After 13 miles, turn right (east) onto the signed, paved Monitor Valley Road. Continue 46.5 miles on this road, which turns to graded dirt after Belmont, then turn left (south) onto the signed, graded Pine Creek Road (FR 009). After 1 mile, turn right (west) at a sign for campground, then drive 2.6 miles to the campground. The trailhead is signed, and is on the north side of the campground as you enter. **Trailhead GPS:** N38 47.734 / W116 51.119

WHAT TO SEE

Four miles of this hike traverses the 11,500–foot-plus Mount Jefferson plateau. The summit plateau is treeless, and there is no shelter from high wind or bad weather. Be prepared for windy, cold conditions; if you plan to camp on the summit plateau, make certain you have a good tent.

Rather than doing a car shuttle between the Pasco Canyon and Pine Creek trailheads, it is easy to walk the foothills from Pine Creek to Pasco Canyon. Starting from the Pine Creek trailhead, walk north, keeping just at the base of the mountains. You'll find the Pasco Canyon trailhead at the mouth of Pasco Canyon on the north side of the creek.

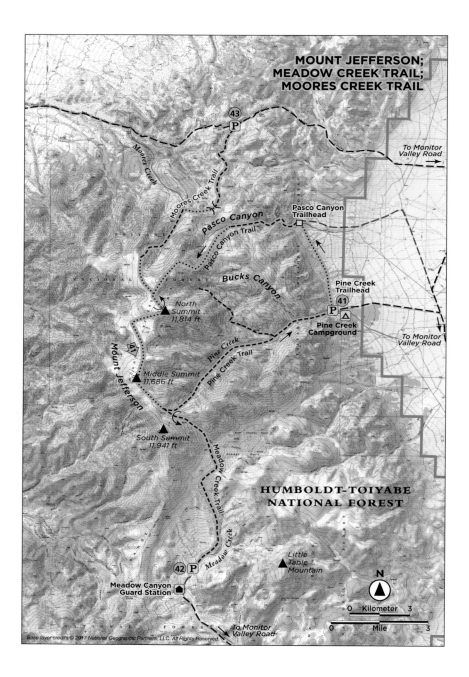

**MOUNT JEFFERSON;
MEADOW CREEK TRAIL;
MOORES CREEK TRAIL**

To Monitor
Valley Road

Moores Creek

Moores Creek Trail

Pasco Canyon

Pasco Canyon
Trailhead

Pasco Canyon Trail

Bucks Canyon

Pine Creek
Trailhead

North
Summit
11,814 ft

Pine Creek

Pine Creek Trail

Pine Creek
Campground

To Monitor
Valley Road

Mount Jefferson

Middle Summit
11,686 ft

South Summit
11,941 ft

Meadow Creek Trail

HUMBOLDT-TOIYABE
NATIONAL FOREST

Little
Table
Mountain

Meadow Creek

N

Meadow Canyon
Guard Station

To Monitor
Valley Road

0   Kilometer   3

0   Mile   3

Aspen and limber pine on the upper slopes of Pasco Canyon, Toquima Range

A sign near the trailhead gives credit to the Tonopah Explorer Scout Post for reconstructing the Pasco Canyon Trail during 1988–89. The trail contours along the slope to reach the bottom of the canyon. For the next mile, the trail stays in the bed through a narrow section hemmed in by high cliffs. The trail is overgrown but easy to follow through this section. As the canyon opens out, aspens appear. The trail continues to the last stand of aspens where there is a spring, then fades out. There is a nice view of the North Summit of Mount Jefferson from this open basin, and this is a good destination for an easy day hike.

There is no reliable water source in Pasco Canyon above this point, so those continuing with the loop over the mountain should pick up enough water for the climb. Stay in the canyon bottom another 0.5 mile to the 8,600-foot contour, then start cross-country southwest up the ridge leading to the elevation marked 11188 on the topographic map. The first mile is moderate; then the ascent becomes much steeper. After the 11188 point, follow the ridgetop west then southwest over the 11,691-foot summit. Although the map shows a trail here, only faint traces exist. The trails across Mount Jefferson apparently don't get enough use to remain distinct, and there are no cairns. However, it is easy to walk cross-country on the broad ridges.

Go south through the broad saddle, then southwest along the side of the North Summit. West of the North Summit, you will come out onto a very flat area at 11,000 feet. A small creek meanders through the alpine tundra, and there are plenty of campsites. The view of the Toiyabe Range to the west is expansive.

Pine Creek Canyon, a classic glacial canyon, is the most popular access to the Alta Toquima Wilderness.

An avalanche path in Pine Creek Canyon

A beautiful mixture of mountain mahogany, quaking aspen, and bristlecone pines cover the upper slopes of Pine Creek Canyon in the Toquima Range.

Hike southeast to regain the ridge crest, then go south, passing east of the Middle Summit. From here, you can look down at a small lake in the South Fork of Pine Creek, and the aspen- and pine-filled basin. Continue southeast, heading for the upper end of Pine Creek, which is just north of the South Summit. Watch for bighorn sheep in this area. As you drop toward the rim, head for the lowest point. A series of rock cairns marks the beginning of the trail descending to Pine Creek, and the trail gets better as you drop over the rim. A sign marks the junction with the south end of the Summit Trail.

Turn left (east) and continue the descent along Pine Creek. After less than a mile, the trail enters a mixed forest of aspen and bristlecone pine, a pleasant sight after the stark summit plateau. In late summer this section of the creek may be dry. There is reliable water where the trail first crosses to the north side of the creek, and a nice campsite in the aspens. Several avalanche paths funnel major winter snowslides down the north wall of the canyon—the destroyed trees attest to their force.

Just as the trail and the creek enter the lower, craggy section of the canyon (about 1 mile from the trailhead), there is a cairn marking the trail to Bucks Canyon. Continue down the Pine Creek Trail to the trailhead.

MILES AND DIRECTIONS

0.0 Pine Creek trailhead; hike north, cross-country, along foot of range.

2.5 Pasco Canyon trailhead.

4.0 Trail fades out at spring in aspen grove; continue up main canyon.

4.5 Start up ridge leading to 11188 elevation point.

6.1 11188 elevation point; continue up ridge.

8.1 North Summit; head west to unnamed spring and campsites.

9.0 Unnamed spring; go south-southeast back onto main ridge, and continue south to Middle Summit.

10.5 Middle Summit; hike southeast to head of southernmost fork of Pine Creek, and descend to creek to intercept Pine Creek Trail.

11.6 Pine Creek Trail; follow trail east, down Pine Creek.

14.4 Aspen grove with springs and campsites.

16.8 Return to Pine Creek trailhead.

42. **MEADOW CREEK TRAIL**

WHY GO?

A day hike in the Toquima Range, featuring access to the scenic Mount Jefferson crest trail from the south and a remote alpine basin.

THE RUNDOWN

See map on page 138
Start: 83 miles north of Tonopah
Distance: 10.2-mile out and back
Hiking time: About 7 hours
Difficulty: Strenuous
Trail surface: Dirt and rocks
Water: None
Seasons: Summer through fall
Other trail users: Equestrians
Canine compatibility: Dogs allowed under control
Land status: Humboldt-Toiyabe National Forest

Nearest town: Tonopah
Fees and permits: None
USGS topo map: Pine Creek Ranch, Mount Jefferson, and Jefferson
Other maps: Forest Service: Humboldt-Toiyabe National Forest, Tonopah Ranger District
Trail contacts: Humboldt-Toiyabe National Forest, Austin-Tonopah Ranger District, PO Box 3940, 1400 S. Erie Main St., Tonopah, NV 89049-3940; (775) 482-6286; www.fs.fed.us/r4/htnf

FINDING THE TRAILHEAD

From Tonopah, drive east about 6 miles on US 6, then turn left (north) onto NV 376. After 13 miles, turn northeast (right) onto the paved Monitor Valley Road. Continue on this road past Belmont (where it becomes a graded, dirt road) 32.3 miles, then turn left onto the signed, graded Meadow Canyon Road. The road goes through a fine section of narrow canyon; then the canyon opens out into a series of meadows. The road passes the Meadow Canyon Guard Station 8.1 miles from the turnoff; continue on the unmaintained road another 1.2 miles. You will see an unsigned jeep road turning off to the left (north). Park here. **Trailhead GPS:** N38 42.139 / W116 54.852

WHAT TO SEE

Follow the jeep trail as it climbs the ridge just west of the head of Meadow Creek. This section is a steady climb on a moderate grade with panoramic views of the Meadow Creek Basin. After about 2 miles, the jeep trail turns east and contours to Windy Pass, overlooking Andrews Basin. The route becomes a foot trail after the pass, climbing across the upper section of Andrews Basin, then climbing steeply to a saddle on the ridge east of the South Summit of Mount Jefferson. This saddle, your destination, offers sweeping

An old stone cabin in Meadow Creek in the Toquima Range is roofed with timber and sod.

views of Andrews Basin and upper Pine Creek close at hand, and the Monitor Valley and Monitor Range farther to the east.

—USDA Forest Service and Bruce Grubbs

MILES AND DIRECTIONS

0.0 Meadow Creek trailhead; follow jeep trail up ridge just west of head of Meadow Creek.

3.2 Windy Pass; follow foot trail across Andrews Basin.

5.1 Saddle east of South Summit.

10.2 Return to Meadow Creek trailhead.

Option: The Meadow Creek Trail continues into the head of Pine Creek to meet the Pine Creek Trail and the Summit Trail. If a car shuttle is used, a traverse of Mount Jefferson can be done, exiting at Pasco Canyon or Moores Creek.

43. MOORES CREEK TRAIL

WHY GO?

A day hike in the Toquima Range offering access to the north end of the Mount Jefferson Plateau.

THE RUNDOWN

See map on page 138
Start: 83 miles north of Tonopah
Distance: 13.6-mile out and back
Hiking time: About 10 hours
Difficulty: Strenuous
Trail surface: Cross-country
Water: Seasonal in upper Moores Creek
Seasons: Summer through fall
Other trail users: Equestrians
Canine compatibility: Dogs allowed under control
Land status: Humboldt-Toiyabe National Forest

Nearest town: Tonopah
Fees and permits: None
USGS topo map: Mount Jefferson
Other maps: Forest Service: Humboldt-Toiyabe National Forest, Tonopah Ranger District
Trail contacts: Humboldt-Toiyabe National Forest, Austin-Tonopah Ranger District, PO Box 3940, 1400 S. Erie Main St., Tonopah, NV 89049-3940; (775) 482-6286; www.fs.fed.us/r4/htnf

FINDING THE TRAILHEAD

To reach the Moores Creek trailhead from Tonopah, drive east about 6 miles on US 6, then turn left (north) onto NV 376 and drive approximately 62 miles. Turn east onto the signed, graded Toquima Range Road (FR 008), go 5.4 miles, then turn right (signed 008). After another 4.9 miles, turn left (signed Moores Creek and 008). Continue 7.9 miles to Moores Creek Summit (called Charnock Pass on the maps); drive east another 0.9 mile, then turn right (south) at an old jeep road and park. This point is 19.1 miles from NV 376. **Trailhead GPS:** N38 51.358 / W116 55.35

WHAT TO SEE

The trail follows the old jeep road to a pass at the head of Pasco Canyon. From here, work your way south along the ridges, then contour west cross-country into upper Moores Creek, where you will encounter an old trail ascending Moores Creek to the north rim of the Mount Jefferson Plateau. At the rim, the view is open to the north but somewhat restricted by the points to the east and west. Continue cross-country southeast to the 11,814-foot North Summit, for 50-mile views in all directions. This is your destination for the hike.

—USDA Forest Service and Bruce Grubbs

Bighorn sheep can be found near the top of the plateau.
© ISTOCK.COM/MLHARING

MILES AND DIRECTIONS

- **0.0** Moores Creek trailhead.
- **1.8** Pass at head of Pasco Canyon.
- **3.4** Upper Moores Creek; turn left on trail and hike up canyon to south.
- **5.1** Rim of Mount Jefferson Plateau; continue cross-country southeast to North Summit.
- **6.8** North Summit.
- **13.6** Return to Moores Creek trailhead.

Option: This trail could be used for a traverse of Mount Jefferson by using the Pine Creek or Meadow Creek Trail. Note that travel on Mount Jefferson is essentially cross-country; the trails shown on the maps don't get enough use to remain distinct, and they are not marked.

44. MORGAN CREEK TRAIL

WHY GO?

A day hike in the Monitor Range featuring the shortest access to Table Mountain. This is the starting point for crest traverses.

THE RUNDOWN

Start: 70 miles northeast of Tonopah
Distance: 4.0-mile out and back
Hiking time: About 3 hours
Difficulty: Strenuous
Trail surface: Dirt and rocks
Water: Morgan Creek
Seasons: Summer through fall
Other trail users: Equestrians
Canine compatibility: Dogs allowed under control
Land status: Humboldt-Toiyabe National Forest

Nearest town: Tonopah
Fees and permits: None
USGS topo map: Danville
Other maps: Forest Service: Humboldt-Toiyabe National Forest, Tonopah Ranger District
Trail contacts: Humboldt-Toiyabe National Forest, Austin-Tonopah Ranger District, PO Box 3940, 1400 S. Erie Main St., Tonopah, NV 89049-3940; (775) 482-6286; www.fs.fed .us/r4/htnf

FINDING THE TRAILHEAD

From Tonopah, drive east about 6 miles on US 6, then turn left (north) onto NV 376. After 13 miles, turn right (east) onto the signed, paved Monitor Valley Road. Continue 45.3 miles on this road, which turns to graded dirt after Belmont. Turn right (northeast) at the signed, graded Morgan Creek–Mosquito Creek Road and continue 5.7 miles, then turn left (north) onto Morgan Creek Road. Go left at an unsigned fork, then right (east) at the signed turn for Morgan Creek. The trailhead is at the east end of a beautiful stand of aspens, 14.7 miles from Monitor Valley Road. There is good car camping near the trailhead. **Trailhead GPS:** N38 51.596 / W116 36.627

WHAT TO SEE

Follow the jeep trail that leaves the parking area to the south. The trail climbs steeply the first mile, then moderates somewhat. The 10,000-foot north end of Table Mountain is reached 2 miles from the trailhead. This point is the goal for this short but steep hike, where there are good views of the north end of the Monitor Range.

Monitor Valley Road, which you followed on your approach to this hike, passes through the ghost town of Belmont, a National Historic Site. Belmont got its start in 1866 after silver was discovered in the area. Once a town of more than 2,000 residents, Belmont was for a time the county seat. A few people still live there. It has a small mountain stream that runs year-round, and two of the most photographed old buildings in the state—the courthouse and the Cosmopolitan Hotel.

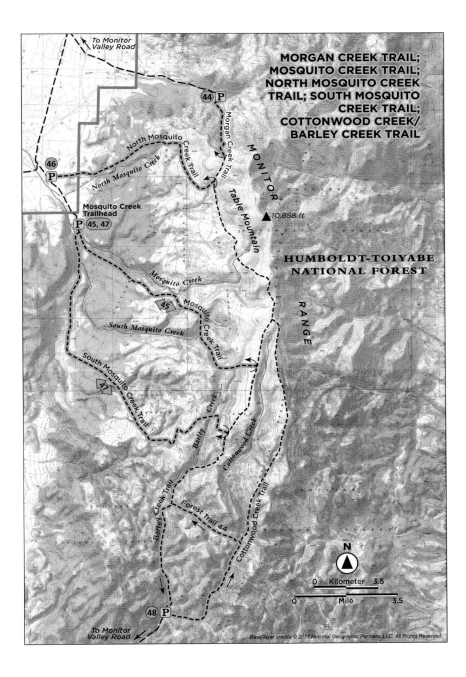

To Monitor
Valley Road

MORGAN CREEK TRAIL;
MOSQUITO CREEK TRAIL;
NORTH MOSQUITO CREEK
TRAIL; SOUTH MOSQUITO
CREEK TRAIL;
COTTONWOOD CREEK/
BARLEY CREEK TRAIL

44 P

North Mosquito Creek Trail

46 P

North Mosquito Creek

Mosquito Creek
Trailhead

P 45, 47

Morgan Creek Trail

MONITOR

Table Mountain

▲10,888 ft

HUMBOLDT-TOIYABE
NATIONAL FOREST

Mosquito Creek

45

South Mosquito Creek

Mosquito Creek Trail

RANGE

47

South Mosquito Creek Trail

Barley Creek

Cottonwood Creek

Barley Creek Trail

Forest Trail 4A

Cottonwood Creek Trail

N

0   Kilometer   3.5

0   Mile   3.5

48 P

To Monitor
Valley Road

BaseTayer credits © 2017 National Geographic Partners, LLC. All Rights Reserved.

Morgan Creek at the north end of the Monitor Range

Manhattan, another mining town, is located about 15 miles west of Belmont and is reached via FR 014. The town started about the same time as Belmont but grew very slowly until 1905, when gold was discovered. By the end of the year, more than 1,000 people were living in Manhattan. The San Francisco earthquake of 1906 jolted Manhattan indirectly—many investors withdrew funds from mining stocks and turned to rebuilding San Francisco. The mines in Manhattan virtually ceased production within a month. Rich strikes later that year and the next revived the district, and prospecting and mining have continued to the present.

—USDA Forest Service and Bruce Grubbs

Option: This trail can be used to start a traverse of Table Mountain, using the Mosquito Creek, South Mosquito Creek, Barley Creek, or Cottonwood Creek Trails as exit points.

45. MOSQUITO CREEK TRAIL

WHY GO?

A long day hike or overnight backpack trip in the Monitor Range offering access to Table Mountain from the west and a possible loop with the South Mosquito Creek Trail.

THE RUNDOWN

See map on page 147
Start: 70 miles northeast of Tonopah
Distance: 14.8-mile out and back
Hiking time: About 10 hours
Difficulty: Strenuous
Trail surface: Dirt and rocks
Water: Numerous springs
Seasons: Summer through fall
Other trail users: Equestrians
Canine compatibility: Dogs allowed under control
Land status: Humboldt-Toiyabe National Forest

Nearest town: Tonopah
Fees and permits: None
USGS topo map: Danville and Mosquito Creek
Other maps: Forest Service: Humboldt-Toiyabe National Forest, Tonopah Ranger District
Trail contacts: Humboldt-Toiyabe National Forest, Austin-Tonopah Ranger District, PO Box 3940, 1400 S. Erie Main St., Tonopah, NV 89049-3940; (775) 482-6286; www.fs.fed.us/r4/htnf

FINDING THE TRAILHEAD

From Tonopah, drive east about 6 miles on US 6, then turn left (north) onto NV 376. After 13 miles, turn right (east) onto the signed, paved Monitor Valley Road. Continue on this road, which turns to gravel after Belmont, for 45.3 miles. Turn right (northeast) at the signed, graded Morgan Creek–Mosquito Creek Road and continue 5.7 miles, then turn right (east) onto Mosquito Creek Road (FR 096). Go 2.1 miles to the Mosquito Creek trailhead, which is signed. **Trailhead GPS:** N38 48.561 / W116 40.869

WHAT TO SEE

The Mosquito Creek Trail is not signed, but you can reach it from the parking area by crossing the creek to the south. Turn left (southeast) at a fork in the trail just after crossing the creek. The trail is used regularly (especially by horse parties) and very easy to follow. It climbs onto the ridge south of Mosquito Creek and follows it southeast about 3.5 miles. It crosses a pass at 9,400 feet, then descends and crosses the South Fork of Mosquito Creek before making the final climb to Table Mountain on its gentle western slope.
—USDA Forest Service and Bruce Grubbs

Mosquito Creek near the
Mosquito Creek trailhead in
the Monitor Range

Table Mountain, Monitor Range

MILES AND DIRECTIONS

0.0 Mosquito Creek trailhead.

4.7 Pass.

5.2 South Fork Mosquito Creek.

7.4 Table Mountain.

14.8 Return to Mosquito Creek trailhead.

Option: An obvious loop could be made with the South Mosquito Creek Trail—but it should start with the South Mosquito Trail, which is the harder trail to find. Other possibilities are traverses of Table Mountain, exiting at Barley Creek or Cottonwood Creek.

46. **NORTH MOSQUITO CREEK TRAIL**

📷 ♨️ 🚶

WHY GO?

A day hike in the Monitor Range on a rarely used trail that accesses the northwest portion of Table Mountain.

THE RUNDOWN

See map on page 147
Start: 70 miles northeast of Tonopah
Distance: 11.6-mile out and back
Hiking time: About 8 hours
Difficulty: Strenuous
Trail surface: Dirt and rocks
Water: Unnamed springs
Seasons: Summer through fall
Other trail users: Equestrians
Canine compatibility: Dogs allowed under control
Land status: Humboldt-Toiyabe National Forest

Nearest town: Tonopah
Fees and permits: None
USGS topo map: Danville and Mosquito Creek
Other maps: Forest Service: Humboldt-Toiyabe National Forest, Tonopah Ranger District
Trail contacts: Humboldt-Toiyabe National Forest, Austin-Tonopah Ranger District, PO Box 3940, 1400 S. Erie Main St., Tonopah, NV 89049-3940; (775) 482-6286; www.fs.fed .us/r4/htnf

FINDING THE TRAILHEAD

From Tonopah, drive east about 6 miles on US 6, then turn left (north) onto NV 376. After 13 miles, turn right (east) onto the signed, paved Monitor Valley Road. Continue 45.3 miles on this road, which turns to graded dirt after Belmont. Turn right (northeast) onto the signed, graded Morgan Creek–Mosquito Creek Road and continue 5.7 miles, then turn right (east) onto Mosquito Creek Road (FR 096). Go 0.5 mile, then turn left onto signed FR 096A and park. FR 096A goes 1 mile farther, but is washed out; it's preferable to park here. **Trailhead GPS:** N38 49.675 / W116 41.755

WHAT TO SEE

Follow FR 096A to the crest of a small hill. The North Mosquito Creek Trail takes off behind a wilderness boundary sign; initially it goes through a field of flat rock, and is hard to follow for about 0.5 mile. After the trail drops off into the creek bottom, it is in a very pretty canyon, which it follows to the top of Table Mountain.
—USDA Forest Service and Bruce Grubbs

The Monitor Range from Monitor Valley

Option: The North Mosquito Creek Trail could be used for a short traverse of the north end of the mountain, exiting at Morgan Creek. Alternatively, a much longer loop trip could be completed using the Mosquito Creek or South Mosquito Creek Trail.

47. SOUTH MOSQUITO CREEK TRAIL

WHY GO?

A 2- or 3-day backpack trip in the Monitor Range following a seldom-used trail through the lower country west of Table Mountain.

THE RUNDOWN

See map on page 147
Start: 70 miles northeast of Tonopah
Distance: 20.6-mile out and back
Hiking time: 2 to 3 days
Difficulty: Strenuous
Trail surface: Dirt and rocks
Water: Springs near Table Mountain
Seasons: Summer through fall
Other trail users: Equestrians
Canine compatibility: Dogs allowed under control
Land status: Humboldt-Toiyabe National Forest
Nearest town: Tonopah

Fees and permits: None
USGS topo map: Green Monster Canyon, Barley Creek, and Mosquito Creek
Other maps: Forest Service: Humboldt-Toiyabe National Forest, Tonopah Ranger District
Trail contacts: Humboldt-Toiyabe National Forest, Austin-Tonopah Ranger District, PO Box 3940, 1400 S. Erie Main St., Tonopah, NV 89049-3940; (775) 482-6286; www.fs.fed.us/r4/htnf

FINDING THE TRAILHEAD

From Tonopah, drive east about 6 miles on US 6, then turn left (north) onto NV 376. After 13 miles, turn right (east) onto the signed, paved Monitor Valley Road. Continue 45.3 miles on this road, which turns to graded dirt after Belmont. Turn right (northeast) onto the signed, graded Morgan Creek–Mosquito Creek Road and continue 5.7 miles, then turn right (east) onto Mosquito Creek Road (FR 096). Go 2.1 miles to the Mosquito Creek trailhead, which is signed. **Trailhead GPS:** N38 48.561 / W116 40.869

WHAT TO SEE

Start by following the unsigned Mosquito Creek Trail south, across the creek from the parking area. The trail goes up a short steep section, and then the South Mosquito Creek Trail branches right (south) at an unsigned junction. It follows the South Fork of Mosquito Creek for a little over a mile. Still heading south, it follows a minor drainage over a saddle, then stays on a bench to the west for another mile before rejoining the South Fork. About 2 miles farther south, the South Fork and the trail both veer east. After a mile, the trail leaves the South Fork to the east and spends about a mile on the slopes northeast of the drainage before descending to cross the head of the South Fork. The trail climbs a ridge upward to the east then crosses the head of Barley Creek before making the final climb to the gentle slopes of Table Mountain. Here the trail turns north to meet the Mosquito Creek Trail in 2 miles.

—USDA Forest Service and Bruce Grubbs

MILES AND DIRECTIONS

0.0 Mosquito Creek trailhead; start on Mosquito Creek Trail.

0.3 Turn right on South Mosquito Creek Trail.

1.2 South Mosquito Creek Trail leaves South Fork Mosquito Creek.

7.1 Trail crosses head of South Fork Mosquito Creek.

9.5 Trail crosses head of Barley Creek.

10.3 Table Mountain.

20.6 Return to Mosquito Creek trailhead.

Option: It is possible to use this trail and the Mosquito Creek Trail to make a loop over Table Mountain. The loop should start with the South Mosquito Creek Trail, which is harder to find than the Mosquito Creek Trail. That way, if you lose the trail, you can return to the trailhead the way you came.

48. COTTONWOOD CREEK/ BARLEY CREEK TRAIL

WHY GO?

A loop hike at the south end of the Monitor Range.

THE RUNDOWN

See map on page 147
Start: 62 miles northeast of Tonopah
Distance: 9.0-mile loop
Hiking time: About 6 hours
Difficulty: Strenuous
Trail surface: Dirt and rocks
Water: Cottonwood Creek, Barley Creek
Seasons: Summer through fall
Other trail users: Equestrians
Canine compatibility: Dogs allowed under control
Land status: Humboldt-Toiyabe National Forest

Nearest town: Tonopah
Fees and permits: None
USGS topo map: Barley Creek and Green Monster Canyon
Other maps: Forest Service: Humboldt-Toiyabe National Forest, Tonopah Ranger District
Trail contacts: Humboldt-Toiyabe National Forest, Austin-Tonopah Ranger District, PO Box 3940, 1400 S. Erie Main St., Tonopah, NV 89049-3940; (775) 482-6286; www.fs.fed .us/r4/htnf

FINDING THE TRAILHEAD

From Tonopah, drive east about 6 miles on US 6, then turn north onto NV 376. After 13 miles, turn northeast (right) onto Monitor Valley Road. Continue 33.3 miles on this road (which becomes graded dirt after Belmont), then turn right onto the graded, signed Barley Creek Road (FR 093) and continue 6.2 miles to the signed Barley Creek turnoff (just past the Barley Creek Ranch). Turn left onto Barley Creek–Cottonwood Creek Road (FR 093) and continue 4 miles to the Cottonwood/ Barley trailhead and the end of the road. **Trailhead GPS:** N38 39.197 / W116 38.374

WHAT TO SEE

You'll be hiking this loop counterclockwise. Go east on the Cottonwood Creek Trail (signed just beyond the trailhead). The well-built trail stays on the north side of the creek for a while. At first the creek is lined only with willow, but soon you come to the first grove of aspen. In the fall these graceful trees turn yellow and orange, adding colorful accents to the gray-green canyon.

One mile from the trailhead, there is a signed junction with the Willow Creek Trail. Stay on the Cottonwood Creek Trail as the creek turns north. The next mile features rugged cliffs on the west side of the canyon. Shortly after this section there is a view of the south rim of Table Mountain, 4 miles to the north.

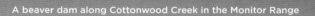

A beaver dam along Cottonwood Creek in the Monitor Range

Fall color in Cottonwood Creek, Monitor Range

The trail up Cottonwood Creek

The trail crosses the little creek many times, encountering a broad-leaved shrub with elliptical, finely toothed leaves that turn red-orange in the fall. This is western choke-cherry, very common along streams in the West, and named because its astringent berries are impossible to eat.

About 3.5 miles from the trailhead, watch for a signed junction with Forest Trail 44 (the sign says "Barley Creek"). Turn left (west) on this trail. It climbs steeply up a side canyon, veering north to switchback up to a ridge. It then crosses a saddle to the west, where there is a fine view of Mount Jefferson in the Toquima Range. Now Trail 44 descends into the broad valley below, staying on the north side of the drainage. Some sections of this trail are faint, but it is marked by large rock cairns. About 3 miles from the junction, the trail ends at a signed junction with the Barley Creek Trail.

Turn left (south) and follow the well-used trail down Barley Creek. This trail is a popular access to Table Mountain, especially for horse packers. For some reason Barley Creek has a lower flow than Cottonwood Creek, and the aspens are absent. The stream course is choked with willow, and the trail crosses it many times. There is a stand of narrowleaf cottonwood about a mile below the junction. Also known as black cottonwood, these water-loving trees are distinguished from the more common Fremont cottonwood by their narrow, willowlike leaves. The leaves of the Fremont cottonwood are triangular and often wider than they are long.

After 3.5 miles, you'll reach the trailhead, completing the loop.

MILES AND DIRECTIONS

0.0   Cottonwood/Barley trailhead.

1.0   Willow Creek Trail; stay left on Cottonwood Creek Trail.

3.5   Forest Trail 44; turn left and hike west, leaving Cottonwood Creek.

3.9   Saddle.

5.9   Barley Creek Trail; turn left and hike south down Barley Creek.

9.0   Return to Cottonwood/Barley trailhead.

Option: Both the Cottonwood and Barley Trails can be used to reach Table Mountain, with the possibility of one-way hikes over the top. This would require a car shuttle to the Mosquito Creek or Morgan Creek trailhead.

49. GREEN MONSTER TRAIL

WHY GO?

A day hike or overnight backpack in the Monitor Range offering access to Table Mountain from the east.

THE RUNDOWN

Start: 81 miles northeast of Tonopah
Distance: 3.6-mile out and back
Hiking time: About 3 hours
Difficulty: Moderate
Trail surface: Dirt and rocks
Water: Green Monster Creek
Seasons: Summer through fall
Other trail users: Equestrians
Canine compatibility: Dogs allowed under control
Land status: Humboldt-Toiyabe National Forest
Nearest town: Tonopah

Fees and permits: None
USGS topo map: Green Monster Canyon and Danville
Other maps: Forest Service: Humboldt-Toiyabe National Forest, Tonopah Ranger District
Trail contacts: Humboldt-Toiyabe National Forest, Austin-Tonopah Ranger District, PO Box 3940, 1400 S. Erie Main St., Tonopah, NV 89049-3940; (775) 482-6286; www.fs.fed .us/r4/htnf

FINDING THE TRAILHEAD

From Tonopah, drive east 34.4 miles on US 6, then turn left (north) onto the signed, graded Little Fish Lake Valley Road (FR 139). Where the road passes a dry lakebed called Squaw Flat, there is an impressive section of old roadway that was built up by hand. Continue 43.8 miles, then turn left (west) onto the un-signed, unmaintained Green Monster Road. This turnoff is just north of a junction along Little Fish Valley Lake Road, where a signed right turn goes to Little Fish Valley Ranch (FR 139 goes left). Now drive 4.3 miles to the trailhead. This road can be driven by passenger cars with care. At the trailhead, two jeep roads branch right just before the main road crosses the creek to the south. Just after the crossing, a closed jeep road turns right, paralleling the creek. This is the unsigned Green Monster Trail. Camping is very limited near the trailhead; there is better camping several miles east along the access road. **Trailhead GPS:** N38 44.458 / W116 32.164

WHAT TO SEE

The old road parallels the creek for about 0.25 mile, then crosses to the north side. It passes through pleasant piñon-juniper woodland. The singleleaf piñon that grows here is easily identified since it is the only pine with its needles growing singly instead of in bunches of two or more. The nuts produced by this tree were highly prized by Native Americans as a food source, and are still valuable today. They are also an important staple for wildlife, especially wood rats.

About 0.5 mile from the trailhead, the jeep track ends abruptly, and the foot trail crosses to the south side of the creek again. It stays on the south side for about 0.25 mile, then crosses to the north side and remains there. There are few signs of trail maintenance, and the trail is confused by the cattle paths along the creek. After passing a fine stand of aspen, the trail crosses the creek to the south but remains there only a few yards before crossing again. At this point a side canyon comes in from the southwest, but the trail continues up the fork to the west, the main creek. The trail climbs more steeply after this side canyon, climbing into the upper basin below the steep eastern slopes of Table Mountain. This basin makes a good stopping point for a moderate day hike.

—Bruce Grubbs and USDA Forest Service

MILES AND DIRECTIONS

0.0   Green Monster trailhead.

1.1   Side canyon.

1.8   Upper basin.

3.6   Return to Green Monster trailhead.

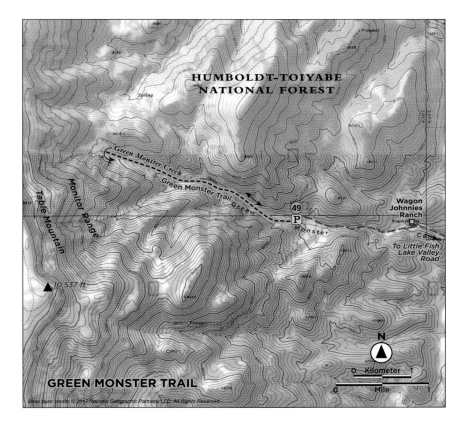

50. **CLEAR LAKE TRAIL**

WHY GO?

A day hike in the Monitor Range featuring a beautiful aspen-filled canyon bottom and access to the country east of Table Mountain.

THE RUNDOWN

Start: 87 miles northeast of Tonopah
Distance: 6.0-mile out and back
Hiking time: About 4 hours
Difficulty: Moderate
Trail surface: Dirt and rocks
Water: Lower Clear Creek near the trailhead, and also near the end of the hike
Seasons: Summer through fall
Other trail users: Equestrians
Canine compatibility: Dogs allowed under control
Land status: Humboldt-Toiyabe National Forest

Nearest town: Tonopah
Fees and permits: None
USGS topo map: Danville
Other maps: Forest Service: Humboldt-Toiyabe National Forest, Tonopah Ranger District
Trail contacts: Humboldt-Toiyabe National Forest, Austin-Tonopah Ranger District, PO Box 3940, 1400 S. Erie Main St., Tonopah, NV 89049-3940; (775) 482-6286; www.fs.fed.us/r4/htnf

FINDING THE TRAILHEAD

From Tonopah, drive east 34.4 miles on US 6, then turn left (north) onto the signed, graded Little Fish Lake Valley Road. Continue 51.1 miles, then turn left onto the signed Clear Lake Road. This junction has four roads and is just after a cattle guard; Clear Creek Road goes west. Continue 2.1 miles to the end of the road. There are several campsites near the end of the road. The last 0.2 mile is more a jeep track than a road, and is not worth driving. **Trailhead GPS:** N38 49.053 / W116 30.526

WHAT TO SEE

The unsigned trail initially follows the south side of Clear Creek, through an open area burned in an old fire. The first 0.5 mile of the trail avoids the willow-choked streambed, but then it crosses to the north side. A section of the creek may be dry, but there is water farther up the trail. Massive limestone cliffs tower above the trail as it drops into the streambed to wind through shady groves of aspen. This section provides very enjoyable walking as the trail climbs gradually. About 2.5 miles from the trailhead, the trail emerges from the aspen, and the canyon begins to open out into a basin with views of Table Mountain to the west and southwest. The foot trail meets an old jeep trail coming in from the north, and crosses Clear Creek again. This marks the end of the hike. There is a good flow of water here, and a few campsites are available.
—Bruce Grubbs and USDA Forest Service

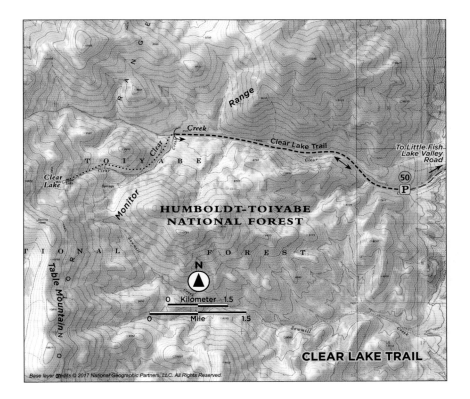

Option: More experienced hikers who have the USGS topographic map may wish to continue the hike to Clear Lake. The map shows the trail continuing to Clear Lake up Clear Creek, which turns to the southwest about 0.2 mile beyond the jeep trail, but I found instead that the trail goes up a shallow drainage, following the jeep trail onto the slope above. Here the trail disappears into cattle paths amid the sage. Go west toward a patch of drab green mountain mahogany that covers the ridge between this point and Clear Creek, and you will encounter the trail again as it contours into Clear Creek. After another 0.5 mile, the trail disappears again in a maze of cattle trails. I stopped here, but Clear Lake should be reachable by walking cross-country on either side of Clear Creek. Except in the mahogany thickets, the slopes are open sage. This optional hike to the lake would add 2 miles, one way, to the described hike.

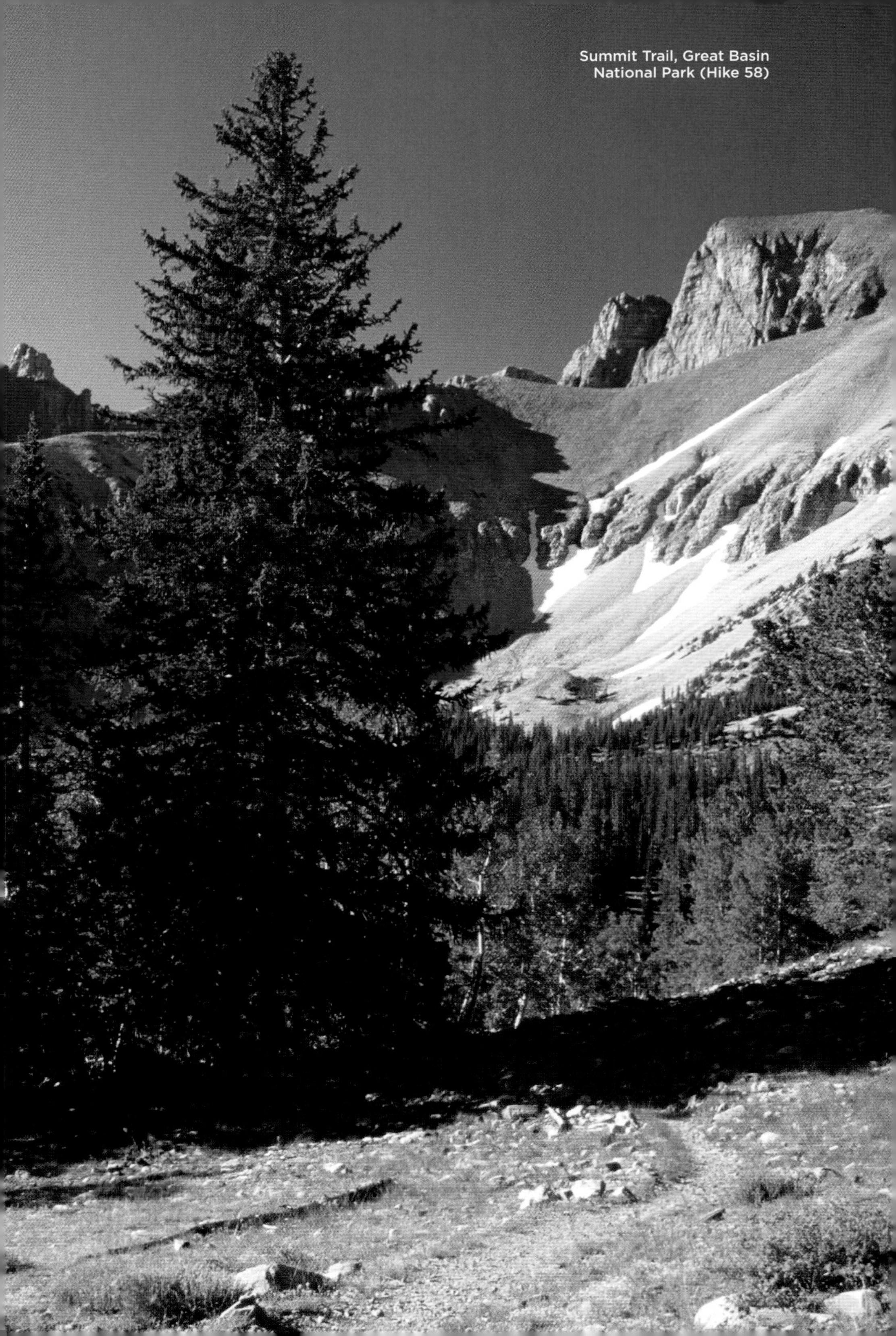

Summit Trail, Great Basin
National Park (Hike 58)

EASTERN NEVADA

LIKE CENTRAL NEVADA, EASTERN NEVADA is dominated by high mountain ranges that tower above the flanking valleys. This elevation contrast reaches a dramatic extreme in the southern Snake Range, where 13,063-foot Wheeler Peak towers more than 7,000 feet above the flat desert valleys to the east and west. Length is present, too, in the magnificent Schell Creek Range that not only reaches nearly to 12,000 feet but is also more than 80 miles long. Like Nevada's other loftiest mountains, the upper reaches of these peaks were carved by glaciers. In fact, the glacial cirque carved into the sheer northeast face of Wheeler Peak has the only permanent icefield between the Colorado Rockies and the California Sierras.

51. SMITH CREEK

WHY GO?

A day hike up a remote canyon with interesting limestone caves and cliffs, in the northern portion of the Mount Moriah Wilderness, in the Snake Range.

THE RUNDOWN

Start: 39 miles north of Baker
Distance: 4.8-mile out and back
Hiking time: About 3 hours
Difficulty: Moderate
Trail surface: Dirt and rocks
Water: Smith Creek
Seasons: Summer through fall
Other trail users: Equestrians
Canine compatibility: Dogs allowed under control
Land status: Humboldt-Toiyabe National Forest

Nearest town: Baker
Fees and permits: None
USGS topo map: Mount Moriah and Little Horse Canyon
Other maps: Forest Service: Humboldt-Toiyabe National Forest, Ely Ranger District
Trail contacts: Humboldt-Toiyabe National Forest, Ely Ranger District, 825 Avenue East, Ely, NV 89301; (775) 289-3031; www.fs.fed.us/r4/htnf

FINDING THE TRAILHEAD

From Baker, drive 5 miles northwest on NV 487, then turn right (east) onto US 6/50. Almost immediately turn left onto Silver Creek Road (CR 41). Drive past an electrical substation. At 10.9 miles from US 6/50, Silver Creek Road ends at the junction of Hendrys Creek Road and Gandy Road. Drive straight ahead onto Gandy Road. Continue northeast to a small ranch 26.9 miles from US 6/50, then turn left onto Smith Creek Road. Follow this minimally maintained dirt road 7.1 miles to its end at the wilderness boundary. There are a couple of rough creek crossings near the end of the road, and their condition changes from year to year. If necessary, park and walk the last part of the road. Smith Creek has water, and there's limited camping (with shade) at a small site 100 yards before the trailhead. **Trailhead GPS:** N39 20.086 / W114 6.696

WHAT TO SEE

The unsigned trail up Smith Creek gets very little use. It starts as an old jeep trail and climbs away from the creek on the north, giving great views of the impressive canyon. Then the trail crosses the creek and enters a cottonwood grove. Deadman Creek enters noisily from the left (south) as it pours over a series of ledges. Continue up Smith Creek on the now much fainter trail. Since it was built as a jeep road, the trail always crosses the creek when the bench peters out. The canyon becomes gradually narrower, and the high cliff on the north side is especially impressive. There are also tantalizing views of the high

country, far above to the south. About 2.4 miles from the trailhead, the old trail drops into the bed of the creek and fades out. Your hike ends here, but experienced hikers can continue to Ryegrass Canyon. Other exploration possibilities are Deadman Creek and its several tributaries.

Option: Smith Creek can be used as a jumping-off point for extended exploration of the northern Mount Moriah Wilderness, using Deep or Deadman Creeks, or the intervening ridges, to hike up to The Table. There are no trails, and all such exploration will require cross-country hiking skills.

52. HENDRYS CREEK

WHY GO?

A very long day hike or overnight backpack trip on a good trail through a scenic canyon offering access to The Table and Mount Moriah, in the Snake Range.

THE RUNDOWN

Start: 17 miles north of Baker
Distance: 18.8-mile out and back
Hiking time: About 12 hours, or 2 days
Difficulty: Strenuous
Trail surface: Dirt and rocks
Water: Hendrys Creek
Seasons: Summer through fall
Other trail users: Equestrians
Canine compatibility: Dogs allowed under control
Land status: Humboldt-Toiyabe National Forest

Nearest town: Baker
Fees and permits: None
USGS topo map: The Cove, Old Mans Canyon and Mount Moriah
Other maps: Forest Service: Humboldt-Toiyabe National Forest, Ely Ranger District
Trail contacts: Humboldt-Toiyabe National Forest, Ely Ranger District, 825 Avenue East, Ely, NV 89301; (775) 289-3031; www.fs.fed.us/r4/htnf

FINDING THE TRAILHEAD

From Baker, drive 5 miles northwest on NV 487, then turn right (east) onto US 6/50. Almost immediately turn left onto Silver Creek Road (CR 41). Drive past an electrical substation. At 10.9 miles from US 6/50, Silver Creek Road ends at the junction of Hendrys Creek Road and Gandy Road. Turn left (northwest) onto Hendrys Creek Road. Drive 3 miles and then turn left at a sign for Hendrys Creek trailhead; go another 0.1 mile then turn right at an unsigned junction. After 0.3 mile, turn left at another sign for the trailhead. In another 0.6 mile, you'll pass the national forest boundary and reach Hendrys Creek trailhead. There is neither shade nor good camping at the trailhead. **Trailhead GPS:** N39 12.599 / W114 4.744

WHAT TO SEE

The well-maintained Hendrys Creek Trail starts along the south side of the creek but soon crosses north to follow an old jeep road. The hillsides are open sage and grass, but the stream course is dense with willow, cottonwood, and a few stately ponderosa pine. Watch for occasional poison ivy along the first mile. As the trail gradually climbs, ponderosa pine becomes more common, and almost dominant for a while. Within a mile of the trailhead, there's plenty of shade along the trail. The dramatic canyon walls, covered with piñon pine and juniper, start to close in. You'll pass the signed wilderness boundary at about 1.5 miles. The creek runs nicely throughout, and this lower section of the canyon

Hendrys Creek,
Snake Range

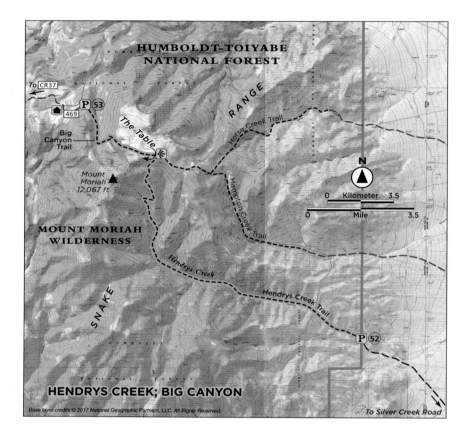

HENDRYS CREEK; BIG CANYON

Base layer credits © 2017 National Geographic Partners, LLC. All Rights Reserved.

has plenty of camping for those who only want to walk a mile or two. After about 2 miles, quaking aspen start to appear, and the canyon walls become more forested. Hendrys Creek has been a popular place for many years, as the multitude of historic inscriptions on the aspen show. At about 9,000 feet, and 5.9 miles, the trail enters an aspen-bordered meadow that offers a glimpse of Mount Moriah high to the northwest. There are several possible campsites. This would be a good destination for the first day of a 2- or 3-day trip. The Table and Mount Moriah are within easy reach from this point.

The good trail continues up Hendrys Creek, climbing more steeply now. At about 10,000 feet and 7.5 miles, the trail enters another, steeper meadow, which offers even better views. This meadow is apparently the lower end of several large snow avalanche paths that start on Mount Moriah's east face. The trail switchbacks to the east, leaving the meadow, and then climbs up a gentle ridge through an open forest. After crossing a couple of canyons on the northeast slopes of Mount Moriah, it climbs up a final slope to the south rim of The Table. This 11,000-foot plateau slopes gently to the north. It's an arctic plain, open and nearly treeless—but not lifeless; during the short growing season a number of alpine flowers including phlox and blue columbine manage to flower. The south edge of The Table is bordered with twisted, picturesque bristlecone pines. By walking a short distance to the north, you can get a view of most of the surrounding ranges, including Jeff Davis and Wheeler Peaks in the south Snake Range. Unlike most high-mountain viewpoints in the Nevada ranges, there isn't a view of the surrounding canyons and ridges. The high rim of The Table blocks the nearer view and makes this vantage point seem especially remote.

MILES AND DIRECTIONS

0.0   Hendrys Creek trailhead.

1.5   Wilderness boundary.

6.0   Aspen meadow.

7.6   Avalanche path.

9.4   The Table.

18.8 Return to Hendrys Creek trailhead.

Option: A sign at the end of the hike on The Table marks the junction with two cairned trails: the trail to Big Canyon on the west, and to Hampton and Horse Creeks on the east. These other trails suggest the possibility of a traverse across the range using a car shuttle. Be warned, however, that most trails shown on the Forest Service and USGS maps are little used, faint, and difficult to find. Most of the Mount Moriah Wilderness should be considered cross-country hiking for those experienced with a map and compass. If you have the skills and experience, there's a lot of wild country to be explored.

53. **BIG CANYON**

📷 🚶 🦴 🏕️

WHY GO?

Easy access to The Table and Mount Moriah from a high trailhead, reached via a scenic road on the west side of the Mount Moriah Wilderness, in the Snake Range.

THE RUNDOWN

See map on page 170
Start: 43 miles northwest of Baker
Distance: 5.8-mile out and back
Hiking time: About 4 hours
Difficulty: Moderate
Trail surface: Dirt and rocks
Water: Spring in Big Canyon
Seasons: Summer through fall
Other trail users: Equestrians
Canine compatibility: Dogs allowed under control
Land status: Humboldt-Toiyabe National Forest

Nearest town: Baker
Fees and permits: None
USGS topo map: Sixmile Canyon and Mount Moriah
Other maps: Forest Service: Humboldt-Toiyabe National Forest, Ely Ranger District
Trail contacts: Humboldt-Toiyabe National Forest, Ely Ranger District, 825 Avenue East, Ely, NV 89301; (775) 289-3031; www.fs.fed.us/r4/htnf

FINDING THE TRAILHEAD

From Baker, drive 5 miles northwest on NV 487, then turn left (west) onto US 6/50. Continue 14.4 miles, crossing over Sacramento Pass, then turn right onto a maintained dirt road (CR 37). This road starts westward but then turns north along the east side of Spring Valley. Go 12.1 miles, turn right (east) onto Fourmile Road (FR 469), an unmaintained dirt road found just before crossing a cattle guard. Drive east 2.6 miles to the foothills, then bear left. The road crosses a drainage, then climbs to reach a small saddle and a cattle guard after 0.3 mile.

To continue beyond this point, you'll probably need a high-clearance, four-wheel-drive vehicle. The road now climbs steeply up a scenic ridge, gaining 2,000 feet in 3 miles. At the top of the climb, several minor roads branch left; stay right on the main road. After another 3.2 miles, a minor road turns left; go straight on the main road. In 0.1 mile you'll pass a small Forest Service cabin on the right in a stand of aspen. The cabin is open to the public and would make a good emergency shelter; please leave it as you found it. Continue 1.9 miles, crossing Deadman Creek, to the signed trailhead at the end of the road. There is a small campsite just north of the trailhead. **Trailhead GPS:** N39 18.086 / W114 12.697

WHAT TO SEE

This hike is worth it just for the view from the trailhead. As you start the walk south into Big Canyon, the rugged northwest face of Mount Moriah is framed in the canyon before you. The trail drops gradually into the bottom of Big Canyon, then follows the bed

Mount Moriah,
Mount Moriah Wilderness,
Snake Range

Bristlecone pine,
The Table,
Snake Range

upstream through aspen, fir, and limber pine forest. Big Canyon is normally dry, but there is a small, unnamed spring (not shown on the USGS topographic map) next to the trail just after it turns sharply left and starts to climb the east slopes of the canyon. Climb this steep, switchbacking section for about a mile to reach the southwest rim of The Table. Continue east as the trail skirts the north ridge of Mount Moriah. At first, The Table is graced with a fine stand of gnarled, timberline bristlecone pine, but it soon becomes a treeless, arctic plateau. After walking across the plateau for a mile, you'll reach a cairn marking the junction with the Hendrys Creek Trail, which drops south into Hendrys Creek.

MILES AND DIRECTIONS

0.0 Big Canyon trailhead.

1.1 Spring where trail starts to climb out of Big Canyon.

2.0 The Table.

2.9 Junction with Hendrys Creek Trail.

5.8 Return to Big Canyon trailhead.

Option: With such an easy approach trail, you should have plenty of time to explore The Table. Mount Moriah is a moderate, 1,000-foot cross-country climb from anywhere along the last mile of this hike. Another great hike is to go out to the north edge of The Table, a walk of about a mile one way. More bristlecone groves skirt the north edge of the plateau, and the view into Deadman Creek and the other tributaries of Smith Creek is excellent. With a car shuttle, you could use the Hendrys Creek Trail to make a 2- or 3-day backpack trip traversing the range.

54. OSCEOLA TUNNEL

WHY GO?

An easy walk to a historic hand-dug tunnel in Great Basin National Park.

THE RUNDOWN

Start: 13.8 miles northwest of Baker
Distance: 1.6-mile out and back
Hiking time: About 1 hour
Difficulty: Easy
Trail surface: Old road
Water: None
Seasons: Summer through fall
Other trail users: None
Canine compatibility: Dogs not allowed on trails or in the backcountry

Land status: Great Basin National Park
Nearest town: Baker
Fees and permits: None
USGS topo map: Windy Peak
Other maps: Forest Service: Humboldt-Toiyabe National Forest, Ely Ranger District
Trail contacts: Great Basin National Park, 100 Great Basin National Park, Baker, NV 89311; (775) 234-7331; www.nps.gov/grba

FINDING THE TRAILHEAD

From Baker, drive 5 miles northwest on NV 487, then turn left onto US 6/50. Go 3.3 miles, then turn left onto an unsigned, paved road that heads toward a maintenance facility. At 0.3 mile, just before reaching the facility, turn right onto a signed dirt road to Strawberry Creek. Continue another 5.2 miles to a Road Closed sign on the right, next to a lone tree. This unsigned trailhead is in the middle of the meadow at the head of Strawberry Creek. **Trailhead GPS:** N39 3.282 / W114 18.411

Osceola Tunnel,
Snake Range
NATIONAL PARK
SERVICE

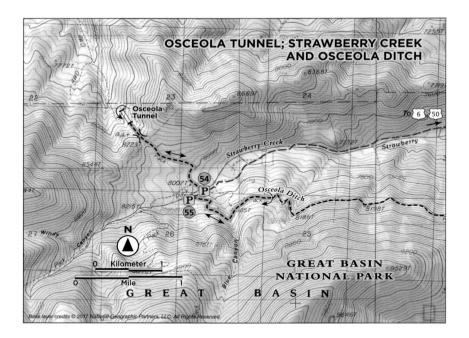

OSCEOLA TUNNEL; STRAWBERRY CREEK AND OSCEOLA DITCH

WHAT TO SEE

This area may be closed due to a large wildfire. Check with Great Basin National Park before planning this hike.

The trail follows the old, closed jeep track across the meadow and up the hillside to the pass visible to the northwest. This is an easy, enjoyable walk with nice views of upper Strawberry Valley and the beautiful, forested slopes of Bald Mountain. When you reach the pass, go through the gate (please leave it as you found it) and walk down the road a short distance to the north. Look for mine tailings below to the left, then drop down the short slope. This is the exit point for a tunnel dug through the rock under the pass you just walked over. This allowed water from the Osceola Ditch to get to this point without having to contour miles around the hill to the east. The continuation of the ditch is visible several hundred feet lower on the hillsides to the northwest. Apparently the water flowed down a wooden chute for about 400 vertical feet before being collected into a ditch again.

55. **STRAWBERRY CREEK AND OSCEOLA DITCH**

WHY GO?

An easy walk to a historic site in Great Basin National Park.

THE RUNDOWN

See map on page 176
Start: 14 miles northwest of Baker
Distance: 1.4-mile out and back
Hiking time: About 1 hour
Difficulty: Easy
Trail surface: Dirt and rocks
Water: None
Seasons: Summer through fall
Other trail users: None
Canine compatibility: Dogs not allowed on trails or in the backcountry

Land status: Great Basin National Park
Nearest town: Baker
Fees and permits: None
USGS topo map: Windy Peak
Other maps: Forest Service: Humboldt-Toiyabe National Forest, Ely Ranger District
Trail contacts: Great Basin National Park, 100 Great Basin National Park, Baker, NV 89311; (775) 234-7331; www.nps.gov/grba

FINDING THE TRAILHEAD

From Baker, drive 5 miles northwest on NV 487, then turn left onto US 6/50. Go 3.3 miles, then turn left onto an unsigned, paved road that heads toward a maintenance facility. At 0.3 mile, just before reaching the facility, turn right onto a signed dirt road to Strawberry Creek. Continue 5 miles, then turn left instead of crossing the creek a final time. Go 0.1 mile to a primitive campsite at the end of the road, which is the trailhead for this hike. **Trailhead GPS:** N39 3.097 / W114 18.806

WHAT TO SEE

This area may be closed due to a large wildfire. Check with Great Basin National Park before planning this hike.

From the trailhead, walk back down the road a few yards to an old, closed jeep trail that climbs the hill to the right (south). Follow this road up the hillside, through an aspen grove, and up a switchback. At a junction, turn left (east) and follow the old road up to the abandoned Osceola Ditch, which is the destination for this easy hike. This vantage point has fine views of Strawberry Valley. You can also see the route of the Osceola Ditch at the head of the valley. If desired, you can follow the old road east along the route of the ditch for several miles.

Osceola Ditch, Great
Basin National Park
NATIONAL PARK SERVICE

56. OSCEOLA DITCH INTERPRETIVE TRAIL

WHY GO?
A very easy interpretive trail to a historic site in Great Basin National Park.

THE RUNDOWN

Start: 10 miles west of Baker
Distance: 0.6-mile out and back
Hiking time: About 1 hour
Difficulty: Easy
Trail surface: Dirt and rocks
Water: None
Seasons: Summer through fall
Other trail users: None
Canine compatibility: Dogs not allowed on trails or in the backcountry

Land status: Great Basin National Park
Nearest town: Baker
Fees and permits: None
USGS topo map: Windy Peak
Trail contacts: Great Basin National Park, 100 Great Basin National Park, Baker, NV 89311; (775) 234-7331; www.nps.gov/grba

FINDING THE TRAILHEAD
From Baker, drive 5 miles west on NV 488. Just after passing the park boundary, turn right onto the paved, signed Wheeler Peak Scenic Drive. Continue 4.6 miles to the signed Osceola Ditch interpretive site, and park on the right side of the highway. **Trailhead GPS:** N39 1.702 / W114 16.026

WHAT TO SEE
The trail may be temporarily closed due to a large wildfire. Check with Great Basin National Park before planning this hike.

A sign at the trailhead briefly explains the history and purpose of the ditch. The trail follows a drainage downhill through the woods a short distance to reach the remains of the ditch, which contours along the hillside. When it was operational, the Osceola Ditch ran 18 miles along the Snake Range to deliver water from Lehman Creek, on the east side of the range, to the town of Osceola on the west.

Why such a massive undertaking? In a word, gold. In 1872 prospectors discovered gold northwest of the present Great Basin National Park. Within 5 years placer deposits were found and the gold mining picked up momentum. Placer mining can be done by hand with a gold pan, but for large-scale work it was more efficient to use hydraulic mining. In the hydraulic process, a jet of water is directed at a hillside to wash out the gravel and dislocate any gold that might be present. The water and gravel are then run through a series of sluices, which separate out the heavier gold. The catch is that a large supply of

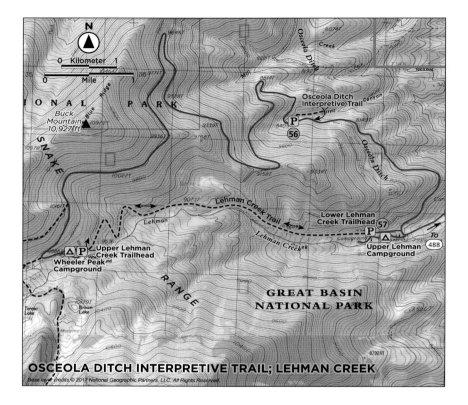

OSCEOLA DITCH INTERPRETIVE TRAIL; LEHMAN CREEK

Base layer Credits © 2017 National Geographic Partners, LLC. All Rights Reserved.

water is required. In 1884 and 1885 a 16-mile ditch was built south along the west slopes of the range to capture water from several creeks and bring it to Osceola. But the amount of water from the west-side streams was disappointing, and the mines were able to operate for only about 2 hours a day. A second ditch, this time to divert water from the larger streams on the east side of the range, was proposed. Though the new ditch would cross more difficult terrain and would be expensive, estimates of the amount of gold that could be recovered with more water seemed to indicate that the venture would be profitable.

Work started in September 1889, and the ditch was finished in July the following year. Several hundred men with pack animals worked on the project, and three sawmills ran full-time to provide lumber. In places where the route traversed cliffs and steep rocky slopes, wooden flumes and chutes were constructed, totaling 11,600 feet. A 632-foot tunnel was blasted through the ridge north of Strawberry Creek. The cost was $108,223, only a few thousand more than originally estimated. At first gold production increased, but there were problems with the new ditch. In the end lawsuits over water rights, water theft, and leaking flumes caused the Osceola Ditch to fail to deliver as much water as anticipated. Dry years, starting in 1893, cut further into the water supply, and by 1901 the ditch was abandoned. Mining activity had almost completely ceased by 1905.

57. LEHMAN CREEK

WHY GO?

A scenic hike along an alpine creek in Great Basin National Park.

THE RUNDOWN

See map on page 180
Start: 17 miles west of Baker
Distance: 6.4-mile out and back
Hiking time: About 4 hours
Difficulty: Strenuous
Trail surface: Dirt and rocks
Water: Upper Lehman Campground, Wheeler Peak Campground, Lehman Creek
Seasons: Summer through fall
Other trail users: None
Canine compatibility: Dogs not allowed on trails or in the backcountry

Land status: Great Basin National Park
Nearest town: Baker
Fees and permits: None
USGS topo map: Windy Peak
Other maps: Earthwalk Press: Great Basin National Park
Trail contacts: Great Basin National Park, 100 Great Basin National Park, Baker, NV 89311; (775) 234-7331; www.nps.gov/grba

FINDING THE TRAILHEAD

From Baker, drive west 5 miles on NV 488, the park approach road. Just past the park entrance, turn right (north) onto the signed, paved Wheeler Peak Scenic Drive. Continue 2.4 miles to Upper Lehman Campground. Turn left at the second campground entrance, then drive to the signed trailhead. The trailhead is on the right just before the road enters the campground loop. **Trailhead GPS:** N39 0.798 / W114 15.202

If you have two vehicles, you can do a shuttle to make this an all-downhill hike. To reach the ending trailhead, continue to the end of the Wheeler Peak Scenic Road and park at the trailhead parking just outside Wheeler Peak Campground. **Trailhead GPS:** N39 0.59 / W114 18.453

WHAT TO SEE

The trail is well maintained and easy to follow as it climbs steadily through a mountain mahogany thicket, away from Lehman Creek. After a while the trail returns to the creek; watch for the remains of the old Osceola Ditch, which the trail crosses. You can follow the ditch to the creek, but there is no trace of the original structure used to divert the creek—it was likely destroyed by a flood. After crossing the old ditch, the trail stays near the creek in a cool, dense fir-and-aspen forest. Then it swings away from the creek and climbs up a ridge to enter a meadow at about 9,100 feet with good views of Jeff Davis and Wheeler Peaks. The Wheeler Glacier is hidden behind a ridge. Above the meadows the trail comes near the creek briefly before finally swinging away and climbing a final

Along the Lehman Creek Trail, Snake Range, Great Basin National Park

Lehman Creek

slope in a wide switchback. The signed trailhead at the east end of Wheeler Peak Campground is your turnaround point.

MILES AND DIRECTIONS

- **0.0** Lower Lehman Creek trailhead (at Upper Lehman Campground).
- **0.7** Osceola Ditch.
- **1.7** Meadow with views.
- **3.2** Upper Lehman Creek trailhead (at Wheeler Peak Campground).
- **6.4** Return to Lower Lehman Creek trailhead.

Option: You can combine this hike with any of the many hikes starting from Wheeler Peak Campground: Bald Mountain, Wheeler Peak, Alpine Lakes, and Bristlecone-Glacier Trail. To reach the trailhead for these hikes from the Upper Lehman Creek trailhead, continue uphill to the west end of the campground and the Alpine Lakes trailhead.

58. BALD MOUNTAIN

📷 🏔 🚶

WHY GO?

A trail and cross-country hike to a rounded summit that offers fine views of Wheeler Peak and Jeff Davis Peak, in Great Basin National Park.

THE RUNDOWN

Start: 17 miles west of Baker
Distance: 5.8-mile out and back
Hiking time: About 5 hours
Difficulty: Moderate
Trail surface: Dirt and rocks, cross-country
Water: Wheeler Peak Campground
Seasons: Summer through fall
Other trail users: None
Canine compatibility: Dogs not allowed on trails or in the backcountry

Land status: Great Basin National Park
Nearest town: Baker
Fees and permits: None
USGS topo map: Windy Peak
Trail contacts: Great Basin National Park, 100 Great Basin National Park, Baker, NV 89311; (775) 234-7331; www.nps.gov/grba

FINDING THE TRAILHEAD

From Baker, drive about 5 miles west on NV 488. Just after passing the park boundary, turn right onto the paved, signed Wheeler Peak Scenic Drive. Continue 12 miles to the signed Bristlecone trailhead just before entering the Wheeler Peak Campground at the end of the road. **Trailhead GPS:** N39 0.59 / W114 18.453

WHAT TO SEE

Bald Mountain is much easier to climb than Wheeler Peak, and may appeal to those with limited time. Start from the trailhead parking at Wheeler Peak Campground by walking across the road to the Alpine Lakes trailhead. The trail crosses Lehman Creek on a footbridge, then climbs gradually through the dense forest. Turn right at the junction with the Bristlecone-Glacier Trail. The trail crosses the creek again, then enters a series of alpine meadows. At the signed junction with the Summit Trail, turn left. After a short distance, turn right onto the Wheeler Peak Trail. Stay on this trail until it reaches Wheeler Saddle, almost directly above Stella Lake. Now turn right (north), and walk cross-country up the easy ridge.

Here, right at timberline, stunted Engelmann spruce and bristlecone pine are the last outposts of the forest. Some of the trees have formed classic *krummholz*—a term that refers to the low, matted forms that timberline trees tend to take. In winter snow covers the krummholz, insulating the trees' foliage from the bitter wind and driven snow.

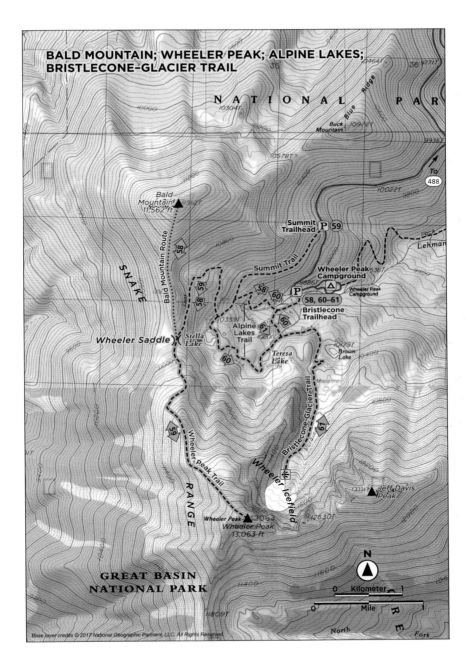

BALD MOUNTAIN; WHEELER PEAK; ALPINE LAKES; BRISTLECONE-GLACIER TRAIL

Summit Trail,
Great Basin
National Park

Your route continues right up the broad ridge as it climbs gently to the rounded sum-mit of Bald Mountain at 11,562 feet. The view takes in the north slopes of the southern Snake Range, the Mount Moriah massif in the northern Snake Range, and the plunging cliffs on Wheeler and Jeff Davis Peaks.

MILES AND DIRECTIONS

0.0   Bristlecone trailhead.

0.2   Junction with Bristlecone-Glacier Trail; turn right.

0.6   Junction with Summit Trail; turn left.

0.8   Junction with Wheeler Peak Trail; turn right.

1.8   Wheeler Saddle; go north, cross-country.

2.9   Bald Mountain.

5.8   Return to Bristlecone trailhead.

**Jeff Davis Peak from Wheeler Peak,
Great Basin National Park**

59. **WHEELER PEAK**

WHY GO?

A trail to the highest summit in the Snake Range and the second highest summit in Nevada, located within Great Basin National Park.

THE RUNDOWN

See map on page 185
Start: 17 miles west of Baker
Distance: 8.0-mile out and back
Hiking time: About 6 hours
Difficulty: Strenuous
Trail surface: Dirt and rocks; may be icy above timberline
Water: Wheeler Peak Campground
Seasons: Summer through fall
Other trail users: None
Canine compatibility: Dogs not allowed on trails or in the backcountry

Land status: Great Basin National Park
Nearest town: Baker
Fees and permits: None
USGS topo map: Wheeler Peak and Windy Peak
Other maps: Earthwalk Press: Great Basin National Park
Trail contacts: Great Basin National Park, 100 Great Basin National Park, Baker, NV 89311; (775) 234-7331; www.nps.gov/grba

FINDING THE TRAILHEAD

From Baker, drive west 5 miles on the Great Basin National Park entrance road (NV 488), then turn right (north) onto Wheeler Peak Scenic Drive. Continue 11.5 miles to the signed Summit trailhead (this trailhead is about 0.5 mile from the end of the road). **Trailhead GPS:** N39 1.039 / W114 18.193

WHAT TO SEE

Follow the Summit Trail as it climbs gradually southwest through stands of aspen along the southern slopes of Bald Mountain. Openings in the forest provide outstanding views of Wheeler and Jeff Davis Peaks. The Alpine Lakes Trail joins from the left; continue a short distance west, then turn sharply right onto the signed Wheeler Peak Trail.

The trail ascends the southeast slopes of Bald Mountain through a broad meadow with more great views of the big peaks to the north. Before long the trail switches back to the south; please do not cut the switchbacks, as the alpine vegetation is very fragile. Continue along the slope until you gain the ridge crest at Wheeler Saddle. Stunted and gnarled limber pine and Engelmann spruce, the last vestiges of forest, struggle to survive at tree line. Views are commanding both to the east and west. The clear, shallow waters of Stella Lake are visible, well below to the east. Above this point, the trail is above timberline and exposed to the high-altitude weather; be certain the weather is good and that you have warm clothing, especially a windbreaker, before you continue.

Wheeler Peak, Snake
Range, Great Basin
National Park

Follow the trail as it climbs south up the broad north ridge of Wheeler Peak. The ridge narrows, and there is a short respite from the climb at about 11,800 feet. The trail becomes steeper as it begins the final ascent. Views down the west slopes are stunning; the entire 7,000-foot sweep of the west ridge is visible from the summit to the floor of Spring Valley. Use care in this section if parts of the trail are snow covered. In early season large snowfields may block parts of the trail. These snowfields may be very dangerous, because the snow is slippery and ends above high cliffs to the north. If necessary, deviate to the right (south) of the trail to avoid the snow.

Views from the summit extend far into Utah to the east, and across a wide sweep of Nevada ranges to the west. To the north, the bulk of Mount Moriah dominates the northern Snake Range.

Surprisingly, there are small patches of alpine plants and flowers growing in sheltered areas all along this ascent, even at the summit, which is 2,000 feet above timberline. Plants growing above tree line must adapt to the arctic environment of strong wind and severe cold.

A number of rock shelters have been built by hikers for protection from the wind. Along the summit ridge to the east, you'll spot several level rock platforms. Look carefully and you'll see that the construction was more than casual. These were tent platforms built by the Wheeler Survey, which occupied the summit during the summer and fall for 4 years starting in 1881. The survey's purpose was to precisely measure the distance and direction to other mountain peaks. This work, coordinated with other federal surveys, resulted in the first accurate network of surveyed points spanning the continent, which were the foundation for accurate mapping of the West.

MILES AND DIRECTIONS

0.0 Summit trailhead.

1.0 Junction with Alpine Lakes Trail; turn right.

1.2 Junction with Wheeler Peak Trail; turn right.

2.2 Wheeler Saddle.

4.0 Wheeler Peak.

8.0 Return to Summit trailhead.

Looking down 7,000 feet from the summit of Wheeler Peak

60. **ALPINE LAKES**

WHY GO?

A day hike past two alpine lakes featuring close-up views of the high peaks in Great Basin National Park's Snake Range.

THE RUNDOWN

See map on page 185
Start: 17 miles from Baker
Distance: 2.3-mile lollipop
Hiking time: About 3 hours
Difficulty: Easy
Trail surface: Dirt and rocks
Water: Wheeler Peak Campground
Seasons: Summer through fall
Other trail users: None
Canine compatibility: Dogs not allowed on trails or in the backcountry

Land status: Great Basin National Park
Nearest town: Baker
Fees and permits: None
USGS topo map: Windy Peak
Other maps: Earthwalk Press: Great Basin National Park
Trail contacts: Great Basin National Park, 100 Great Basin National Park, Baker, NV 89311; (775) 234-7331; www.nps.gov/grba

FINDING THE TRAILHEAD

From Baker, drive west 5 miles on the Great Basin National Park entrance road (NV 488), then turn right (north) onto the signed, paved Wheeler Peak Scenic Drive. Continue 12 miles to the Bristlecone trailhead at the end of the road, just before the Wheeler Peak Campground entrance. **Trailhead GPS:** N39 0.59 / W114 18.453

WHAT TO SEE

Although the Alpine Lakes Trail is relatively short with little elevation gain, it lies at 10,000 feet. Most people, especially those who live at sea level, will have less hiking ability at this altitude. The signed trail crosses Lehman Creek on a small footbridge, then forks after a short distance. Turn right onto the Alpine Lakes Trail, which climbs through Engelmann spruce–limber pine forest to the north of the creek. After crossing the creek again, the pleasant trail switchbacks to the right through meadows bordered with quaking aspen. There are fine views of Wheeler Peak. Stay left at the signed junction with the Summit Trail. A short distance farther, the signed Wheeler Peak Trail turns sharply right; continue straight ahead to the first lake.

Stella Lake is a typical glacial lake formed in the cirque created by a glacier. The moving ice "grinds down at the heel" and forms a depression in the floor of the steep–walled valley at its head. After the ice melts, a deep, cold lake is often left behind. Erosion of the steep mountainsides above the lake gradually fills it in. Stella Lake is in the last stages of fill; it is shallow and freezes almost solid in the winter.

Stella Lake, Alpine Lakes Loop, Great Basin National Park

Teresa Lake, Alpine Lakes Loop, Great Basin National Park

Stella Lake, Alpine Lakes Loop, Great Basin National Park

Day hiking at Stella Lake, Alpine Lakes Loop, Great Basin National Park

The trail skirts the east side of Stella Lake, then wanders through uneven, hummocky terrain. A glacier once covered this area; when it melted, it dropped its mixed load of dirt, sand, rocks, and boulders in a jumbled heap. Sometimes large blocks of ice are left behind and isolated from the retreating mass of the main glacier, and later melt to form kettle lakes in depressions in the moraine. There are a number of depressions along this section of the trail that could contain small lakes, but don't. This is probably because of the present dryness of the climate.

The trail now descends in a single switchback and follows a small stream to Teresa Lake. The depth of this lake varies greatly, depending on the amount of snowmelt. The trail skirts the west side of the lake then continues down the drainage. Just north of the lake, turn left at a signed junction with the Bristlecone–Glacier Trail. (This trail can be done as a side trip; it adds 3.2 miles to the length.) The trail continues north down the slope, and soon reaches the junction with the Alpine Lakes Trail, where you started the loop. Stay right to reach the trailhead.

MILES AND DIRECTIONS

0.0 Bristlecone trailhead.

0.2 Bristlecone-Glacier Trail; turn right.

0.5 Junction with Summit Trail; turn left.

0.7 Junction with Wheeler Peak Trail; stay left.

0.8 Stella Lake.

1.5 Teresa Lake.

1.8 Bristlecone-Glacier Trail; stay left.

2.1 Alpine Lakes Trail; stay right.

2.3 Return to Bristlecone trailhead.

61. BRISTLECONE-GLACIER TRAIL

WHY GO?

This day hike in Great Basin National Park features the Wheeler Glacier, which is the only permanent body of ice between the Sierra Nevada and the Wasatch Mountains, and a bristlecone pine interpretive trail through the oldest living trees on earth.

THE RUNDOWN

See map on page 185
Start: 17 miles west of Baker
Distance: 4.0-mile out and back
Hiking time: About 3 hours
Difficulty: Moderate
Trail surface: Dirt and rocks
Water: Wheeler Peak Campground
Seasons: Summer through fall
Other trail users: Equestrians
Canine compatibility: Dogs not allowed on trails or in the backcountry

Land status: Great Basin National Park
Nearest town: Baker
Fees and permits: None
USGS topo map: Windy Peak
Other maps: Earthwalk Press: Great Basin National Park
Trail contacts: Great Basin National Park, 100 Great Basin National Park, Baker, NV 89311; (775) 234-7331; www.nps.gov/grba

FINDING THE TRAILHEAD

From Baker, drive west 5 miles on the Great Basin National Park entrance road (NV 488), then turn right (north) onto the signed, paved Wheeler Peak Scenic Drive. Continue 12 miles to the Bristlecone trailhead at the end of the road, just before the Wheeler Peak Campground entrance. **Trailhead GPS:** N39 0.59 / W114 18.453

WHAT TO SEE

The trail crosses Lehman Creek then reaches a signed trail junction. Turn left here onto the signed Bristlecone-Glacier Trail, which climbs steadily through dense limber pine–Engelmann spruce forest then meets the Alpine Lakes Trail at a signed junction. (Teresa Lake is a short distance up the Alpine Lakes Trail.) Turn left (east) and follow the Bristlecone-Glacier Trail as it first crosses over a low ridge, then climbs out across a shady north-facing slope. Where the trail turns right around the ridge, there is a good view of the upper Lehman Creek drainage and the Wheeler Peak Campground. Now the trail starts climbing gently along the slope. A switchback leads onto the rough, jumbled terrain of the moraine left by the retreat of the Wheeler Glacier. A short, signed interpretive trail here explains the bristlecone pines. It is certainly worth the time and adds almost nothing to the hike distance.

The Wheeler Icefield is the
only permanent icefield in
the vast Great Basin region.

Bristlecone pine,
Bristlecone-
Glacier Trail,
Great Basin
National Park

The bristlecone pine is a gnarled, tough tree found near timberline in the mountains of Colorado, Utah, Nevada, eastern California, and northern Arizona. It is easily recognized by its short, stiff needles growing five to a bundle; the branches resemble neat bottle brushes. Bristlecones are among the oldest living things on earth, reaching ages of greater than 4,500 years.

Researchers determine the ages of the trees using tree ring dating. A slender cylinder is screwed into the heart of the tree, a process that leaves the tree unharmed. The cylinder is removed and the wood core extracted. Bands along the core are sections of the tree rings, and each ring represents a period of growth. Since bristlecones have one short period of growth each year, the rings can be counted and correlated with other tree ring data to accurately determine the tree's age, as well as indicate climate changes affecting the tree's growth rate. By correlating overlapping sections from older and dead trees, the tree ring record has been extended back 9,000 years.

The two trails rejoin at a signed junction, and the Bristlecone-Glacier Trail continues up the moraine. The only trees that survive now are low mats of bristlecone pine, limber pine, and Engelmann spruce. The trail ends at the foot of the Wheeler rock glacier. In this stark canyon carved by ice and frost, life is reduced to a few hardy tundra plants growing in places where the rocks are stable. But even on the snow of the glacier there is life. In late summer you may notice a red stain on the old snow. This is caused by algae that live on snowfields.

Glaciers form when the annual snowfall exceeds that lost to melting and evaporation. As the layers of snow pile up year after year, their weight compresses the lowest layers into ice. Under such great pressure, ice becomes fluid and begins to flow down the mountainside. The moving ice scours its bed, wearing away the bedrock and moving it downhill. The lower end of the glacier is at the elevation where the ice melts faster than it is replaced. Even a slight change in the climate can cause a rapid retreat or expansion of a glacier, so scientists study glaciers worldwide as a sensitive indicator of climate change. When a glacier retreats, it drops its immense load of rock, forming a moraine, a distinctive heap of dirt, gravel, and rocks of all sizes.

MILES AND DIRECTIONS

0.0 Bristlecone trailhead.

0.2 Bristlecone-Glacier Trail; go left.

0.5 Alpine Lakes Trail; go left.

1.4 Bristlecone interpretive loop.

2.0 Glacier viewpoint.

4.0 Return to Bristlecone trailhead.

62. MOUNTAIN VIEW NATURE TRAIL

WHY GO?

An easy interpretive nature trail in Great Basin National Park that explains the piñon-juniper plant community and the geology of the Snake Range.

THE RUNDOWN

Start: 6 miles west of Baker
Distance: 0.5-mile loop
Hiking time: About 0.5 hour
Difficulty: Easy
Trail surface: Dirt
Water: Visitor center
Seasons: All year
Other trail users: None
Canine compatibility: Dogs not allowed on trails or in the backcountry

Land status: Great Basin National Park
Nearest town: Baker
Fees and permits: None
USGS topo map: None
Other maps: A guide leaflet is available at the visitor center.
Trail contacts: Great Basin National Park, 100 Great Basin National Park, Baker, NV 89311; (775) 234-7331; www.nps.gov/grba

FINDING THE TRAILHEAD

From Baker, drive 5.5 miles west on NV 488 and park at the visitor center.
Trailhead GPS: N39 0.344 / W114 13.17

WHAT TO SEE

This nature trail is a good way to become familiar with the piñon–juniper plant community. It starts at the north end of the visitor center at the old log cabin. The cabin was a guest lodge during the early days of Lehman Cave National Monument. The trail continues behind the cabin, gradually climbing the slope until a viewpoint is reached. Interpretive signs point out typical plants common in the Great Basin.

63. LEHMAN CAVE

WHY GO?
An easy, ranger-guided walk through Lehman Cave in Great Basin National Park, one of the most highly decorated caves of its size in the world.

THE RUNDOWN
Start: 6 miles west of Baker
Distance: 0.6-mile loop
Hiking time: About 1 to 1.5 hours
Difficulty: Easy
Trail surface: Paved
Water: Visitor center
Seasons: All year
Other trail users: None
Canine compatibility: Dogs not allowed
Land status: Great Basin National Park

Nearest town: Baker
Fees and permits: Fees for cave tours
USGS topo map: None
Other maps: Lehman Cave park brochure
Trail contacts: Great Basin National Park, 100 Great Basin National Park, Baker, NV 89311; (775) 234-7331; www.nps.gov/grba

FINDING THE TRAILHEAD
From Baker, drive 5.5 miles west on NV 488 and park at the visitor center. **Trailhead GPS:** N39 0.344 / W114 13.17

THE HIKE
Lehman Cave, though small compared with famous caves such as Carlsbad Caverns, is highly decorated with cave formations—well worth the visit. For the protection of these resources, park rangers lead guided walks through the cave. Check at the visitor center for walk times, fees, and advance ticket sales. Groups are limited to thirty. Some of the cave passages are narrow; camera tripods and backpacks are not allowed. Sections of the trail through the cave may be wet and slippery—the path ascends and descends several sets of stairs.

Lehman Cave,
Great Basin National Park

64. BAKER AND JOHNSON LAKES

WHY GO?

A long but very scenic day hike or backpack trip, with a short section of cross-country, to a pair of alpine lakes set in glacial basins located high in Great Basin National Park's Snake Range.

THE RUNDOWN

Start: 9 miles west of Baker
Distance: 11.4-mile loop
Hiking time: About 8 hours, or 2 days
Difficulty: Strenuous
Trail surface: Dirt and rocks
Water: Baker Creek, Baker Lake, Johnson Lake, South Fork Baker Creek
Seasons: Summer through fall
Other trail users: None
Canine compatibility: Dogs not allowed on trails or in the backcountry

Land status: Great Basin National Park
Nearest town: Baker
Fees and permits: None
USGS topo map: Wheeler Peak and Kious Spring
Other maps: Earthwalk Press: Great Basin National Park
Trail contacts: Great Basin National Park, 100 Great Basin National Park, Baker, NV 89311; (775) 234-7331; www.nps.gov/grba

FINDING THE TRAILHEAD

From Baker, drive west 5.2 miles on NV 488, the entrance road to the park. Just after passing the park boundary sign, turn left (south) onto the signed, maintained dirt Baker Creek Road. Follow this road 4 miles to its end at the signed Baker trailhead. **Trailhead GPS:** N38 58.614 / W114 14.705

WHAT TO SEE

Start on the signed Baker Lake Trail. The trail climbs along the north side of boisterous Baker Creek, sometimes swinging to the north in a series of switchbacks. There are varied views of the canyon walls and the high country, especially when the trail temporarily leaves the creek and its dense riparian vegetation. Other sections of the trail stay near the creek in fine aspen groves. After a long climb, the trail passes the ruins of an old cabin. It was probably used by Peter Deishman, a prospector who was active in the early 20th century. Continue on the main trail, which climbs the steep slope below Baker Lake in a series of switchbacks. Watch for a faint, unsigned trail (the Baker-Johnson Trail to Baker-Johnson Pass) going left, but stay on the main trail (right) and continue to Baker Lake. This small, scenic alpine lake is backdropped by the rugged cliffs of the Snake Range crest and Baker Peak.

Baker Lake, Great Basin National Park,
set in a circle of rugged peaks

Baker Lake occupies a cirque left
over from the last glacial period

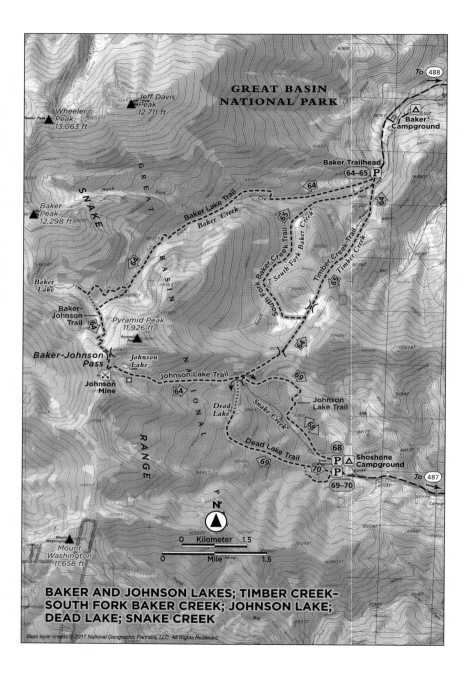

GREAT BASIN NATIONAL PARK

BAKER AND JOHNSON LAKES; TIMBER CREEK-SOUTH FORK BAKER CREEK; JOHNSON LAKE; DEAD LAKE; SNAKE CREEK

Base layer credits © 2017 National Geographic Partners, LLC. All Rights Reserved.

Baker Creek, Great Basin National Park

Baker-Johnson Pass, Snake Range, Great Basin National Park

After enjoying the lake, start back down the trail, but watch for a cairned cross-country route going right (southeast) before the main trail starts its steep descent. Follow the cairns as they contour southeast a short distance to join the faint Baker-Johnson Trail in the open valley above timberline. If you don't find the trail along the creek, just follow the drainage and the cairns uphill. The route finally reaches the broad Baker-Johnson Pass at 11,294 feet. There are sweeping views, including Baker Peak, Jeff Davis Peak, and, close at hand, Pyramid Peak. Look for a few cairns, and use them to descend south from the pass.

The trail becomes well defined on the steep slope below the pass. Early-season hikers will have to avoid one or more steep snowfields. If the trail is lost under snow, pick it up farther down the slope. It soon joins a much better (but still little-used) trail, which goes right (southwest) to the old Johnson tungsten mine, established by Alfred Johnson in the fall of 1909. From this mine, ore was brought down to Johnson Lake via aerial tram, then transported on mules to the mill. After the tungsten ore was concentrated, mules carried it down the mountain and eventually to the railhead at Frisco, Utah. Transportation costs would have been high, which probably contributed to the mine's financial struggles.

Turn left, downhill, and continue to the south shore of Johnson Lake. You'll pass more mine relics, including the aerial tram cable spanning the talus slope up to the mine. Timbers and other old mining gear are scattered along the east shore of the lake, apparently brought down by a major snow avalanche in 1935. This event destroyed most of the mine workings and put an end to this already marginal venture.

The Johnson Lake Trail, now an old jeep road, continues down the drainage east of the lake and gradually becomes more distinct. Watch for the ruins of several old cabins used by the mining operation. There are numerous good camping spots in this area, and water is available in the creek. The trail descends steeply after the cabins. About a mile below Johnson Lake, the trail passes the ruins of a large log structure, the old Johnson mill.

There is more camping in the forest below the mill, on the south side of the trail, though water would have to be carried down from the creek. About 0.25 mile after the mill, you'll pass an old road closure gate; this is the signal to start watching on the left for the trail to the Snake-Baker Pass. The foot trail is little used and easy to miss. It climbs steadily through aspens to reach the pass, where the trail becomes faint. Turn left (north), and descend the trail below the pass, northeast through the forest.

Shortly, the trail emerges into a broad meadow. A wide pass is visible above to the right. Before the trail reaches the pass, turn left onto the South Fork Baker Creek Trail at a signed junction. (This junction is shown incorrectly on the USGS map.) The trail is faint until it nears the creek. You'll pick up the trail again as it nears the right side of the creek, where it enters the trees. From the junction, hike down the South Fork to a signed junction with the Timber Creek Trail. Turn left and follow the South Fork Trail to the Baker trailhead.

MILES AND DIRECTIONS

0.0 Baker trailhead—start on the Baker Lake Trail.

3.4 Old cabin.

3.6 Junction with Baker-Johnson Trail; turn right.

4.5 Baker Lake; retrace your steps to a cairned shortcut to Baker-Johnson Trail.

4.7 Cross-country route to Baker-Johnson Trail; contour southeast.

4.9 Baker-Johnson Trail; turn right.

5.6 Baker-Johnson Pass.

6.1 Johnson Lake—the trail becomes the Johnson Lake Trail.

7.5 Junction with trail to Snake-Baker Pass; turn left.

8.2 Snake-Baker Pass.

8.6 Junction with South Fork Baker Creek Trail; turn left.

11.3 Junction with Timber Creek Trail; turn left.

11.4 Return to Baker trailhead.

65. TIMBER CREEK AND SOUTH FORK BAKER CREEK

WHY GO?

A little-used trail to a high pass and scenic alpine meadows in Great Basin National Park.

THE RUNDOWN

See map on page 202
Start: 9 miles west of Baker
Distance: 4.8-mile loop
Hiking time: About 5 hours
Difficulty: Strenuous
Trail surface: Dirt and rocks
Water: Timber Creek, South Fork Baker Creek
Seasons: Summer through fall
Other trail users: None
Canine compatibility: Dogs not allowed on trails or in the backcountry

Land status: Great Basin National Park
Nearest town: Baker
Fees and permits: None
USGS topo map: Wheeler Peak and Kious Spring
Other maps: Earthwalk Press: Great Basin National Park
Trail contacts: Great Basin National Park, 100 Great Basin National Park, Baker, NV 89311; (775) 234-7331; www.nps.gov/grba

FINDING THE TRAILHEAD

From Baker, drive west 5.2 miles on NV 488, the entrance road to the park. Just after passing the park boundary sign, turn left (south) onto the signed, maintained dirt Baker Creek Road. Follow this road 4 miles to its end at the signed Baker trailhead. **Trailhead GPS:** N38 58.614 / W114 14.705

WHAT TO SEE

Two trails leave the Baker trailhead, the Baker Lake Trail and South Fork Baker Creek Trail. To start the clockwise loop, take the South Fork Baker Creek Trail, which is signed "Johnson Lake," on the left. Cross Baker Creek on a couple of footbridges and then turn left onto the Timber Creek Trail. Follow the sometimes faint trail as it crosses a meadow into Timber Creek Canyon. The trail begins to climb steeply, and continues through a beautiful fir-and-aspen forest. A set of log steps marks the point where the climb starts to relent, and soon afterward the trail comes out onto a wide sage-covered saddle, framed by aspens. Cross the saddle and descend west to the head of the South Fork Baker Creek. There are great views of the east side of Pyramid Peak. The trail is faint across the meadow; just head down into the South Fork. The trail becomes obvious again as it enters the aspens, following the right (east) side of the

**Pyramid Peak,
Great Basin National Park**
© BRUCE GRUBBS

creek. The South Fork Trail is better maintained than the Timber Creek Trail. It's also slightly longer, so the descent is more gradual. A steeper descent in the lower part of the canyon leads to the junction with the Timber Creek Trail; turn left and follow the South Fork Trail to the Baker trailhead.

MILES AND DIRECTIONS

- **0.0** Baker trailhead.
- **0.1** Timber Creek Trail junction; turn left.
- **1.9** Timber Creek Pass.
- **2.0** South Fork Baker Creek Trail junction; turn right.
- **4.7** Timber Creek Trail junction; turn left.
- **4.8** Return to Baker trailhead.

66. **POLE CANYON**

WHY GO?

An easy day hike on a little-used trail in Great Basin National Park. This is a low-elevation hike that is good in early season.

THE RUNDOWN

Start: 7 miles west of Baker
Distance: 4.4-mile out and back
Hiking time: About 3 hours
Difficulty: Easy
Trail surface: Old road, dirt and rocks
Water: Pole Creek
Seasons: All year
Other trail users: None
Canine compatibility: Dogs not allowed on trails or in the backcountry

Land status: Great Basin National Park
Nearest town: Baker
Fees and permits: None
USGS topo map: Kious Spring
Trail contacts: Great Basin National Park, 100 Great Basin National Park, Baker, NV 89311; (775) 234-7331; www.nps.gov/grba

FINDING THE TRAILHEAD

From Baker, drive west 5.2 miles on NV 488, the entrance road to the park. Just after passing the park boundary sign, turn left (south) onto the signed, maintained dirt Baker Creek Road. Follow this road 1.6 miles, then turn left onto Gray Cliffs Road, which is also maintained dirt. Almost immediately, turn left again onto an unmaintained road. Go 0.6 mile, just past a cattle guard, then park on the right at the unsigned trailhead. The trail is an old, closed jeep road that immediately crosses Baker Creek. **Trailhead GPS:** N38 59.394 / W114 12.414

WHAT TO SEE

Due to its low elevation, this is a good hike for early season when the high country is still snow covered; it's also great in the fall when the aspens are changing. The old jeep road crosses Baker Creek, which will probably have to be waded. Use caution; in the spring or after heavy rain, Baker Creek can be too high to cross safely. On the far side of the creek, the trail turns right and follows the left side of the creek through open piñon–juniper country. Soon the loud rush of Baker Creek fades away, to be replaced by the gentle murmur of Pole Creek, a much smaller stream. The old road enters groves of aspen and becomes crisscrossed with deadfall. Persistence will pay off, though. Just as the deadfall is getting really annoying, the trail climbs out on the left and skirts the sage–covered slope. It passes through an aspen grove at about 7,600 feet and emerges into the upper basin of

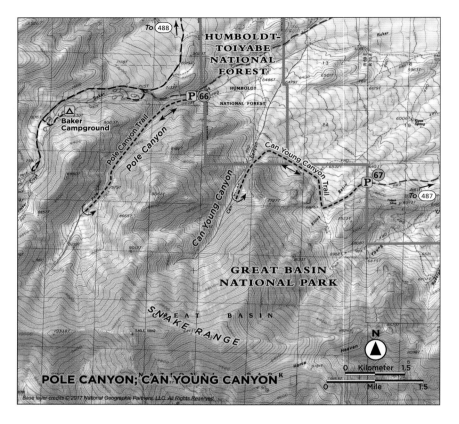

Pole Canyon. The trail fades away here, though with care it could probably be followed to the spring shown on the USGS topographic map. But this makes an excellent destination for the hike, with scenic views all around.

67. **CAN YOUNG CANYON**

WHY GO?
An easy, low-elevation hike in Great Basin National Park that's great in early season.

THE RUNDOWN
See map on page 208
Start: 5 miles southwest of Baker
Distance: 4.8-mile out and back
Hiking time: About 3 hours
Difficulty: Easy
Trail surface: Old roads, dirt and rocks
Water: Can Young Canyon
Seasons: All year
Other trail users: None
Canine compatibility: Dogs not allowed on trails or in the backcountry

Land status: Great Basin National Park
Nearest town: Baker
Fees and permits: None
USGS topo map: Kious Spring
Other maps: Earthwalk Press: Great Basin National Park; Forest Service: Humboldt-Toiyabe National Forest, Ely Ranger District
Trail contacts: Great Basin National Park, 100 Great Basin National Park, Baker, NV 89311; (775) 234-7331; www.nps.gov/grba

FINDING THE TRAILHEAD
From Baker, drive 1 mile southeast on NV 487, then turn right onto a maintained dirt road. The road goes past a large water tank. At 2.4 miles from the highway, turn right onto an unmaintained road, which requires a high-clearance vehicle. Go right at a minor fork 2.7 miles from the highway, and continue to the national park boundary at 3.5 miles. It's advisable to park here, because the road becomes much rougher ahead. **Trailhead GPS:** N38 58.47 / W114 10.172

WHAT TO SEE
This is a good hike for early season, before the snow has melted from the high country. Walk up the road from the park boundary. The road appears to be used very occasionally, so it makes a nice footway. You'll have a good view of the impressive cliffs to the left of the road. The road reaches a T-intersection at a cattle watering trough in Kious Basin. Turn right, downhill, and follow the old road as it swings around another impressive cliff. A road forks right; turn left, uphill to the northwest. Within a few yards the road goes over a saddle formed by a large rock knob. Shortly after leaving the saddle, the road goes through a gate, temporarily leaving the park. After this, the road climbs slowly along the foothills, then more steeply into the mouth of Can Young Canyon. Cross the flowing creek, then, at another T-intersection, turn left and walk past the park boundary sign into the canyon. The road is closed to vehicles at this point. The old road continues along the

Bristlecone Pine, Great Basin National Park
© ISTOCK.COM/ JOE_GUETZLOFF

creek, past fine aspen stands, before fading and becoming blocked by deadfall. This makes a good turnaround point.

MILES AND DIRECTIONS

- **0.0** Trailhead at park boundary.
- **0.7** T-junction at water trough; turn right.
- **1.1** Junction below saddle; stay left.
- **2.1** Can Young Canyon; turn left.
- **2.4** End of hike.
- **4.8** Return to trailhead.

68. **JOHNSON LAKE**

WHY GO?

A day hike or backpack trip on a less used trail to an alpine lake and historic mining district in Great Basin National Park.

THE RUNDOWN

See map on page 202
Start: 18 miles southwest of Baker
Distance: 6.6-mile out and back
Hiking time: About 5 hours, or 2 days
Difficulty: Strenuous
Trail surface: Dirt and rocks
Water: Snake Creek, Johnson Lake
Seasons: Summer through fall
Other trail users: None
Canine compatibility: Dogs not allowed on trails or in the backcountry

Land status: Great Basin National Park
Nearest town: Baker
Fees and permits: None
USGS topo map: Wheeler Peak
Other maps: Earthwalk Press: Great Basin National Park
Trail contacts: Great Basin National Park, 100 Great Basin National Park, Baker, NV 89311; (775) 234-7331; www.nps.gov/grba

FINDING THE TRAILHEAD

From Baker, drive south 5.2 miles on NV 487, then turn right (west) onto the signed, graded Snake Creek Canyon Road. Follow this road 13 miles to its end. (There are numerous primitive campsites along the road.) Just before the end of the road, a jeep road goes left—stay on the main road. The trailhead has a primitive campground with picnic tables, in a fine aspen grove surrounding Snake Creek.
Trailhead GPS: N38 55.693 / W114 15.228

WHAT TO SEE

The Johnson Lake Trail follows an old jeep trail that is closed to vehicles. It is not marked or maintained, so you should have the USGS topographic map. Start from the upper end of the parking lot and follow the unsigned old road directly up the hill. After a few hundred yards, another jeep road comes in from the left, and the trail turns right and crosses Snake Creek. It stays north of Snake Creek all the way to Johnson Lake. After crossing the creek, the trail parallels it on the right, climbing through alpine meadows bordered with aspen and white fir.

After following the creek for a while, the trail veers away to the north and descends to cross a drainage. It then climbs out onto a sage-covered slope, which it ascends in a couple of switchbacks. Notice the contrast between this dry south-facing slope, covered with sage and mountain mahogany, and the moist north-facing slope you just descended, which is covered with fir and aspen.

A young Englemann spruce growing through an old gold sluice, Johnson Lake Trail, Basin National Park

Aspens, Johnson Lake Trail, Snake Range

Above the switchbacks, the trail climbs steeply through forest in which limber pine start to appear. You will also see Engelmann spruce, whose needles grow singly like the firs, but are square in cross section so that they roll easily between your fingers. You may notice a faint, unsigned trail heading right. This trail climbs to the Snake–Baker Pass; stay left on the Johnson Lake Trail. The trail now heads a minor drainage in the forest, and climbs onto a point where the forest takes on a decidedly more alpine appearance. There are a number of campsites here but no water after the snow melts. In another 0.5 mile the trail passes an old cabin. There are a few campsites here, and water in the creek. Be sure to camp at least 100 feet from the water.

After the cabin, the old road becomes rougher and steeper for about 0.5 mile, then moderates a bit for the final climb to the lake. More cabins, one of them fairly elaborate, are located just below the lake. Various cut logs and rusty pieces of equipment are strewn around the cabins and the lake, indicating that a lot of activity took place here. There is even a cable strung from one of the mines high on the talus slope. Some of the cut timber might have been used to support a tramway. The lake itself is small, but the west end is deep. It is a true alpine tarn—a lake created by a glacier.

The forest type found throughout the Snake Range is well represented along the Johnson Lake Trail. Great Basin trees such as curlleaf mountain mahogany grow next to Rocky Mountain white fir and Engelmann spruce. Douglas fir is also common, as is limber pine. Along this section of the trail, you should be able to identify white fir by its flat needles that will not roll in your fingers, and its spongy, corklike bark. The needles of Douglas fir are similar, but the bark is gray and more deeply furrowed. Limber pine has 2–inch–long needles growing five to a bunch, and the limbs are very flexible, helping the tree to survive heavy alpine snow loads.

MILES AND DIRECTIONS

0.0   Snake Creek trailhead.

2.0   Trail to Snake-Baker Pass; stay left.

3.3   Johnson Lake Trail.

6.6   Return to Snake Creek trailhead via Johnson Lake Trail.

Johnson Lake,
Snake Range

69. **DEAD LAKE**

WHY GO?

A cross-country and on-trail day hike in Great Basin National Park featuring an alpine creek and meadows in a seldom-visited area.

THE RUNDOWN

See map on page 202
Start: 18 miles southwest of Baker
Distance: 4.3-mile loop
Hiking time: About 3 hours
Difficulty: Strenuous
Trail surface: Cross-country, old roads, dirt and rocks
Water: Snake Creek
Seasons: Summer through fall
Other trail users: None
Canine compatibility: Dogs not allowed on trails or in the backcountry

Land status: Great Basin National Park
Nearest town: Baker
Fees and permits: None
USGS topo map: Wheeler Peak
Other maps: Earthwalk Press: Great Basin National Park
Trail contacts: Great Basin National Park, 100 Great Basin National Park, Baker, NV 89311; (775) 234-7331; www.nps.gov/grba

FINDING THE TRAILHEAD

From Baker, drive south 5.2 miles on NV 487, then turn right (west) onto the signed, graded Snake Creek Canyon Road. Follow this road 13 miles to its end. (There are numerous primitive campsites along the road.) Just before the end of the road, a jeep road goes left—stay on the main road. The trailhead has a primitive campground with picnic tables, in a fine aspen grove surrounding Snake Creek.
Trailhead GPS: N38 55.693 / W114 15.228

WHAT TO SEE

Walk up the old road you were just driving. You soon pass the limit of vehicle use, and the road starts to climb steadily. Piñon-juniper and ponderosa pine give way to fir and aspen. There are occasional great views to the east. The old jeep trail swings right; watch for a foot trail that branches right. A short, steep climb on this trail leads to a flat bench where the central fork of Snake Creek flows through small alpine meadows. Dead Lake is about 300 yards farther northeast.

From the lake, contour north cross-country through the alpine forest. After about 0.6 mile, you will meet the Johnson Lake Trail, an old jeep road. Turn right and follow this good trail 2 miles downhill to Shoshone Campground. To return to the trailhead, walk down the main road to the faint road at Snake Creek, then turn right and walk uphill a short distance to your vehicle.

Ponderosa pine can be found at lower elevations. © ISTOCK.COM/REX_WHOLSTER

MILES AND DIRECTIONS

0.0 Trailhead on unmaintained road.

1.7 Dead Lake; hike north, cross-country.

2.1 Johnson Lake Trail; turn right and hike downhill.

4.1 Shoshone Campground.

4.3 Return to trailhead on unmaintained road.

70. SNAKE CREEK

WHY GO?
An easy cross-country and trail day hike along Snake Creek in Great Basin National Park.

THE RUNDOWN
See map on page 202
Start: 18 miles southwest of Baker
Distance: 1.1-mile loop
Hiking time: About 2 hours
Difficulty: Easy
Trail surface: Old roads
Water: Snake Creek
Seasons: Summer through fall
Other trail users: Equestrians
Canine compatibility: Dogs not allowed on trails or in the backcountry

Land status: Great Basin National Park
Nearest town: Baker
Fees and permits: None
USGS topo map: Wheeler Peak
Trail contacts: Great Basin National Park, 100 Great Basin National Park, Baker, NV 89311; (775) 234-7331; www.nps.gov/grba

FINDING THE TRAILHEAD
From Baker, drive south 5.2 miles on NV 487, then turn right (west) onto the signed, graded Snake Creek Canyon Road. After 13 miles, the main road veers right, away from Snake Creek. Turn left onto a faint, unmaintained road. Take the first left turn, cross the creek, and park in the primitive campsite. **Trailhead GPS:** N38 55.543 / W114 15.255

WHAT TO SEE
This short trail is worthwhile because it takes you to a tributary of Snake Creek. You'll be hiking it clockwise. Cross the campground and follow the old road that climbs left (southwest) out of the camp area. Several switchbacks lead to the road's abrupt end. Now turn right and drop directly downhill, cross-country, to the creek. Cross this waterway, then turn right onto the Dead Lake Trail, an old road, and follow it back to the trailhead. Or you can just follow the creek downhill to the trailhead.

MILES AND DIRECTIONS

- **0.0** Trailhead at primitive campsite.
- **0.6** End of old road.
- **0.7** Dead Lake Trail.
- **1.1** Return to trailhead at primitive campsite.

Pyramid Peak, Snake
Range, Great Basin
National Park

71. SOUTH FORK BIG WASH

WHY GO?
A day hike on a seldom-used trail in a remote section of Great Basin National Park.

THE RUNDOWN
Start: 24 miles southwest of Baker
Distance: 10.4-mile out and back
Hiking time: About 6 hours
Difficulty: Strenuous
Trail surface: Old roads, dirt, and rocks
Water: Springs at old boiler, along traverse above gorge, and at end of hike
Seasons: Summer through fall
Other trail users: None
Canine compatibility: Dogs not allowed on trails or in the backcountry

Land status: Great Basin National Park
Nearest town: Baker
Fees and permits: None
USGS topo map: Arch Canyon and Kious Spring
Other maps: Earthwalk Press: Great Basin National Park
Trail contacts: Great Basin National Park, 100 Great Basin National Park, Baker, NV 89311; (775) 234-7331; www.nps.gov/grba

FINDING THE TRAILHEAD
From Baker, drive southeast 10.7 miles on NV 487 (the road becomes UT 21 at the state line), then turn right onto the first dirt road past Pruess Lake (signed Lexington Arch). Go west 9.6 miles, then turn right (the left fork is signed for Lexington Arch). You may want a high-clearance vehicle for this section, though most cars should be able to continue, if driven with care. Continue 3.8 miles, then park at the unsigned trailhead. The trail is an old jeep road on the right (north). **Trailhead GPS:** N38 51.361 / W114 13.2

Old boiler, South Fork Big Wash, Great Basin National Park

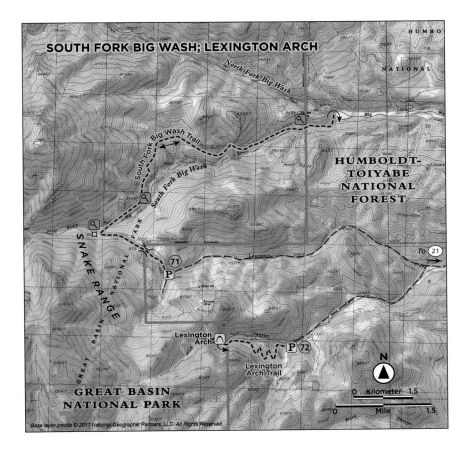

WHAT TO SEE

The old jeep road climbs steeply to a broad saddle, entering the park at a signed gate. It then descends through fir-aspen forest, switches back sharply to the right (northeast), and descends to the dry bed of South Fork Big Wash. An old steam boiler remains from an old sawmill. The trail continues as a footpath and climbs out on the left (north) slope. This section is faint, but once you're on the trail it is easy to follow. Initially the trail goes around a juniper and crosses the flow from a spring. It climbs through dense stands of mountain mahogany, with occasional tantalizing glimpses of the narrow limestone gorge below. After leveling off, the trail passes another spring, then continues around the slope to the north. An open section of ponderosa pine and manzanita afford a great view down South Fork Big Wash.

After rounding a broad basin, the trail turns east and begins to descend rapidly. It reaches the creekbed below Castle Butte, a prominent limestone cliff, then crosses to the south side. Shortly a fine spring enters from the north, and the creek runs steadily. Below this point, the trail goes through a narrow slot in the limestone, made narrower still by a huge fallen boulder. This marks the approximate park boundary. The canyon opens out into a broad flat at the confluence of North Fork Big Wash, which is the end of your hike.

MILES AND DIRECTIONS

0.0   Trailhead at old jeep road.

0.5   Park boundary.

1.3   Sawmill site in South Fork Big Wash.

4.1   Trail returns to South Fork Big Wash.

4.7   Park boundary.

5.2   North Fork Big Wash.

10.4 Return to trailhead.

72. LEXINGTON ARCH

WHY GO?

A day hike to a unique limestone natural arch in Great Basin National Park.

THE RUNDOWN

See map on page 219
Start: 22 miles southwest of Baker
Distance: 3.2-mile out and back
Hiking time: About 2 hours
Difficulty: Moderate
Trail surface: Dirt and rocks
Water: None
Seasons: Summer through fall
Other trail users: None
Canine compatibility: Dogs not allowed on trails or in the backcountry

Land status: Great Basin National Park
Nearest town: Baker
Fees and permits: None
USGS topo map: Arch Canyon
Other maps: Earthwalk Press: Great Basin National Park; Forest Service: Humboldt-Toiyabe National Forest, Ely Ranger District
Trail contacts: Great Basin National Park, 100 Great Basin National Park, Baker, NV 89311; (775) 234-7331; www.nps.gov/grba

FINDING THE TRAILHEAD

From Baker, drive southeast 10.7 miles on NV 487 (the road becomes UT 21), then turn right onto the first dirt road past Pruess Lake (signed Lexington Arch). Go west 11.7 miles, following the signs for Lexington Arch. This road is minimally maintained, and a high-clearance vehicle is recommended. Please leave all gates as you find them, to help keep livestock on the correct ranges. **Trailhead GPS:** N38 50.54 / W114 11.526

WHAT TO SEE

At first the trail follows the drainage, but after about 200 yards it turns left and climbs the sage slope to the west in a series of broad switchbacks. It then traverses the forested south slopes of the canyon. The trail returns to the bed of the canyon at the south buttress of the arch, and finally climbs into the arch itself.

Rising high above the floor of the canyon, this imposing natural arch was created by the forces of weather working slowly over a span of centuries. Lexington Arch is unusual in one important respect: It is carved from limestone. Most of the natural arches of the western United States are composed of sandstone. The fact that Lexington Arch is made of limestone leads to speculation that it was once a passage in a cave system. Flowstone—a smooth, glossy deposit that forms in caves—has been found at the base of the opening, lending support to this theory.

Lexington Arch, Great
Basin National Park

It is even possible that Lexington "Arch" is actually a natural bridge. An arch is formed by the forces of weathering, such as ice, wind, and chemical breakdown of the rock. A natural bridge, by contrast, is formed by the flowing waters of a stream. It could be that long ago, when the canyon was less deep, the waters of Lexington Creek flowed through a cave in its wall, in the process enlarging the tunnel that later became Lexington Arch. If this happened then the "arch" is truly a bridge.

TRAIL ETIQUETTE

Leave no trace. Always leave an area just like you found it—if not better than you found it. Avoid camping in fragile, alpine meadows and along the banks of streams and lakes. Use a camp stove versus building a wood fire. Pack up all of your trash and extra food. Bury human waste at least 100 feet from water sources under 6 to 8 inches of topsoil. Don't bathe with soap in a lake or stream—use prepackaged moistened towels to wipe off sweat and dirt, or bathe in the water without soap.

Stay on the trail. It's true, a path anywhere leads nowhere new, but purists will just have to get over it. Paths serve an important purpose; they limit impact on natural areas. Straying from a designated trail may seem innocent, but it can cause damage to sensitive areas—damage that may take years to recover, if it can recover at all. Even simple shortcuts can be destructive. So, please, stay on the trail.

Leave no weeds. Noxious weeds tend to overtake other plants, which in turn affects animals and birds that depend on them for food. To minimize the spread of noxious weeds, hikers should regularly clean their boots, tents, packs, and hiking poles of mud and seeds. Also brush your dog to remove any weed seeds before heading off into a new area.

ISTOCK.COM/MARGARETW

Crest of the Spring Range south of Mount Charleston, as seen from the North Loop Trail

SOUTHERN NEVADA

ALTHOUGH STILL IN THE BASIN-AND-RANGE geological province, southern Nevada is lower in elevation than the rest of the state, and the Great Basin desert, dominated by sagebrush, gives way to the hotter and drier Mojave Desert in this region. Still, there are plenty of mountains to explore. The Sheep Range reaches almost to 10,000 feet, and the highest point of the Spring Mountains, Mount Charleston, reaches 11,918 feet. Lower ranges and the foothills of the high ranges offer great hiking even in the winter, and there are slick-rock canyons, a unique feature of southern Nevada.

73. CATHEDRAL GORGE

WHY GO?
A series of easy trails in Cathedral Gorge State Park.

THE RUNDOWN

Start: 15 miles north of Caliente
Distance: About 6 miles of trails in park
Hiking time: About 3 hours
Difficulty: Easy
Trail surface: Dirt and rocks
Water: At Regional Visitor Center and campground
Seasons: Fall through spring
Other trail users: None

Canine compatibility: Dogs allowed on leashes
Land status: State park
Nearest town: Caliente
Fees and permits: Entrance fee
USGS topo map: Panaca
Trail contacts: Cathedral Gorge State Park, PO Box 176, Panaca, NV 89042; (775) 728-4460; http://parks.nv.gov

FINDING THE TRAILHEAD
From Caliente, drive north on US 93 for 15 miles and then turn left into Cathedral Gorge State Park. Trails start at the campground and the two picnic areas, as well as at Miller Point Overlook, which is a short distance north on US 93. **Trailhead GPS:** N37 49.291 / W114 24.918

WHAT TO SEE
Cathedral Gorge was formed from layers of ancient lake deposits known as the Panaca formation. These sediments were deposited on the bed of an ancient lake approximately 1 million years ago. As the climate changed and the lake dried up, erosion exposed the soft siltstone and clay shales and began to carve them into the fluted shapes seen today.

The state park features several easy, nearly level trails that wind through the eroded formations that give the park its name. From either of the picnic areas, you can walk the 0.5-mile Nature Loop Trail, which is an interpretive trail with signs explaining the plants and animals of the area.

The Miller Point Trail starts from the CCC Picnic Area and runs 1 mile to the Miller Point Overlook. This trail not only gives you a close-up view of the Panaca formation, but also an overview of the area from the viewpoint at the north end of the trail.

The 4-mile Juniper Draw Trail starts from the campground and joins the Miller Point Trail to return to the CCC Picnic Area. The 0.5-mile Nature Loop Trail can be used to complete the loop and return to the campground. The loop can also be hiked from either of the picnic areas.

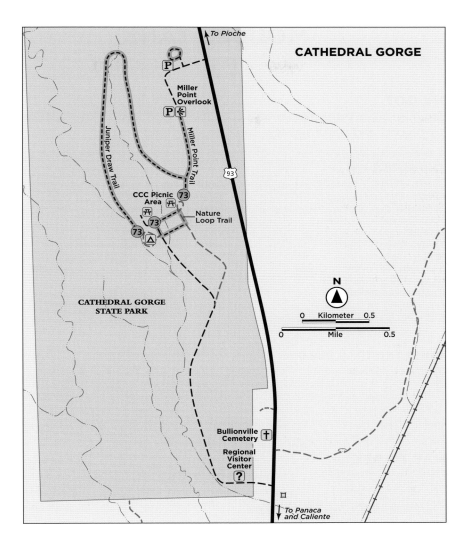

CATHEDRAL GORGE

To Pioche

P

Miller
Point
Overlook

P

Juniper Draw Trail

Miller Point Trail

93

CCC Picnic
Area

73

73

73

Nature
Loop Trail

CATHEDRAL GORGE
STATE PARK

N

0   Kilometer   0.5

0   Mile   0.5

Bullionville
Cemetery

Regional
Visitor
Center

To Panaca
and Caliente

74. MOUSES TANK

WHY GO?
A day hike on an interpretive trail in Valley of Fire State Park, featuring petroglyphs and natural water tanks.

THE RUNDOWN
Start: 74 miles northeast of Las Vegas
Distance: 0.8-mile out and back
Hiking time: About 1 hour
Difficulty: Easy
Trail surface: Sand and rocks
Water: None
Seasons: Fall through spring
Other trail users: None
Canine compatibility: Dogs not allowed on trails or in the backcountry

Land status: State park
Nearest town: Las Vegas
Fees and permits: None
USGS topo map: Valley of Fire East, Valley of Fire West
Trail contacts: Valley of Fire State Park, PO Box 515, Overton, NV 89040; (702) 397-2088; http://parks.nv.gov

FINDING THE TRAILHEAD
From Las Vegas, drive northeast on I-15 approximately 55 miles, then turn right on NV 169 which is signed for Valley of Fire State Park. Continue into the park, and turn left at the visitor center, approximately 18 miles from I-15. After 0.2 mile, turn left (before reaching the visitor center), and continue about 1 mile to the signed Mouses Tank parking area on the right. **Trailhead GPS:** N36 26.496 / W114 30.98

WHAT TO SEE
The trail follows Petroglyph Canyon east from the parking area. Brochures are available at the trailhead explaining various features along this short walk. It points out a couple of petroglyphs along the way, but sharp-eyed hikers will see several more. The striking red rocks of the Valley of Fire are the Aztec sandstone, which is composed of petrified sand dunes. Tiny grains of windblown sand make up the rock, and the sloping surfaces of the ancient sand dunes are clearly visible in the rock faces along the trail. The forces of erosion, primarily that of water, have acted over millions of years to sculpt the soft rock into the weird shapes found in the park.

After a relatively straight section, the wash veers sharply left, and in a few dozen yards drops into the first of several natural water tanks. In 1897 Mouse, a Paiute Indian who was suspected of several crimes, hid out in the intricate Valley of Fire area to avoid capture. He used this water tank and probably others to survive in this nearly waterless area. This water may seem stagnant and uninviting (and is not presently safe to drink), but it would become infinitely more valuable if one were on foot many miles from civilization.

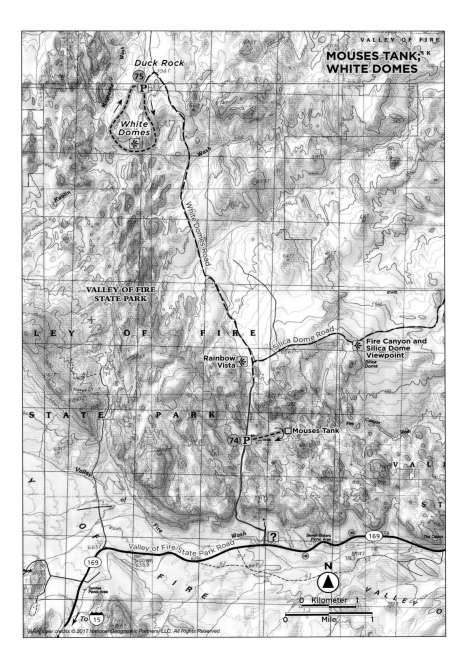

MOUSES TANK;
WHITE DOMES

Duck Rock

75
P

White
Domes

Wash

Kaolin

White Domes Road

VALLEY OF FIRE
STATE PARK

L E Y   O F   F I R E

Silica Dome Road

Fire Canyon and
Silica Dome
Viewpoint

Silica
Dome

Rainbow
Vista

S T A T E   P A R K

74
P

Mouses Tank

Valley

of

Fire

Fire   Canyon

Wash

V A L

S T

Wash

?

Seven Sisters
Picnic Area

169

The Cabins

169

Valley of Fire State Park Road

N

169

To 15

Sunrise
Picnic Area

F I R E

V A L L E Y

0   Kilometer   1
0   Mile   1

Baselayer credits © 2017 National Geographic Partners, LLC. All Rights Reserved.

**Mouses Tank, Valley
of Fire State Park**

MILES AND DIRECTIONS

0.0   Mouses Tank trailhead.

0.4   Mouses Tank.

0.8   Return to trailhead.

75. **WHITE DOMES**

📷 🚶 🦴

WHY GO?
A day hike in Valley of Fire State Park featuring access to the primitive northern area of the park.

THE RUNDOWN
See map on page 229
Start: 55 miles northeast of Las Vegas
Distance: 1.3-mile loop
Hiking time: About 1 hour
Difficulty: Easy
Trail surface: Dirt and rocks
Water: None
Seasons: Fall through spring
Other trail users: None

Canine compatibility: Dogs allowed on leashes
Land status: State park
Nearest town: Las Vegas
Fees and permits: Entrance fee
USGS topo map: Valley of Fire East and Valley of Fire West
Trail contacts: Valley of Fire State Park, PO Box 515, Overton, NV 89040; (702) 397-2088; http://parks .nv.gov

FINDING THE TRAILHEAD
From Las Vegas, drive northeast on I-15 approximately 55 miles, then turn right onto NV 169 (Valley of Fire State Park Road), which is signed for Valley of Fire State Park. Continue into the park, turning left at the visitor center, approximately 18 miles from I-15. After 0.2 mile, turn left (before reaching the visitor center), and continue about 5.5 miles to the end of the road and the White Domes trailhead. **Trailhead GPS:** N36 29.268 / W114 31.952

WHAT TO SEE
Hike the loop clockwise starting at the south side of the parking lot. The rock formations just south of the trailhead are composed of the remains of ancient sand dunes, and the crossbedded layers are clearly visible in the eroding rock. A little farther on, you'll pass the remains of an old movie set. The dramatic rock formations in the park have been the setting for numerous movies. At the south end of the loop, you'll walk along the rim of Kaolin Wash, which has been carved into a slot canyon. Sudden runoff from thunderstorms tends to carve the soft sandstone into deep, narrow canyons, known locally as "slot canyons." On the return part of the loop, as you head north back toward the trailhead, you'll pass an area of "Indian marbles." These are nodules of harder rock that were embedded in the sandstone and were left behind as the parent rock eroded away.

Note the nearly white sandstone in this area, in contrast to the deep red sandstone near the visitor center. The red color in the rock near the visitor center is caused by traces of iron minerals that have oxidized or, literally, rusted. Subtle changes in the colors, from white to tan, purple, maroon, and red, are thought to be caused by underground water movement that leached the oxidized iron.

Many believe that wind erodes desert landscapes such as this one. Wind plays a minor part, however, and mainly moves loose sand and heaps it into small sand dunes. Water is actually responsible for most of the landforms within the park. That seems fantastic in this arid landscape, especially if one has only seen the rare and gentle winter rains. But every few years the area is subjected to heavy rains from strong summer thunderstorms, and even more rarely, prolonged winter rain, such as the 2-week rain of January 1993. The power of water becomes more apparent when one multiplies the effects of one of these storms by millions of storms occurring over many millions of years.

Fire Canyon Trail, Valley of Fire State Park

76. CHARLESTON PEAK NATIONAL SCENIC TRAIL

WHY GO?

A day hike in the Spring Mountains along a high ridge with spectacular alpine views.

THE RUNDOWN

Start: 33 miles northwest of Las Vegas
Distance: 15.4-mile loop
Hiking time: About 10 hours
Difficulty: Strenuous
Trail surface: Dirt and rocks; paved road for 1.3 miles
Water: Unnamed spring on Mummy Mountain
Seasons: Summer through fall
Other trail users: Equestrians
Canine compatibility: Dogs allowed under control

Land status: Spring Mountain National Recreation Area
Nearest town: Las Vegas
Fees and permits: None
USGS topo map: Charleston Peak
Other maps: Forest Service: Humboldt-Toiyabe National Forest, Las Vegas Ranger District
Trail contacts: Humboldt-Toiyabe National Forest, Spring Mountain National Recreation Area, 4701 N. Torrey Pines Dr., Las Vegas, NV 89130-2301; (702) 515-5400; www.fs.fed.us/r4

FINDING THE TRAILHEAD

From Las Vegas, drive northwest on US 95 approximately 13 miles and turn left (west) onto the signed and paved Kyle Canyon Road, NV 157. Continue 19 miles to the summer home area, then continue straight on Echo Road (NV 157 turns sharply left and crosses the creek). After 0.5 mile, turn right (staying on Echo Road) and go 0.1 mile to the North Loop trailhead. **Trailhead GPS:** N36 16.054 / W116 39.472

WHAT TO SEE

Use caution if you attempt this hike in late spring or early summer: The higher sections of the trail may be covered with snow, especially the North Loop near Charleston Peak. It may not be possible to traverse the steep slopes safely without technical climbing equipment and experience.

You'll be hiking this loop counterclockwise. The North Loop Trail climbs steeply north up a drainage as it heads toward the crest of the range. A beautiful forest of ponderosa pine and quaking aspen gives way to a more open view in an old burn on the southwest slopes of Mummy Mountain. A series of switchbacks lead to the unsigned junction with the Deer Creek Trail in a saddle. Swinging northwest, the trail climbs

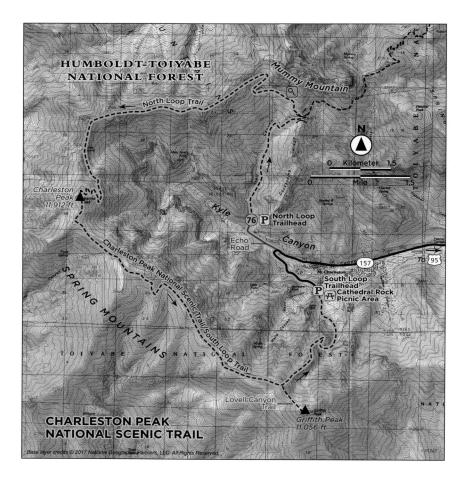

HUMBOLDT-TOIYABE
NATIONAL FOREST

North Loop Trail

Mummy Mountain

N

0   Kilometer   1.5

0   Mile   1.5

Charleston
Peak
11,912 ft

Kyle

Canyon

76 P North Loop
Trailhead

Echo
Road

157

To 95

South Loop
Trailhead

P Cathedral Rock
Picnic Area

Charleston Peak National Scenic Trail South Loop Trail

SPRING MOUNTAINS

TOIYABE   NATIO   FO EST

Lovell Canyon
Trail

NATI

Griffith Peak
11,056 ft

CHARLESTON PEAK
NATIONAL SCENIC TRAIL

Base layer credits © 2017 National Geographic Partners, LLC. All Rights Reserved

across Mummy Mountain past the spring shown on the USGS topographic map. After
the spring, the trail swings southwest and west and gradually climbs to the crest, where
there are views of the Lee Canyon area to the north.

Staying near the crest but skirting minor peaks to the left, the trail traverses limestone
slopes forested with bristlecone pine and finally reaches the east slope of Charleston Peak,
where it switchbacks upward to the summit.

The South Loop Trail descends the treeless west slopes of the peak from just north
of the summit, then follows the long, nearly level crest through a fine bristlecone forest. About 0.5 mile before reaching Peak 11072, the trail turns left (north) at the signed
junction with the Lovell Canyon Trail, and descends via numerous switchbacks toward
the floor of Kyle Canyon. Near the bottom, the trail drops into a drainage to avoid high
limestone cliffs; this spectacular area is a major snow avalanche path in winter. Notice that

Mount Charleston,
Spring Range

Along the crest of
the Spring Range

there are few trees in the drainage, and the trees near the sides are all of the same size and age. This is due to the regular occurrence of snowslides that destroy the trees.

At the bottom of the drainage, there is a choice of a left and right fork; stay right on the newer trail to reach the South Loop Trailhead at the Cathedral Rock Picnic Area. Walk down the road to Echo Road, turn left, and walk up the road to the North Loop trailhead.

MILES AND DIRECTIONS

0.0 North Loop trailhead.

4.1 Trail reaches crest.

7.3 Charleston Peak; the trail becomes the South Loop Trail; continue south.

11.5 Lovell Canyon Trail; turn left and descend east.

13.5 Unsigned junction; stay left.

13.9 South Loop Trailhead; walk down the road.

14.8 Turn left on Echo Road.

15.4 Return to North Loop Trailhead.

77. **JOE MAY CANYON**

📷 🧗

WHY GO?
A day hike in the Desert National Wildlife Refuge offering a good opportunity to observe bighorn sheep, including lambs.

THE RUNDOWN
Start: 35 miles north of Las Vegas
Distance: 8.0-mile out and back
Hiking time: About 5 hours
Difficulty: Strenuous
Trail surface: Dirt and rocks
Water: None
Seasons: Spring
Other trail users: None
Canine compatibility: Dogs not allowed on trails or in the backcountry

Land status: Desert National Wildlife Refuge
Nearest town: Las Vegas
Fees and permits: None
USGS topo map: Black Hills and Corn Creek Springs
Trail contacts: Desert National Wildlife Refuge, 16001 Corn Creek Rd., Las Vegas, NV 89124; (702) 879-6110; www.fws.gov/refuge/desert/

FINDING THE TRAILHEAD
From Las Vegas, drive northwest 20 miles on US 95, then turn right (east) onto Corn Creek Springs Road (signed "Desert National Range"). After 4 miles, turn left (north) onto Alamo Road at the Corn Creek Field Station. Drive north 3 miles, then turn right (east) onto Joe May Canyon Road and continue 3.7 miles to the proposed wilderness boundary, identified by a No Vehicles sign. Joe May Canyon Road is unimproved, and a high-clearance vehicle is recommended. Four-wheel drive is not needed. **Trailhead GPS:** N36 30.444 / W115 18.844

WHAT TO SEE
Walk north up Joe May Canyon to Wildhorse Pass, which provides an excellent panoramic view into scenic Picture Canyon. The east side of Joe May Canyon is an excellent lambing area, and you may be able to observe large groups of bighorn ewes and lambs in this area. Good binoculars will be useful. About 1.5 miles from the No Vehicles sign is the Joe May Guzzler in a small side canyon—one method used to provide water for bighorn sheep and other wildlife.

Desert bighorn sheep prefer rugged mountains and negotiate steep terrain with impressive agility for their somewhat bulky appearance. The size of small deer, they have gray-brown coats that blend nicely with the desert tones, making them difficult to spot. Males are distinguished by their massive curling horns, while the females have much smaller horns. It is thought that the bighorns once ranged much more widely, but pressure from humans has limited them to more rugged terrain. Although they cannot survive without

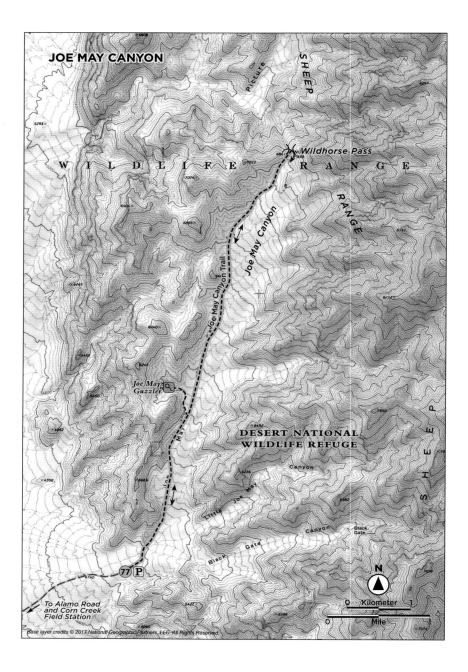

JOE MAY CANYON

SHEEP RANGE

Wildhorse Pass

WILDLIFE RANGE

Joe May Canyon

Joe May Canyon Trail

Joe May Guzzler

DESERT NATIONAL WILDLIFE REFUGE

Joe May Canyon

Little Joe May Canyon

Black Gate Canyon

Black Gate

77 P

To Alamo Road and Corn Creek Field Station

SHEEP

N

0 Kilometer 1

0 Mile 1

Base layer credits © 2017 National Geographic Partners, LLC. All Rights Reserved.

Desert bighorn sheep
© ISTOCK.COM/TWILDLIFE

liquid water, the sheep do obtain enough moisture from green vegetation to enable them to go without water 3 to 5 days in hot weather, and 10 to 14 days in cold weather.

The Corn Creek Field Station, which you passed on the way to the trailhead, has an interesting history. It has seen use as a campsite, stagecoach stop, and ranch. Corn Creek Springs and part of the surrounding land was purchased in 1939 for use as a field station for the wildlife refuge. The station, with its trees, pasture, and spring-fed ponds, attracts a wide variety of migrating birds not commonly observed in such an arid environment. The ponds also provide habitat for the endangered Pahrump poolfish. Evidence of earlier human occupation of this site is provided by Native American arrowhead and tool flakes that litter the surrounding grounds, and the historical buildings located at the northern side of the field station.

—US Fish and Wildlife Service and Bruce Grubbs

MILES AND DIRECTIONS

0.0 Joe May Canyon trailhead.

1.5 Spur trail to Joe May Guzzler on left; stay right.

4.0 Wildhorse Pass.

8.0 Return to Joe May Canyon trailhead.

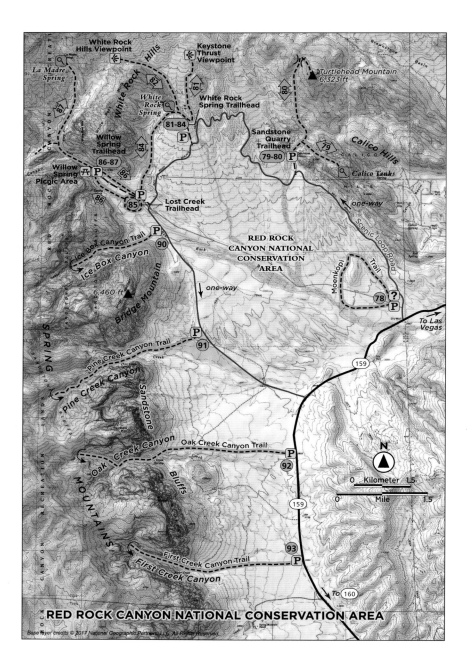

La Madre Spring

White Rock Hills Viewpoint

Keystone Thrust Viewpoint

White Rock Hills

Turtlehead Mountain 6,323 ft

White Rock Spring

White Rock Spring Trailhead

Willow Spring Trailhead

86-87

81-84

84

Sandstone Quarry Trailhead

79-80

Calico Hills

79

Willow Spring Picnic Area

86

85

86

Lost Creek Trailhead

Calico Tanks Spring

one-way

Scenic Loop Road

Ice Box Canyon Trail

Ice Box Canyon

90

RED ROCK CANYON NATIONAL CONSERVATION AREA

Moenkopi Trail

78

To Las Vegas

6,460 ft

Bridge Mountain

one-way

91

159

Pine Creek Canyon Trail

Pine Creek Canyon

Sandstone

SPRING

N

Oak Creek Canyon

Oak Creek Canyon Trail

92

0   Kilometer   1.5

0   Mile   1.5

MOUNTAINS

Bluffs

159

First Creek Canyon Trail

First Creek Canyon

93

To 160

RED ROCK CANYON NATIONAL CONSERVATION AREA

Base layer credits © 2017 National Geographic Partners, LLC. All Rights Reserved

78. MOENKOPI TRAIL

WHY GO?

An easy day hike on an interpretive trail in the Red Rock Canyon National Conservation Area.

THE RUNDOWN

See map on page 240
Start: 15 miles west of Las Vegas
Distance: 2.2-mile loop
Hiking time: About 1 hour
Difficulty: Easy
Trail surface: Dirt and rocks
Water: None
Seasons: Fall through spring
Other trail users: None
Canine compatibility: Dogs allowed under control

Land status: Red Rock Canyon National Conservation Area
Nearest town: Las Vegas
Fees and permits: None
USGS topo map: La Madre Mtn
Trail contacts: Bureau of Land Management, Southern Nevada District Office, 4701 N. Torrey Pines Dr., Las Vegas, NV 89130-2301; (702) 515-5000; www.blm.gov

FINDING THE TRAILHEAD

From Las Vegas, drive west on Charleston Boulevard (NV 159) to reach the start of Red Rock Scenic Loop, which is 10.7 miles from the intersection of Charleston and Rainbow Boulevards. Turn right (north) onto Scenic Loop Road, then immediately left to the Bureau of Land Management visitor center. Here you can obtain general information on the Red Rock area and check on the road and trail conditions. **Trailhead GPS:** N36 7.986 / W115 25.541

WHAT TO SEE

The Moenkopi Trail starts southwest of the visitor center near the weather station. Along the way, watch for creosote, blackbrush, and yucca—typical members of this desert plant community. The trail leads to the crest of the hill west of the visitor center. At the crest, cottontop barrel cactus and Triassic fossils can be seen.

Creosote bush, found along this trail and common in southern Nevada and the rest of the Mojave Desert, is an outstanding example of the extreme methods desert plants use to survive drought. During dry periods, the bush sheds its mature leaves as well as whole twigs and branches, retaining only the new leaves. These leaves can lose well over half their water and still survive. In comparison, humans are seriously ill after a water loss of only a few percent.

—Bureau of Land Management and Bruce Grubbs

Rock climbers in
the Calico Hills

79. **CALICO TANKS**

WHY GO?

An easy day hike to natural water tanks in the redrock Calico Hills in the Red Rock Canyon National Conservation Area.

THE RUNDOWN

See map on page 240
Start: 15 miles west of Las Vegas
Distance: 2.0-mile out and back
Hiking time: About 1 hour
Difficulty: Easy
Trail surface: Dirt and slickrock
Water: None
Seasons: Fall through spring
Other trail users: None
Canine compatibility: Dogs allowed under control

Land status: Red Rock Canyon National Conservation Area
Nearest town: Las Vegas
Fees and permits: None for day hikes; register at visitor center for overnight trips
USGS topo map: La Madre Mtn
Trail contacts: Bureau of Land Management, Southern Nevada District Office, 4701 N. Torrey Pines Dr., Las Vegas, NV 89130-2301; (702) 515-5000; www.blm.gov

FINDING THE TRAILHEAD

From Las Vegas, drive west on Charleston Boulevard (NV 159) to reach the start of Red Rock Scenic Loop, which is 10.7 miles from the intersection of Charleston and Rainbow Boulevards. Turn right (north) onto Scenic Loop Road (one way), drive 2.7 miles to Sandstone Quarry on the right, and park. **Trailhead GPS:** N36 9.801 / W115 27.022

WHAT TO SEE

Follow the wash north 0.25 mile, then turn right (east) at the third canyon and continue up a side canyon through the red slickrock to a large natural water tank (*tinaja*). When they have water, this and other tinajas in the Calico Hills are important sources of water for the area's wildlife.

Tinaja is Spanish for "tank." Most natural desert water tanks are smaller than this one, and tend to form where cascading floodwaters have scoured out deep basins in the rock. They tend to occur in deep canyons where the additional shade helps keep the water from evaporating. In many desert ranges, tinajas are the only year-round source of water for wildlife. Hikers can use the water as well, but should observe a few courtesies. Take only the water you need, and use it sparingly for all purposes except drinking. Never bathe in a tinaja or pollute it with soap or food scraps. Others will need the water. Avoid camping nearby: Your presence will scare away the animals that normally come to drink

Along the trail to Calico Tanks,
Red Rock Canyon National
Conservation Area

during the night. Finally, water from a tinaja should always be purified before drinking or cooking with it.

The origin and exact meaning of the term *slickrock* is unclear. It is generally used in the American Southwest to describe areas of exposed sandstone such as this. From a distance the term is descriptive, because in arid climates sandstone erodes to form sleekly rounded domes and turrets. Up close, however, you'll discover that the rock is anything but slick. It is nature's sandpaper, consisting of billions of grains of sand cemented together by heat and pressure. Contrary to popular opinion, slickrock country is primarily eroded by water during the rare desert storms. Wind plays a very minor role.

—Bureau of Land Management and Bruce Grubbs

80. TURTLEHEAD MOUNTAIN

WHY GO?

A cross-country day hike to a 6,323-foot summit offering spectacular views of the red rocks and Spring Mountains in the Red Rock Canyon National Conservation Area.

THE RUNDOWN

See map on page 240
Start: 15 miles west of Las Vegas
Distance: 4.0-mile out and back
Hiking time: About 3 hours
Difficulty: Strenuous
Trail surface: Cross-country
Water: None
Seasons: Fall through spring
Other trail users: None
Canine compatibility: Dogs allowed under control

Land status: Red Rock Canyon National Conservation Area
Nearest town: Las Vegas
Fees and permits: None for day hikes; register at visitor center for overnight trips
USGS topo map: La Madre Mtn
Trail contacts: Bureau of Land Management, Southern Nevada District Office, 4701 N. Torrey Pines Dr., Las Vegas, NV 89130-2301; (702) 515-5000; www.blm.gov

FINDING THE TRAILHEAD

From Las Vegas, drive west on Charleston Boulevard (NV 159) to reach the start of Red Rock Scenic Loop, which is 10.7 miles from the intersection of Charleston and Rainbow Boulevards. Turn right (north) onto Scenic Loop Road (one way), drive 2.7 miles to Sandstone Quarry on the right, and park. **Trailhead GPS:** N36 9.801 / W115 27.022

WHAT TO SEE

Follow the Calico Tanks Trail until the trail turns east, then leave the trail and hike north up the wash. Once you're north of the Calico Hills with a clear view of Turtlehead Mountain to the north, head up the ravine to the left (west) of the peak. Ascend this ravine to its head, then turn right and follow the ridge a short distance to the summit.

The spectacular views are well worth the long climb. You can see a representative sample of the Mojave Desert, which encompasses the southern tip of Nevada, most of southeastern California, and a bit of western Arizona. The Mojave's symbol is the Joshua tree, a large yucca. Joshua trees tend to grow on the higher slopes of the valleys, with creosote bush dominating at lower elevations, a yucca belt at higher elevations, and, above the yuccas, a piñon life zone where the dominant plants are the piñon pines and juniper trees.

—Bureau of Land Management and Bruce Grubbs

**Turtlehead Peak, Red
Rock Canyon National
Conservation Area**

MILES AND DIRECTIONS

0.0 Sandstone Quarry trailhead; start on Calico Tanks Trail.

0.3 Leave Calico Tanks Trail and hike north up wash.

1.2 Enter ravine west of Turtlehead Mountain.

1.6 Head of ravine; turn right and hike southeast to summit.

2.0 Turtlehead Mountain.

4.0 Return to Sandstone Quarry trailhead.

81. **KEYSTONE THRUST**

WHY GO?

An easy day hike to a unique geological feature, the Keystone Thrust Fault Zone, in the Red Rock Canyon National Conservation Area.

THE RUNDOWN

See map on page 240
Start: 15 miles west of Las Vegas
Distance: 2.0-mile out and back
Hiking time: About 1 hour
Difficulty: Easy
Trail surface: Dirt and rocks
Water: None
Seasons: Fall through spring
Other trail users: None
Canine compatibility: Dogs allowed under control

Land status: Red Rock Canyon National Conservation Area
Nearest town: Las Vegas
Fees and permits: None for day hikes; register at visitor center for overnight trips
USGS topo map: La Madre Mtn
Trail contacts: Bureau of Land Management, Southern Nevada District Office, 4701 N. Torrey Pines Dr., Las Vegas, NV 89130-2301; (702) 515-5000; www.blm.gov

FINDING THE TRAILHEAD

From Las Vegas, drive west on Charleston Boulevard (NV 159) to reach the start of Red Rock Scenic Loop, which is 10.7 miles from the intersection of Charleston and Rainbow Boulevards. Turn right (north) onto Scenic Loop Road (one way), then drive 5.9 miles to White Rock Spring parking area and turn right. Follow the dirt road 0.9 mile to the White Rock Spring trailhead, at road's end, and park. **Trailhead GPS:** N36 10.376 / W115 28.643

WHAT TO SEE

Walk 100 yards back down the road (east) to a closed dirt road now on your left (north). Follow the old road across the wash, where it turns left and starts to climb the ridge opposite the trailhead. After approximately 0.75 mile, the trail crosses a wash and climbs into a small saddle. Just up the ridge, the trail forks, with the right fork descending off the ridge into a small canyon. The contact of the Keystone Thrust Fault is visible below, where the older gray limestone has been forced over the top of the much younger red and white Aztec sandstone.

This is a fine example of a thrust fault—a fracture in the earth's crust where one rock layer is thrust horizontally over another. Normally, younger rocks are found on top of older rocks, because they are deposited in layered succession. But here the older limestone has been pushed over the top of the younger sandstone. It is believed that this occurred about 65 million years ago when two continental plates collided to

The Keystone Thrust, where the older gray limestone has been pushed on top of the younger red sandstone

create the present North American continent. The thrust contact is clearly defined by the sharp contrast between the gray limestones and the red sandstones. The Keystone Thrust Fault extends from the Cottonwood Fault (along the Pahrump Highway) 13 miles northward to the vicinity of La Madre Mountain, where it is obscured by more complex faulting.

—Bruce Grubbs and Bureau of Land Management

82. **WHITE ROCK HILLS**

WHY GO?

A cross-country day hike in the Red Rock Canyon National Conservation Area featuring a dramatic view of La Madre Spring Valley.

THE RUNDOWN

See map on page 240
Start: 15 miles west of Las Vegas
Distance: 2.6-mile out and back
Hiking time: About 2 hours
Difficulty: Easy
Trail surface: Dirt and rocks
Water: None
Seasons: Fall through spring
Other trail users: None
Canine compatibility: Dogs allowed under control

Land status: Red Rock Canyon National Conservation Area
Nearest town: Las Vegas
Fees and permits: None for day hikes; register at visitor center for overnight trips
USGS topo map: La Madre Mtn
Trail contacts: Bureau of Land Management, Southern Nevada District Office, 4701 N. Torrey Pines Dr., Las Vegas, NV 89130-2301; (702) 515-5000; www.blm.gov

FINDING THE TRAILHEAD

From Las Vegas, drive west on Charleston Boulevard (NV 159) to reach the start of Red Rock Scenic Loop, which is 10.7 miles from the intersection of Charleston and Rainbow Boulevards. Turn right (north) onto Scenic Loop Road (one way), then drive 5.9 miles to White Rock Spring parking area and turn right. Follow the dirt road 0.9 mile to the White Rock Spring trailhead, at road's end, and park. **Trailhead GPS:** N36 10.376 / W115 28.643

WHAT TO SEE

Go west down a short closed road, which drops into the wash to the right of the White Rock Hills. Then continue up the wash along the base of the sandstone bluffs. After about 0.5 mile, a faint trail veers out of the wash to the right. A few cairns mark the route as it parallels the wash. A little over 1 mile from the trailhead, the route reaches a saddle with excellent views of the west side of the White Rock Hills and the valley above La Madre Spring. The towering limestone cliffs on the right make a somber contrast with the bright sandstone to the left.
—Bruce Grubbs

MILES AND DIRECTIONS

0.0   White Rock Spring trailhead.

0.5   Trail veers out of wash on right.

1.3   Saddle overlooking La Madre Spring Valley.

2.6   Return to White Rock Spring trailhead.

White Horse Hills Trail,
Red Rock Canyon
National Conservation
Area

83. WHITE ROCK SPRING

WHY GO?
A day hike in the Red Rock Canyon National Conservation Area that offers an opportunity to observe bighorn sheep.

THE RUNDOWN

See map on page 240
Start: 15 miles west of Las Vegas
Distance: 0.6-mile out and back
Hiking time: About 0.5 hour
Difficulty: Easy
Trail surface: Dirt and rocks
Water: None
Seasons: Fall through spring
Other trail users: None
Canine compatibility: Dogs allowed under control

Land status: Red Rock Canyon National Conservation Area
Nearest town: Las Vegas
Fees and permits: None
USGS topo map: La Madre Mtn
Trail contacts: Bureau of Land Management, Southern Nevada District Office, 4701 N. Torrey Pines Dr., Las Vegas, NV 89130-2301; (702) 515-5000; www.blm.gov

FINDING THE TRAILHEAD
From Las Vegas, drive west on Charleston Boulevard (NV 159) to reach the start of Red Rock Scenic Loop, which is 10.7 miles from the intersection of Charleston and Rainbow Boulevards. Turn right (north) onto Scenic Loop Road (one way), then drive 5.9 miles to White Rock Spring parking area and turn right. Follow the dirt road 0.9 mile to the White Rock Spring trailhead, at road's end, and park. **Trailhead GPS:** N36 10.376 / W115 28.643

White Rock Spring, Red Rock Canyon National Conservation Area

Red Rock Canyon National Conservation
Area, as seen from above.
SKIP MOORE/FLICKR

WHAT TO SEE

The trail is a closed dirt road on the left (west). Follow the old road to the White Rock
Spring water catchment constructed by the Civilian Conservation Corps. This is a good
place to observe bighorn sheep in season. Water catchments such as this one are intended
to expand the range of the desert bighorn sheep by providing additional permanent
water sources. This enables the animals to use more of their natural habitat.
—Bruce Grubbs and Bureau of Land Management

84. **WHITE ROCK SPRING TO WILLOW SPRING**

WHY GO?

A day hike connecting White Rock Spring and Willow Spring, in the Red Rock Canyon National Conservation Area.

THE RUNDOWN

See map on page 240
Start: 15 miles west of Las Vegas
Distance: 3.0-mile out and back
Hiking time: About 2 hours
Difficulty: Easy
Trail surface: Dirt and rocks
Water: None
Seasons: Fall through spring
Other trail users: None
Canine compatibility: Dogs allowed under control

Land status: Red Rock Canyon National Conservation Area
Nearest town: Las Vegas
Fees and permits: None
USGS topo map: La Madre Mtn
Trail contacts: Bureau of Land Management, Southern Nevada District Office, 4701 N. Torrey Pines Dr., Las Vegas, NV 89130-2301; (702) 515-5000; www.blm.gov

FINDING THE TRAILHEAD

From Las Vegas, drive west on Charleston Boulevard (NV 159) to reach the start of Red Rock Scenic Loop, which is 10.7 miles from the intersection of Charleston and Rainbow Boulevards. Turn right (north) onto Scenic Loop Road (one way), then drive 5.9 miles to White Rock Spring parking area and turn right. Follow the dirt road 0.9 mile to the White Rock Spring trailhead, at road's end, and park. **Trailhead GPS:** N36 10.376 / W115 28.643

WHAT TO SEE

The trail is the closed dirt road on the left (west). Follow this road toward the White Rock Spring water catchment; just before you reach it, look for the trail to Willow Spring on the left, heading in a southwesterly direction. The trail follows along the base of the White Rock Hills, and joins the Willow Spring Trail across from the Lost Creek parking area. This hike ends at the Lost Creek trailhead.

Along this trail, or almost anywhere in the Nevada desert, you are likely to see one of the American desert's most common mammals: the jackrabbit, with its large, black-tipped ears. It is commonly seen bounding across roads, and in good years is unusually numerous. The large ears contain many blood vessels and serve to radiate heat to the environment.

—Bureau of Land Management and Bruce Grubbs

85. **LOST CREEK LOOP**

WHY GO?

A day hike to a box canyon with a seasonal waterfall in the Red Rock Canyon National Conservation Area.

THE RUNDOWN

See map on page 240
Start: 15 miles west of Las Vegas
Distance: 0.7-mile loop
Hiking time: About 1 hour
Difficulty: Easy
Trail surface: Dirt and rocks
Water: Lost Creek
Seasons: Fall through spring
Other trail users: None
Canine compatibility: Dogs allowed under control

Land status: Red Rock Canyon National Conservation Area
Nearest town: Las Vegas
Fees and permits: None
USGS topo map: USGS: La Madre Mtn
Trail contacts: Bureau of Land Management, Southern Nevada District Office, 4701 N. Torrey Pines Dr., Las Vegas, NV 89130-2301; (702) 515-5000; www.blm.gov

FINDING THE TRAILHEAD

From Las Vegas, drive west on Charleston Boulevard (NV 159) to reach the start of Red Rock Scenic Loop, which is 10.7 miles from the intersection of Charleston and Rainbow Boulevards. Turn right (north) onto Scenic Loop Road (one way), then drive 7 miles to the Lost Creek trailhead, on the right, and park.
Trailhead GPS: N36 9.271 / W115 29.284

WHAT TO SEE

Take either the right or left loop to the creek, with its permanent water. You can continue upstream to a box canyon with a seasonal waterfall.

A box canyon is a canyon with no outlet at its upper end. Usually the obstacle is a dry waterfall that runs only after storms.

—Bureau of Land Management and Bruce Grubbs

Falls in Lost Creek, Red Rock Canyon
National Conservation Area

86. WILLOW SPRING LOOP

WHY GO?

A day hike through a variety of plant communities, including riparian, pines, oaks, and desert, in the Red Rock Canyon National Conservation Area.

THE RUNDOWN

See map on page 240
Start: 15 miles west of Las Vegas
Distance: 1.5-mile loop
Hiking time: About 1 hour
Difficulty: Easy
Trail surface: Dirt and rocks
Water: None
Seasons: Fall through spring
Other trail users: None
Canine compatibility: Dogs allowed under control

Land status: Red Rock Canyon National Conservation Area
Nearest town: Las Vegas
Fees and permits: None
USGS topo map: La Madre Mtn
Trail contacts: Bureau of Land Management, Southern Nevada District Office, 4701 N. Torrey Pines Dr., Las Vegas, NV 89130-2301; (702) 515-5000; www.blm.gov

FINDING THE TRAILHEAD

From Las Vegas, drive west on Charleston Boulevard (NV 159) to reach the start of Red Rock Scenic Loop, which is 10.7 miles from the intersection of Charleston and Rainbow Boulevards. Turn right (north) onto Scenic Loop road (one way), then drive 7 miles to the Willow Spring Picnic Area turnoff and turn right. Continue 0.7 mile to the Willow Spring Picnic Area and trailhead. **Trailhead GPS:** N36 9.631 / W115 29.91

WHAT TO SEE

You'll hike this loop clockwise, first following the left (northeast) side of the canyon past Native American roasting pits to the Lost Creek parking area. The right-hand trail then crosses Red Rock Wash, branches to the right, and parallels the Red Rock Escarpment to return to Willow Spring.

Roasting pits were used by the ancient inhabitants for slow-cooking. Agave plants, other vegetables, and meats were placed in a bed of hot coals mixed with cobbles and covered with plant materials and earth. After enough time had passed, the cooked food, ash, and fire-cracked rock were dug out. The discarded rock and ash forms a doughnut-shaped ring often several feet high. Also known as mescal pits, these cooking sites are common in the Southwest.

—Bureau of Land Management and Bruce Grubbs

87. LA MADRE SPRING

WHY GO?

A day hike in the Red Rock Canyon National Conservation Area offering an opportunity to view bighorn sheep and other wildlife.

THE RUNDOWN

See map on page 240
Start: 15 miles west of Las Vegas
Distance: 3.8-mile out and back
Hiking time: About 2 hours
Difficulty: Easy
Trail surface: Dirt and rocks
Water: None
Seasons: Fall through spring
Other trail users: None
Canine compatibility: Dogs allowed under control

Land status: Red Rock Canyon National Conservation Area
Nearest town: Las Vegas
Fees and permits: None
USGS topo map: La Madre Mtn, La Madre Spring, and Mountain Springs
Trail contacts: Bureau of Land Management, Southern Nevada District Office, 4701 N. Torrey Pines Dr., Las Vegas, NV 89130-2301; (702) 515-5000; www.blm.gov

FINDING THE TRAILHEAD

From Las Vegas, drive west on Charleston Boulevard (NV 159) to reach the start of Red Rock Scenic Loop, which is 10.7 miles from the intersection of Charleston and Rainbow Boulevards. Turn right (north) onto Scenic Loop Road (one way), then drive 7 miles to the Willow Spring Picnic Area turnoff and turn right. Continue 0.7 mile to the Willow Spring Picnic Area and trailhead. **Trailhead GPS:** N36 9.631 / W115 29.91

WHAT TO SEE

Walk up Rocky Gap Road, an unsigned jeep road that begins at the end of the pavement. Just after crossing the wash, turn right at an unsigned fork. A more interesting way to reach this junction is to walk up the wash to the south of the road. After the fork, remain on the main road, which stays left (west) of the wash. Numerous unsigned roads branch off on either side.

The road ends at a small dam, and a footpath leads up the creek to the spring. Bighorn sheep and other wildlife rely on the water from this spring.

This valley is higher and more sheltered than the open desert east of the White Rock Hills, and so supports a pygmy forest of juniper and singleleaf piñon pine. The singleleaf piñon is easily recognized since it is the only pine with needles growing singly rather than in bunches of two or more. Like its cousin the Colorado piñon, it has edible seeds and used to be an important food source for the Native Americans. It is still an important food source for birds and small mammals.

—Bureau of Land Management and Bruce Grubbs

88. TOP OF THE ESCARPMENT

WHY GO?

A day hike to a 7,208-foot summit in the Red Rock Canyon National Conservation Area featuring excellent views of the Red Rock Escarpment.

THE RUNDOWN

Start: 15 miles west of Las Vegas
Distance: 2.0-mile out and back
Hiking time: About 2 hours
Difficulty: Moderate
Trail surface: Dirt and rocks
Water: None
Seasons: Fall through spring
Other trail users: None
Canine compatibility: Dogs allowed under control
Land status: Red Rock Canyon National Conservation Area

Nearest town: Las Vegas
Fees and permits: None for day hikes; register at visitor center for overnight trips
USGS topo map: La Madre Mtn, La Madre Spring, and Mountain Springs
Trail contacts: Bureau of Land Management, Southern Nevada District Office, 4701 N. Torrey Pines Dr., Las Vegas, NV 89130-2301; (702) 515-5000; www.blm.gov

FINDING THE TRAILHEAD

From Las Vegas, drive west on Charleston Boulevard (NV 159) to reach the start of Red Rock Scenic Loop, which is 10.7 miles from the intersection of Charleston and Rainbow Boulevards. Turn right (north) onto Scenic Loop Road (one way), then drive 7 miles to the Willow Spring Picnic Area turnoff and turn right. Continue 0.7 mile to the Willow Spring Picnic Area. Drive up Rocky Gap Road, a rough, rocky road that requires a high-clearance, four-wheel-drive vehicle. This road begins at the end of the pavement. After 0.5 mile, stay left at a fork. Continue 3.5 miles to Red Rock Summit and park. **Trailhead GPS:** N36 7.834 / W115 32.009

Alternatively, Red Rock Summit can be approached from the west. From Las Vegas, drive 27 miles west on NV 160 to Mountain Springs. Continue about 3 miles, then turn right (north) onto Lovell Canyon Road. In approximately 8 miles, the road to Red Rock Summit turns right (east). It is about 3 miles and 1,200 feet in elevation gain to the summit.

The Escarpment, Red Rock Canyon National Conservation Area

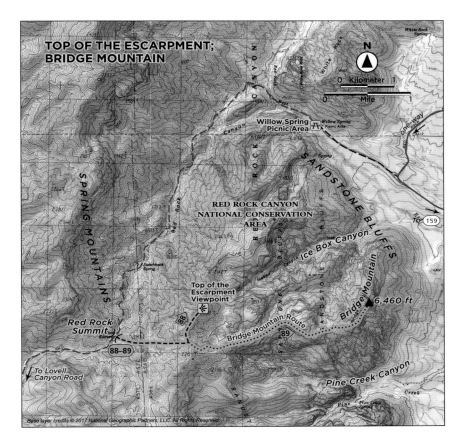

WHAT TO SEE

The trail begins at Red Rock Summit and leaves the road to the east. It winds up around the head of a basin that drains to the west, and eventually reaches the crest of the escarpment. Now follow the ridge east–northeast to a spectacular viewpoint overlooking Red Rock Canyon. From this 7,208-foot summit the view encompasses the Spring Mountains

Another view of the Red Rock Canyon National Conservation Area. © BLM/FLICKR

to the north, the entire Red Rock Canyon National Conservation Area, Blue Diamond Mountain, the Las Vegas Valley, Lake Mead, the Mormon Mountains, and Mount Potosi.

—Bureau of Land Management

MILES AND DIRECTIONS

0.0 Trailhead at Red Rock Summit.

0.7 Crest of escarpment; turn left and follow ridge to peak marked 7208 on USGS topo.

1.0 Peak 7208.

2.0 Return to trailhead.

89. **BRIDGE MOUNTAIN**

WHY GO?

A cross-country day hike to a natural bridge and great views of the Red Rock Canyon National Conservation Area.

THE RUNDOWN

See map on page 259
Start: 15 miles west of Las Vegas
Distance: 5.8-mile out and back
Hiking time: About 4 hours
Difficulty: Strenuous
Trail surface: Cross-country, with a steep exposed system of joints and ledges near the end of the hike. This section does not require technical climbing equipment or skills, but it does demand extreme care. Only hikers experienced in cross-country travel should attempt this hike.
Water: None
Seasons: Fall through spring
Other trail users: None

Canine compatibility: Dogs allowed under control
Land status: Red Rock Canyon National Conservation Area
Nearest town: Las Vegas
Fees and permits: None for day hikes; register at visitor center for overnight trips
USGS topo map: Mountain Springs, La Madre Mtn, and La Madre Spring
Trail contacts: Bureau of Land Management, Southern Nevada District Office, 4701 N. Torrey Pines Dr., Las Vegas, NV 89130-2301; (702) 515-5000; www.blm.gov

FINDING THE TRAILHEAD

From Las Vegas, drive west on Charleston Boulevard (NV 159) to reach the start of Red Rock Scenic Loop, which is 10.7 miles from the intersection of Charleston and Rainbow Boulevards. Turn right (north) onto Scenic Loop Road (one way), then drive 7 miles to the Willow Spring Picnic Area turnoff and turn right. Continue 0.7 mile to the Willow Spring Picnic Area. Drive up Rocky Gap Road, a rough, rocky road that requires a high-clearance, four-wheel-drive vehicle. This road begins at the end of the pavement. After 0.5 mile, stay left at a fork. Continue 3.5 miles to Red Rock Summit and park. **Trailhead GPS:** N36 7.834 / W115 32.009

Alternatively, Red Rock Summit can be approached from the west. From Las Vegas, drive 27 miles west on NV 160 to Mountain Springs. Continue about 3 miles, then turn right (north) onto Lovell Canyon Road. In approximately 8 miles, the road to Red Rock Summit turns right (east). It is about 3 miles and 1,200 feet in elevation gain to the summit.

WHAT TO SEE

Although this is a day hike of moderate length, the trail is minimal, and the last 400-foot climb to the natural bridge on Bridge Mountain is along a steep exposed system of joints and ledges. This section does not require technical climbing equipment or skills, but does require extreme care. Only hikers experienced in cross-country travel should attempt this hike.

The trail begins at Red Rock Summit and leaves the road to the east. It winds up around the head of a basin that drains to the west, and eventually reaches the crest of the escarpment after a mile walk with approximately 700 feet of elevation gain.

Now the trail turns south along the ridgeline for approximately 0.25 mile. It descends around the heads of two small drainages to the east then climbs a steep sidehill to the top of a long, narrow ridge that runs off to the east into Pine Creek. No trail exists in the resistant sandstone, but the route is intermittently marked by two parallel black lines of paint.

This ridge offers an excellent view of the Keystone Thrust Fault Zone. Tremendous forces associated with the movement of the earth's crustal plates have forced the dark gray limestones to ride up over the red and white sandstones that were formed later, and were originally positioned above the limestone. The limestone weathers into fairly large blocks that remain in place, trapping sand, silt, and plant debris that develops into soil supporting a heavy cover of shrubs and small trees. The sandstone weathers differently, breaking down into sand grains that are easily washed and blown away, constantly exposing a new surface of solid rock that is bare of all plants except lichens and a few shrubs growing in cracks. The contrast between the brush-covered limestone and the bare sandstone beneath it clearly delineates the Keystone Thrust Fault Zone.

The trail becomes poorly defined as it snakes down the crest of the ridge to the east. Stay on the crest as much as possible—the going is easier there than it is on the sidehill. Soon after the limestone rock disappears and exposes the sandstone, the route drops off the ridge to the north into a small basin that empties into Pine Creek. At the lower edge of the basin, a sheer cliff descends into the depths of Pine Creek 1,500 feet below. Rising air currents are attractive to soaring birds, which ride along the cliffs; the rising air also carries flying insects to the higher elevations. Small insect-eating birds such as the white-throated swift and violet-green swallow swoop along the edge, buzzing hikers and snapping up bugs on the wing.

From the head of Pine Creek, the route winds off through a slickrock bench studded with numerous small catch basins that hold water after a rain. Some of these basins are quite large; the largest is located in the extreme southeast corner of section 8 on the Mountain Springs USGS topographic map, near the edge. Water trapped in these tanks, or tinajas as the Spanish termed them, supports a diverse and fragile community of plants and animals. Ponderosa pines, junipers, piñon pines, and smaller bushes provide shelter for birdlife. Amphibians such as frogs and toads breed in the ponds, and ravens, hawks, deer, bighorn sheep, and hundreds of other animals rely on the tinajas for water. Never camp within 0.25 mile of such water sources, as the presence of humans will scare the wildlife away. Also remember that since there is no outlet from the tanks, pollutants from soap, human wastes, or litter will remain in them indefinitely, poisoning the creatures that depend on these natural reservoirs.

From the large tank mentioned above, the trail becomes a mere route across the slickrock bench. The correct route is marked intermittently with small patches of orange paint in the shape of bighorn sheep tracks. If you don't follow the correct route carefully, you'll find yourself perched on the edge of a sheer drop with no way down. In many areas the route is broken by short vertical pitches that must be carefully negotiated. It is

The bridge on Bridge Mountain
STAN SHEBS

approximately 0.5 mile from the big tank to the bottom of the saddle that leads up to Bridge Mountain, with a drop of 350 feet.

To reach the bridge near the summit of Bridge Mountain, the route leads straight up a system of joints and ledges for a distance of 400 feet. The path is not as sheer as it appears during the approach, and there are plenty of holds for hands and feet. Still, this climb is relatively exposed; exercise extreme care. A misstep could plunge you hundreds of feet into Pine Creek. Climbing within the joints offers more security, but climbing the faces alongside is slightly easier.

Once the bridge has been reached and explored, a further route leads up onto the bench above, from inside the alcove near the pine tree. Just 100 yards north of the bridge is a large, deep, nearly circular tinaja nearly 80 feet across and 60 feet deep. Over the bench to the east is a large alcove that shelters a hidden forest of ponderosa pines. Trees grow very slowly in this area because of the dry conditions. Wood is relatively scarce, slowly replaced, and absolutely should not be used to build fires. A fire in the hidden forest could cause damage that would not heal in 1,000 years. Note that all wood gathering and ground fires are prohibited in the Red Rock backcountry.

Return to Red Rock Summit by retracing your route. Do not attempt to take shortcuts or alternate routes.

—Bureau of Land Management

MILES AND DIRECTIONS

0.0 Trailhead at Red Rock Summit.

0.7 Crest of escarpment.

2.9 Bridge Mountain.

5.8 Return to trailhead.

90. **ICE BOX CANYON**

WHY GO?

A day hike in the Red Rock Canyon National Conservation Area featuring a seasonal waterfall and box canyon.

THE RUNDOWN

See map on page 240
Start: 15 miles west of Las Vegas
Distance: 2.8-mile out and back
Hiking time: About 2 hours
Difficulty: Easy
Trail surface: Dirt and rocks; cross-country in wash
Water: None
Seasons: Fall through spring
Other trail users: None
Canine compatibility: Dogs allowed under control

Land status: Red Rock Canyon National Conservation Area
Nearest town: Las Vegas
Fees and permits: None (day use only)
USGS topo map: La Madre Mtn and Mountain Springs
Trail contacts: Bureau of Land Management, Southern Nevada District Office, 4701 N. Torrey Pines Dr., Las Vegas, NV 89130-2301; (702) 515-5000; www.blm.gov

FINDING THE TRAILHEAD

From Las Vegas, drive west on Charleston Boulevard (NV 159) to reach the start of Red Rock Scenic Loop, which is 10.7 miles from the intersection of Charleston and Rainbow Boulevards. Turn right (north) onto Scenic Loop Road (one way), then drive 7.4 miles to the Ice Box Canyon Overlook and trailhead, which is on the right. **Trailhead GPS:** N36 9.021 / W115 28.893

WHAT TO SEE

Follow the trail across the wash. The trail stays on the bench on the right (north) side of the canyon until the canyon narrows, then ends as it drops into the wash. Follow the wash (boulder-hopping is required) to a seasonal waterfall and box canyon. The narrow Ice Box Canyon derives its name from the cooler temperatures found in it. These cooler temperatures create what are called microclimates: small areas where the year-round climate is different enough from the surrounding area to support a plant and animal community normally found at higher elevations.

—Bureau of Land Management and Bruce Grubbs

Ice Box Canyon
© JOE O'KELLEY/FLICKR

MILES AND DIRECTIONS

0.0 Ice Box Canyon trailhead.

0.2 Trail ends; follow wash upstream.

1.4 Seasonal waterfall.

2.8 Return to Ice Box Canyon trailhead.

91. PINE CREEK CANYON

WHY GO?

A day hike in the Red Rock Canyon National Conservation Area featuring an unusual low-elevation pine forest.

THE RUNDOWN

See map on page 240
Start: 15 miles west of Las Vegas
Distance: 5.0-mile out and back
Hiking time: About 3 hours
Difficulty: Moderate
Trail surface: Old road, dirt and rocks, cross-country with some rock scrambling
Water: None
Seasons: Fall through spring
Other trail users: None
Canine compatibility: Dogs allowed under control

Land status: Red Rock Canyon National Conservation Area
Nearest town: Las Vegas
Fees and permits: None (day use only)
USGS topo map: Blue Diamond, La Madre Mtn, and Mountain Springs
Trail contacts: Bureau of Land Management, Southern Nevada District Office, 4701 N. Torrey Pines Dr., Las Vegas, NV 89130-2301; (702) 515-5000; www.blm.gov

FINDING THE TRAILHEAD

From Las Vegas, drive west on Charleston Boulevard (NV 159) to reach the start of Red Rock Scenic Loop, which is 10.7 miles from the intersection of Charleston and Rainbow Boulevards. Turn right (north) onto Scenic Loop Road (one way), then drive 9 miles to the Pine Creek Canyon Overlook and Trailhead, which is on the right. **Trailhead GPS:** N36 7.699 / W115 28.393

WHAT TO SEE

Follow the trail downhill to the closed dirt road that leads to the old Horace Wilson homestead site; nothing remains except the foundation. The canyon divides above the homestead site. You can take either fork, but the left is preferable. Pine Creek was named for the unusual occurrence of ponderosa pines at this elevation in the desert. The trees thrive here because of the moisture and cooler temperatures.

The microclimate supporting these tall pines is caused by the high canyon walls (which increase the amount of shade), the moisture from the Pine Creek drainage, and the cool air flowing down the canyon at night. After sunset on calm clear nights, the ground in the high mountains rapidly cools by radiating its heat to the open sky. This in turn cools the air in contact with the earth. The cool air is heavier than warmer air and starts to flow downward, collecting in the drainages and moving toward the valleys via the canyons. This is why there is often a downcanyon breeze or even a wind in desert canyons and mountain valleys after sunset.

—Bureau of Land Management and Bruce Grubbs

Hikers on Pine Creek
Canyon Trail

MILES AND DIRECTIONS

0.0 Pine Creek Canyon trailhead.

0.7 Horace Wilson homestead site.

1.2 Mouth of Pine Creek Canyon.

1.5 Pine Creek Canyon forks; turn left onto left fork.

2.5 Trail fades out.

5.0 Return to Pine Creek Canyon trailhead.

92. **OAK CREEK CANYON**

WHY GO?

A Red Rock Canyon National Conservation Area day hike that features stands of live shrub oak and sandy "beaches" along the wash.

THE RUNDOWN

See map on page 240
Start: 15 miles west of Las Vegas
Distance: 6.0-mile out and back
Hiking time: About 4 hours
Difficulty: Moderate
Trail surface: Old road, dirt and rocks, cross-country with some rock scrambling
Water: None
Seasons: Fall through spring
Other trail users: None
Canine compatibility: Dogs allowed under control

Land status: Red Rock Canyon National Conservation Area
Nearest town: Las Vegas
Fees and permits: None (day use only)
USGS topo map: Blue Diamond
Trail contacts: Bureau of Land Management, Southern Nevada District Office, 4701 N. Torrey Pines Dr., Las Vegas, NV 89130-2301; (702) 515-5000; www.blm.gov

---

FINDING THE TRAILHEAD

From Las Vegas, drive west on Charleston Boulevard (NV 159) to reach the start of Red Rock Scenic Loop, which is 10.7 miles from the intersection of Charleston and Rainbow Boulevards. Continue south on NV 159 another 2.6 miles, passing the lower end of Red Rock Scenic Loop, then turn right (west) onto a dirt road and park at the Oak Creek trailhead. **Trailhead GPS:** N36 6.18 / W115 26.989

WHAT TO SEE

Hike up the old road to its end. Now follow the trail around "Potato Knoll" to the left. Oak Creek Canyon is known for its nice stands of live shrub oak and the sandy "beaches" along the wash. Seasonal waterfalls can be found in the canyon.

The term *live oak* means that a plant is evergreen—it keeps its leaves all year. Shrub oaks often grow in thick stands with mountain mahogany and manzanita, creating formidable obstacles to cross–country hikers. However, the dense brush provides important cover for wildlife.

—Bureau of Land Management and Bruce Grubbs

Oak Creek Canyon.
© DARYL GRIFFITH/FLICKR

MILES AND DIRECTIONS

0.0 Oak Creek trailhead.

1.8 End of old road and mouth of canyon.

2.5 Canyon forks; stay right on main fork.

3.0 End of hike.

6.0 Return to Oak Creek trailhead.

93. FIRST CREEK CANYON

WHY GO?

A day hike to a scenic canyon with seasonal waterfalls in the Red Rock Canyon National Conservation Area.

THE RUNDOWN

See map on page 240
Start: 15 miles west of Las Vegas
Distance: 5.0-mile out and back
Hiking time: About 3 hours
Difficulty: Moderate
Trail surface: Old road, dirt and rocks, cross-country with some rock scrambling
Water: None
Seasons: Fall through spring
Other trail users: None
Canine compatibility: Dogs allowed under control

Land status: Red Rock Canyon National Conservation Area
Nearest town: Las Vegas
Fees and permits: None (day use only)
USGS topo map: Blue Diamond and Mountain Springs
Trail contacts: Bureau of Land Management, Southern Nevada District Office, 4701 N. Torrey Pines Dr., Las Vegas, NV 89130-2301; (702) 515-5000; www.blm.gov

FINDING THE TRAILHEAD

From Las Vegas, drive west on Charleston Boulevard (NV 159) to reach the start of Red Rock Scenic Loop, which is 10.7 miles from the intersection of Charleston and Rainbow Boulevards. Continue south on NV 159 another 4.1 miles, passing the lower end of Red Rock Scenic Loop, and then turn right (west) onto a dirt road and park at the First Creek trailhead. **Trailhead GPS:** N36 4.875 / W115 26.891

WHAT TO SEE

Follow the closed dirt road to the mouth of the canyon. A trail follows the left side of the canyon for a distance; some rock scrambling is required thereafter.

Seasonal waterfalls are found all over Nevada in the numberless canyons that cut into the flanks of the mountains. At higher elevations the falls run during the snowmelt during late spring and early summer, and sometimes briefly after heavy thunderstorms. At lower elevations such as these, runoff tends to occur during wet storms, which primarily occur in winter. The best chance to see the falls running is in late winter or early spring.

—Bureau of Land Management and Bruce Grubbs

94. SPIRIT PEAK

WHY GO?

A cross-country day hike to the summit of 5,535-foot Spirit Peak, the highest peak in the Newberry Mountains.

THE RUNDOWN

Start: 10 miles northwest of Laughlin
Distance: 3.2-mile out and back
Hiking time: About 4 hours
Difficulty: Strenuous
Trail surface: Cross-country
Water: None
Seasons: Fall through spring
Other trail users: None
Canine compatibility: Dogs allowed under control

Land status: Lake Mead National Recreation Area
Nearest town: Laughlin
Fees and permits: None
USGS topo map: Spirit Mountain
Trail contacts: Lake Mead National Recreation Area, 601 Nevada Hwy., Boulder City, NV 89005; (702) 293-8990; www.nps.gov/lame

FINDING THE TRAILHEAD

From Laughlin, drive west on NV 163 for 6 miles to the signed turnoff for Christmas Tree Pass. Turn right onto this graded dirt road and continue for 6.2 miles, then turn right and continue 0.2 mile to the end of the road.

This same turnoff can be reached from the west by leaving US 95 about 1 mile south of Cal-Nev-Ari and turning east onto the signed Christmas Tree Pass Road, which is maintained gravel. It is 10 miles to the trailhead turnoff, which is just past the first units of the Christmas Tree Pass Campground. **Trailhead GPS:** N35 15.473 / W114 42.484

WHAT TO SEE

Although the summit can be reached in many different ways, this is the most direct route. From the parking area, go generally north, angling up the east-facing talus slope toward the last of the granite outcrops on the skyline above. Stay below the steepest terrain near the top of the ridge until you're nearly to the northernmost visible outcrop, then climb an easy gully just to the south of this last outcrop. The top of the ridge is broad and gentle when you reach it, with pleasant little basins.

Notice the gradual change from mesquite desert to piñon–juniper woodland as you ascend. After wet winters, the ground will be covered with cheatgrass, an exotic plant that cures rapidly when the temperature starts to rise in the summer. Once it is completely dry, it turns a pale yellow or straw color and becomes extremely flammable. On any slope or with the slightest breeze a wildfire will spread rapidly, burning not only the cheatgrass but also the shrubs and trees. Most of the native plants are very slow growing and take many years to replace once burned. In dry years, however, there may be almost no cheatgrass, leaving the desert nearly fireproof, its more natural state.

Spirit Peak,
Newberry Mountains

Looking north along the
Newberry Mountains toward
Lake Mohave

Continue directly up the ridge above, going generally west and avoiding rock outcrops to either side. As this ridge joins the main north–south summit ridge, angle northwest to reach another pleasant ridgetop. From here, it appears that the summit is the peak to the northeast, but it is actually to the northwest at the end of the very rugged granite ridge. The easiest way to the highest point is to stay below the summits to the north and head diagonally northwest. Skirt the massive granite fins at their southern ends then walk up a gully to a saddle just below the summit. The highest point is marked by an old survey post.

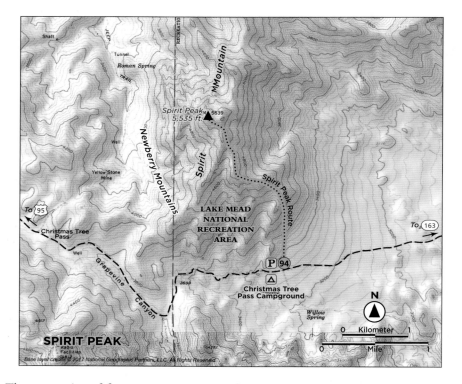

The mountains of four states are spread before you. To the south are the low ranges near Needles, California. The 8,000-foot Hualapai Mountains are visible southeast near Kingman, Arizona. To the northeast, the 8,000-foot Virgin Mountains mark the extreme northwest corner of Arizona. Just beyond the Virgins, the Pine Valley Mountains rise to 10,000 feet above St. George, Utah. Finally, to the northwest, the 11,000-foot Spring Range towers above Las Vegas.

MILES AND DIRECTIONS

0.0 Parking.

1.0 Top of east ridge; follow ridge west, avoiding granite outcrops to either side.

1.3 Crest of main north–south ridge; head northwest to Spirit Peak.

1.6 Spirit Peak.

3.2 Return to vehicle.

AFTERWORD: NEVADA'S WILDERNESS CHALLENGE

Nevada is the most mountainous state, the driest state, and the fastest-growing state in the country. When the first edition of *Hiking Nevada* was published, its vast wild places were relatively unknown except to a few hikers, horsemen, and hunters. But now, thanks to the work of the Nevada Wilderness Coalition, Nevada is no longer a "black hole" in the wilderness map of the West. Growing numbers of outdoor enthusiasts are discovering the magnificent expanses of Nevada's high desert and unique mountain ranges and the wonderful wildlife habitat to be found there.

In addition to the 777,000 acres of USDA Forest Service land and National Park Service land that Congress designated as wilderness by the end of 1994, an additional 1,994,000 acres of Bureau of Land Management areas were added in 2000, 2002, and 2004. These lands range from the huge Black Rock Desert wilderness in northwestern Nevada to the desert ranges of Lincoln County in the southeast, as well as the areas near Las Vegas, the fastest-growing city in the United States. In 2006, twelve new wilderness areas, totaling 558,000 acres, were added in White Pine County, protecting the high Schell Range and Mount Grafton area, among others. And in 2014, portions of the Pine Forest Range were designated as wilderness. Currently, 3.44 million acres of Nevada are protected as part of the National Wilderness System.

In December 2016, President Obama used the Antiquities Act to protect 297,000 acres in southeast Nevada as Gold Butte National Monument. This national monument protects the area west of Arizona's Grand Canyon–Parashant National Monument, from the Virgin Mountains on the north to Lake Mead National Recreation Area on the south and west, and includes the Jumbo Springs and Lime Canyon Wildernesses.

The effort to protect Nevada's wild country continues, and every region in Nevada has lands that qualify in every way as wilderness. It will take a strong and united effort on the part of conservationists and outdoor enthusiasts to achieve wilderness status for these remote lands. Local leaders and the congressional delegation need to be educated about the valuable legacy that these wild lands offer to us and to future generations.

We need wilderness enthusiasts to get out and enjoy Nevada's wild places and to spread the word to others. To learn what you can do, please contact Friends of Nevada Wilderness via their website, www.nevadawilderness.org.

—Marjorie Sill and Bruce Grubbs

Bristlecone pines,
Spring Range

APPENDICES

HIKERS' CHECKLISTS

The following checklists may be useful for ensuring that you forget nothing essential on your hiking trips. Of course, these lists contain far more items than you'll need on any individual trip!

CLOTHING

- ❑ Shirt
- ❑ Pants
- ❑ Underwear (extra)
- ❑ Swimsuit
- ❑ Walking shorts
- ❑ Belt or suspenders
- ❑ Windbreaker
- ❑ Jacket or parka
- ❑ Rain gear
- ❑ Gloves or mittens
- ❑ Sun hat
- ❑ Warm cap for cold
- ❑ Bandanna
- ❑ Sweater

FOOTWEAR

- ❑ Boots
- ❑ Socks (extra)
- ❑ Boot wax
- ❑ Camp shoes

SLEEPING

- ❑ Tarp or tent with fly
- ❑ Groundsheet
- ❑ Sleeping pad
- ❑ Sleeping bag

PACKING

- ❑ Backpack
- ❑ Day pack or fanny pack

COOKING

- ❑ Matches or lighter
- ❑ Waterproof match case
- ❑ Fire starter
- ❑ Stove
- ❑ Fuel
- ❑ Stove maintenance kit
- ❑ Cooking pot(s)
- ❑ Cup
- ❑ Bowl or plate
- ❑ Utensils
- ❑ Pot scrubber
- ❑ Plastic water bottles
- ❑ Collapsible water containers

FOOD

- ❑ Cereal
- ❑ Bread
- ❑ Crackers
- ❑ Cheese
- ❑ Margarine
- ❑ Dry soup
- ❑ Packaged dinners
- ❑ Snacks
- ❑ Hot chocolate
- ❑ Tea
- ❑ Powdered milk
- ❑ Powdered drink mixes

NAVIGATION

- ❑ Topographic maps
- ❑ Compass

EMERGENCY/REPAIR

- ❑ Pocketknife
- ❑ First-aid kit
- ❑ Snakebite kit
- ❑ Nylon cord
- ❑ Plastic bags
- ❑ Wallet or ID card
- ❑ Space blanket
- ❑ Emergency fishing gear
- ❑ Signal mirror
- ❑ Pack parts
- ❑ Stove parts
- ❑ Tent parts
- ❑ Flashlight bulbs, batteries
- ❑ Scissors
- ❑ Safety pins

MISCELLANEOUS

- ❑ Fishing gear
- ❑ Photographic gear
- ❑ Sunglasses
- ❑ Flashlight
- ❑ Candle lantern
- ❑ Sunscreen
- ❑ Insect repellent
- ❑ Toilet paper and trowel
- ❑ Binoculars
- ❑ Trash bags
- ❑ Notebook and pencils
- ❑ Field guides
- ❑ Book or game
- ❑ Dental and personal items
- ❑ Towel
- ❑ Water purification tablets
- ❑ Car key
- ❑ Watch
- ❑ Calendar

CAR

- ❑ Extra water
- ❑ Extra food
- ❑ Extra clothes

RESOURCES

CONSERVATION ORGANIZATIONS AND HIKING CLUBS

Desert Trail Association, www.thedeserttrail.org

Friends of Nevada Wilderness, www.nevadawilderness.org

Great Basin Association, Baker, NV 89311; (775) 234-7270; www.nps.gov/grba/gbnha/gba.htm

Sierra Club, www.sierraclub.org

Sierra Club, Toiyabe Chapter, http://nevada.sierraclub.org

Tahoe Rim Trail Association, www.tahoerimtrail.org

MAPS AND MAPPING/GPS APPS

AllTrails.com: subscription website with some Nevada trails and maps, plus iPhone and Android apps

Backcountry Navigator Pro: Android GPS and topo map app

ExpertGPS.com: computer topo maps and satellite images with GPS and mapping tools

GaiaGPS.com: digital maps for iPhone and Android devices

Garmin: www.garmin.com; DeLorme, www.delorme.com (maps for Garmin trail GPS receivers)

GPSFileDepot.com: free topo and other maps for Garmin trail GPS receivers

Maptech: www.maptech.com

National Geographic Maps (Trails Illustrated waterproof paper hiking map series) Topo! digital state maps, http://maps.nationalgeographic.com/topo; https://shop.national geographic.com/category/maps/trail-maps/nevada

Topozone.com: free online topo maps

USGS Topographic Maps: 1400 Independence Rd., Rolla, MO 65401; (573) 308-3500; http://topomaps.usgs.gov; https://nationalmap.gov/ustopo/index.html

FURTHER READING

Cline, Gloria Griffen. *Exploring the Great Basin*. University of Nevada Press, 1963.

Elliott, Russel R. *History of Nevada*. University of Nebraska Press, 2015.

Fiero, G. William. *Nevada's Valley of Fire*. KC Publications, 1997.

Hart, John. *Hiking the Great Basin*. Sierra Club Books, 1992.

Houghton, Samuel G. *A Trace of Desert Waters: The Great Basin Story*. Howe Brothers, 1986.

Larson, Peggy. *The Sierra Club Naturalist's Guide to the Deserts of the Southwest*. Sierra Club Books, 1977.

Perry, John, and Jane Greverus. *Guide to the Natural Areas of New Mexico, Arizona, and Nevada*. Sierra Club Books, 1986.

Redfern, Ron. *The Making of a Continent*. Times Books, 1983.

Trimble, Stephen. *The Sagebrush Ocean*. University of Nevada Press, 1999.

Waring, Gwendolyn. *A Natural History of the Intermountain West: Its Ecological and Evolutionary Story*. University of Utah Press, 2011.

Wilkerson, James. *Medicine for Mountaineering*. Mountaineers Books, 2010.

HIKE INDEX

Alpine Lakes, 191
Arc Dome, 122
Baker and Johnson Lakes, 200
Bald Mountain, 184
Berlin-Ichthyosaur State Park, 114
Big Canyon, 172
Blue Lakes, 29
Bridge Mountain, 261
Bristlecone-Glacier Trail, 194
Buckskin Mountain, 34
Calico Tanks, 243
Can Young Canyon, 209
Cathedral Gorge, 226
Charleston Peak National Scenic
    Trail, 233
Clear Lake Trail, 162
Cold Springs Pony Express Station, 112
Cottonwood Creek/Barley Creek
    Trail, 156
Cow Canyon Trail, 136
Dead Lake, 214
Desert Trail: High Rock Canyon
    Section, 18
Desert Trail: Sheldon National Wildlife
    Refuge Section, 23
Duffer Peak, 32
Echo Lake, 82
Falls Canyon Trail, 48
First Creek Canyon, 271
Granite Peak, 38
Green Monster Trail, 160
Grimes Point Archaeological Area, 107
Hendrys Creek, 168
Hobart Creek Reservoir, 90
Horse Canyon Trail, 46
Ice Box Canyon, 264
Island Lake, 73

Jett Canyon Trail, 130
Joe May Canyon, 237
Johnson Lake, 211
Jones Creek/Whites Creek Trail, 98
Keystone Thrust, 247
La Madre Spring, 257
Lehman Cave, 199
Lehman Creek, 181
Lexington Arch, 221
Lost Creek Loop, 254
Lye Creek Basin, 36
Marlette Lake, 96
Matterhorn Loop, 66
McConnell Creek Trail, 45
Meadow Creek Trail, 142
Moenkopi Trail, 241
Moores Creek Trail, 144
Morgan Creek Trail, 146
Mosquito Creek Trail, 149
Mount Jefferson, 137
Mount Rose, 101
Mountain View Nature Trail, 198
Mouses Tank, 228
North Mosquito Creek Trail, 152
North Twin River Loop, 125
Oak Creek Canyon, 269
Ophir Creek Trail, 104
Osceola Ditch Interpretive Trail, 179
Osceola Tunnel, 175
Overland Lake, 85
Peavine Canyon Trail, 134
Pine Creek Canyon, 266
Pole Canyon, 207
Rebel Creek Trail, 41
Ruby Crest National Recreation
    Trail, 78
Sand Springs Desert Study Area, 108

Santa Rosa Summit Trail: Buffalo Canyon, 50

Santa Rosa Summit Trail: North Hanson Creek, 54

Santa Rosa Summit Trail: Singas Creek, 52

Smith Creek, 166

Snake Creek, 216

Soldier Creek, 70

South Fork Big Wash, 218

South Mosquito Creek Trail, 154

South Twin River Overlook, 128

Spirit Peak, 272

Spooner Lake, 93

Star Peak, 60

Strawberry Creek and Osceola Ditch, 177

Timber Creek and South Fork Baker Creek, 205

Toiyabe Crest National Recreation Trail, 116

Toms Canyon Trail, 132

Top of the Escarpment, 258

Turtlehead Mountain, 245

Water Canyon, 56

Wheeler Peak, 188

White Domes, 231

White Rock Hills, 249

White Rock Spring, 251

White Rock Spring to Willow Spring, 253

Willow Spring Loop, 256